Leaders Who
Make a Difference

Burt Nanus
Stephen M. Dobbs

Leaders Who Make a Difference

Essential Strategies for Meeting the Nonprofit Challenge

Jossey-Bass Publishers
San Francisco

Jossey-Bass books and products are available through most bookstores. To contact Jossey-Bass directly, call (888) 378-2537, fax to (800) 605-2665, or visit our website at www.josseybass.com.

Substantial discounts on bulk quantities of Jossey-Bass books are available to corporations, professional associations, and other organizations. For details and discount information, contact the special sales department at Jossey-Bass.

TCF Manufactured in the United States of America on Lyons Falls Turin Book. This paper is acid-free and 100 percent totally chlorine-free.

Library of Congress Cataloging-in-Publication Data

Nanus, Burt.
     Leaders who make a difference : essential strategies for
meeting the nonprofit challenge / Burt Nanus, Stephen M. Dobbs—
1st ed.
        p. cm.
     Includes bibliographical references and index.
     ISBN 0-7879-4665-6 (alk. paper)
     1. Nonprofit organizations—Management.   2. Leadership.
3. Executive ability.   I. Dobbs, Stephen M.   II. Title.
     HD62.6.N36   1999
     658.4'012—dc21   99-6757

HB Printing   10 9 8 7 6 5 4 3 2 1   FIRST EDITION

Contents

97512

Part Four: Making a Difference

Preface

Nonprofit organizations make numerous and significant contributions to American society and in the international arena. They provide invaluable services to individuals and groups in such areas as education, health, human services, arts and humanities, housing, transportation, and the environment. They support institutions carrying out medical research, public policy initiatives, and programs of international affairs. Nonprofits offer opportunities for those who are more fortunate to assist their neighbors in need, and to help build and sustain community assets like libraries, museums, parks, and recreational facilities. They direct talent and financial resources to help meet community needs and to increase the quality of life for everyone. They act as advocacy groups at every point of the political spectrum.

The special roles played by nonprofit organizations in our national life are acknowledged and valued in several ways. Millions of individuals and thousands of foundations, corporations, and other diverse groups contribute an aggregate of tens of billions of dollars annually to support nonprofit organizations, and taxpayers support such groups through nonprofits' exemptions from federal and state taxation. Many of our most esteemed fellow citizens, the people in the community cherished for their generosity and selflessness, are frequently affiliated with nonprofit organizations as board members, volunteers, or donors.

People are at the heart of the nonprofit enterprise, and none more so than the staff or professional leader, who may be called an executive director, president, executive vice president, or chief executive officer (CEO). This individual has the responsibility to provide the inspiration, direction, and strategic guidance that enables the organization to fulfill its mission and to move forward and make a difference. The leader is the central figure, the operational and administrative head of the nonprofit organization. Situated between the board and the rest of the staff and other members of the family, the leader carries on his or her shoulders the burdens and the challenges of being in charge.

In our view, nothing is more important to improving the ability of nonprofit organizations to serve their clients and communities than improving the effectiveness of their leaders. We're convinced that there is much that can be done to increase the number, quality, and performance of nonprofit leaders, and we hope that this book will contribute to that end.

Leaders Who Make a Difference had its genesis at a conference of the Larger Community Foundations Group in Phoenix in early 1997. In attendance were the presidents and board chairs of the thirty largest community foundations in the United States, among them Stephen Dobbs, then the CEO of the $800 million Marin Community Foundation. Burt Nanus was invited to speak on leadership and to facilitate the meeting. We met for the first time at that conference and shared our concern for the paucity of practical professional guidance available to leaders of nonprofit organizations. In subsequent months we remained in touch, sharing our thoughts about nonprofit leadership and eventually deciding to collaborate on this book.

We bring different and complementary backgrounds and experiences to this task. Nanus is an emeritus professor who has researched, taught, and consulted in the leadership arena for over thirty-five years. Dobbs has served as CEO for two large philanthropic entities and has other extensive experience with community organizations. Our collaboration brings together a seasoned academic theorist with an experienced practitioner of nonprofit leadership.

Overview of the Contents

To improve nonprofit leadership, one needs to understand how effective leaders approach their jobs and specifically how their actions contribute to human betterment in the community. To explore these subjects, this book is divided into four parts.

Part One sets the stage and provides the basic premises for our exposition of leadership in nonprofit organizations. Chapter One defines leadership; describes the distinctive characteristics, roles, and qualities of successful nonprofit leaders; and discusses how a leader earns the right to lead. Chapter Two explores what leadership is for—namely, to achieve a greater good, a significant improvement in the services the organization provides for its clients and the community. This chapter offers a conceptual framework that leads directly to measures of leadership and organizational effectiveness. Chapter Three furnishes useful advice about getting started as a leader, including valuing the legacy of predecessors, building new relationships, and establishing values and expectations.

Part Two examines the three roles of the nonprofit leader that are essential to building a strong nonprofit organization: the leader as visionary, as strategist, and as change agent. Chapter Four outlines the critical importance of vision, how new vision statements are formulated, and how the leader plays a major role in moving from vision to action. Chapter Five is about creating the strategic framework that will govern the decisions and actions through which a nonprofit can realize its vision and mission. The leader's role in defining strategic issues, guiding the strategy process, and communicating the strategy to others is also discussed. Chapter Six explores the leader's role as change agent in transforming the organization and building the community. The nature of organizational change and renewal and the impact of strategic alliances are also examined.

Part Three concentrates on the three roles of the nonprofit leader that are needed to build and sustain strong relationships with others: the leader as coach, as politician, and as campaigner. Chapter Seven covers the leader's role in fashioning and coaching an effective team, including igniting the passion of colleagues, designing the right kind of organization and culture, developing the board-staff relationship, and encouraging high performance. Chapter Eight shows how the leader acts as a politician, advocate, troubleshooter, and spokesperson for the organization, dealing with a wide variety of stakeholders and interests. Chapter Nine is about the financial lifeline needed to sustain nonprofit organizations and the leader's role as campaigner in developing and maintaining it.

The final part of this book contains two chapters devoted to how a nonprofit leader makes a real difference in the community. Chapter Ten treats the twin challenges of accountability and measurement, describing the various types of audits that can be used to assess the performance of nonprofit leaders and their organizations. Finally, Chapter Eleven positions the leader as a bridge to the future, leaving a legacy for the benefit of the organization and those who will follow in his or her footsteps.

Intended Audience

Leaders Who Make a Difference was written to assist individuals who need to understand the complexity, the challenge, and the fulfillment of the nonprofit leader. The primary audience is intended to be practicing and aspiring leaders of small, medium, and large nonprofit organizations. Members of boards of directors and others who have a strong need to assess the quality of leadership in their organizations and develop plans for improvement will find many helpful suggestions. The book should also be of interest to organizational development consultants, both those inside community-based organizations and those affiliated with independent firms, who will be able to use it as a resource for executive development, leadership assessment, and other services offered to the social sector.

We are mindful of our responsibility to the next generation of nonprofit leaders and hope that this book also will prove useful in university, college, and community college classes on nonprofit leadership and in continuing education programs for those with an interest in community and philanthropic organizations.

How to Read This Book

There is a growing literature on leadership and nonprofit organizations. We have tried to be quite broad in our coverage of the significant leadership issues, but we also wanted to keep this book to a manageable length for the reader-practitioner. Fortunately, many of the subjects treated in this book, such as advocacy, strategic planning, and fundraising, have large literatures of their own. We distill some of the essential lessons of these studies for nonprofit leaders and then offer references and suggestions for additional readings at the end of the book.

Each of the eleven chapters begins with a vignette about a man or woman somewhere in the United States who has been an effective nonprofit leader. We think that we can learn the most from those who have been widely acclaimed for their success, those who have been among the very best. Some are national figures, such as Marian Wright Edelman of the Children's Defense Fund, whereas others are similarly remarkable individuals whose reputations are for leadership in a local or regional setting, like Adam Hamilton, senior pastor at the Church of the Resurrection in Leawood, Kansas. They all have had their setbacks, of course, but what makes them suitable exemplars for our chapters is their overall success in leading nonprofit organizations.

Wherever possible we allude to the actual experiences of nonprofit organizations and their leaders. These experiences are drawn from a wide range of organizations in terms of both size and type of mission. They emphasize what a nonprofit leader actually can do, the key considerations that lead to top performance. A number of lists, exhibits, and diagrams cite and summarize practical ideas that have worked well for these leaders as well as new ideas and applications that are being reported in leadership studies.

For reasons of consistency and ease of discussion we have kept the focus on the leader at the top of the organization, the president or chief executive officer. However, there are important leaders at every level of a nonprofit organization, including leaders of volunteers, leaders on the board, leaders of programs, and so forth, and they will find many of the same lessons applicable to their roles.

Acknowledgments

Given the importance of nonprofit organizations and the widespread impact some one million of them have on the texture of life throughout this society, the nonprofit leaders at the heart of such enterprises bear a heavy burden of responsibility. The well-being and fate of nonprofit organizations is likely to rise and fall with the quality, efficiency, and durability of their staff and professional leadership. This book recognizes those tens of thousands of executive directors and CEOs who have labored, sometimes under exceedingly adverse circumstances, for their vision of a better society and the greater good. All Americans are greatly in their debt.

We wish to express special appreciation to Alan Shrader, senior editor at Jossey-Bass, for his indispensable care and guidance during the process of creating this book. We are also grateful to the nonprofit leaders featured in the chapter vignettes for their permission to use their stories to illustrate successful nonprofit leadership. Thanks also to Lovett H. Weems Jr. and to John Stewart for their timely suggestions for nonprofit leaders to profile. Finally, we appreciate the assistance of our colleagues who read the manuscript and offered helpful suggestions: Clark Blasdell, Leilani Lattin Duke, Wayne Feinstein, Howard Gardner, and Tom Ruppanner.

We would be grateful if readers would share their experiences in applying the ideas and practices in this book by e-mailing their thoughts to Burt Nanus at nanusburt@hotmail.com or Stephen Dobbs at smdobbs@aol.com.

July 1999   Burt Nanus
                                                     Santa Cruz, California

                                                     Stephen M. Dobbs
                                                     San Rafael, California

To our parents—
Max & Mollie Nanus
and
Harold & Annette Dobbs—
who gave service to the community
and inspired our interest in and practice of leadership
and of working toward the greater good

Leaders Who
Make a Difference

Part I

Leadership in Nonprofit Organizations

1

The Leadership Challenge

Lives of great men all remind us
We can make our lives sublime,
And, departing, leave behind us
Footprints on the sands of time.

Henry Wadsworth Longfellow

I. Donald Terner had been teaching urban planning and archi-tecture at Harvard, MIT, and Berkeley for many years. His research and writings revealed a deep concern about the scarcity of affordable housing in the United States. He would often decry the "unspeakable" (his word) conditions under which many poor fami-lies were living in a country that was the richest in the world. He knew that in some areas, like San Francisco, housing prices had risen so high that even schoolteachers and police officers couldn't afford to live in the communities they served.

Terner thought he might be able to do something about this problem. He accepted a position as director of New York City's Urban Homesteading Assistance Board, and later served as Cali-fornia's director of housing and community development under Governor Jerry Brown.

In 1983, Terner launched BRIDGE Housing Corporation, a non-profit development company. The name is significant. Terner sought to create a bridge between the private, public, and philanthropic sectors in order to build high-quality housing for people in the $12,000 to $25,000 income range, who would otherwise be unable to afford it.

Starting as a two-person operation with a small, anonymous grant, BRIDGE Housing went on to become one of the great success stories in low-income housing in the United States. Terner was able in a brief thirteen-year period to build more than six thousand housing units representing over $600 million in value. More than that, these units were exceptionally well designed, environmentally responsible, and conveniently located near job centers. This was housing that made the residents and neighbors proud. How was he able to accomplish so much in so short a time under difficult economic circumstances?

Extraordinary leadership was the key. Don Terner was a man constantly in motion, bringing people together, finding partners, developing new sources of funding, enrolling others in his cause. Often he'd encounter obstacles that others called impossible. There were occasional setbacks, of course, but most of the time he prevailed. Many of his colleagues were convinced that he could be depended upon reliably to produce a miracle a day, more on some days. One Ford Foundation official acknowledged that Terner was so persuasive that the foundation may have given him more than he asked for.

He inspired others with his vision, passion, and focus. As a professor, he steered many urban planning students toward a career in affordable housing. At BRIDGE Housing he infected others with his enthusiasm and can-do attitude. One manager of a BRIDGE facility said Terner made him proud of the work he did. Terner inspired hope and optimism when problems seemed insurmountable and others were ready to give up.

He was a social entrepreneur, guided by his personal motto that he would do whatever it takes to build homes for those who couldn't get them any other way. In 1994, for example, he found a way into the largest untapped source of new funding for affordable housing in the United States—pension funds. With a challenge loan from

World Savings and Loan, he persuaded the California State Teachers and California Public Employee Retirement Systems to commit $225 million in loans. He matched these funds with another $100 million from two large banks, thereby creating the financing for thousands of units of housing for low- and moderate-income workers.

He was truly innovative as well. Consider Marin City, USA, an outstanding residential, commercial, and community project in northern California. By designing a mixed-use development, he was able to use rents from commercial properties and office space to support job training and other social goals. He also innovated in social services, providing day-care centers, miniparks, and health clinics in some of his developments.

Terner's personal story ended tragically. He died in a fiery plane crash in April 1996, near Dubrovnic, that also claimed the lives of Secretary of Commerce Ron Brown and thirty-three other business and government leaders. But the legacy of Don Terner lives on in the leadership he inspired in the BRIDGE Housing Corporation, and in the thousands of families who live in homes that would not have existed if not for his persistence and dedication.

Don Terner was a strong and effective leader, but his story is hardly unique. Think of any great nonprofit organization that has survived and prospered for over a hundred years—Harvard University, the Art Institute of Chicago, the Mormon Church, the International Red Cross, the Salvation Army, or the Metropolitan Opera Association, for example. To be sure, these organizations have been blessed by generous donors, dedicated and capable professional staff, and good timing. But it is important to note that they wouldn't have had any of these advantages, or wouldn't have benefited much from them if they did, without exceptional leadership at critical times in their history.

Look at any successful organization and the answer will be much the same. They couldn't have done it without effective leadership, the *great enabler* that energizes an organization, allowing it to attain its full potential and make a real difference in its community.

What Is Leadership?

Ask a hundred leaders to define what they mean by the term *leadership* and no two of them will respond exactly alike. Still, they will voice some common themes. For example, in the eight well-regarded definitions of leadership shown in Exhibit 1.1, certain themes keep recurring—purpose, hope, inspiration, influence, marshaling resources, and effecting change.

We also offer our own definition: a leader of a nonprofit organization is a person who marshals the people, capital, and intellectual resources of the organization to move it in the right direction. More precisely:

- *Marshaling resources* means collecting them, focusing their attention, and inspiring or empowering their use.

- *Moving an organization* means energizing it, removing obstacles to progress, making the changes necessary to improve performance, and enabling it to learn and grow.

- *The right direction* is the one that makes the greatest possible contribution over the long term to society or to the particular clients or community that the organization was created to serve. The right direction is *toward the greater good,* which we explore at some length in the next chapter.

Our characterization of leadership is also the emphasis of this book. It focuses squarely on the main purpose of nonprofit leadership, which is moving the organization in the right direction. We agree with Kouzes and Posner's statement (in Exhibit 1.1) that the main reason leaders are needed is to move the organization forward, to make progress. Leadership is where tomorrow begins.

In a small nonprofit organization the top leadership usually is exercised by the president, CEO, or executive director, although it

Exhibit 1.1. Some Definitions of Leadership.

"My own definition of leadership is this: The capacity and the will to rally men and women in a common purpose, and the character which inspires confidence."

—Field Marshall Bernard Montgomery

"A leader is a dealer in hope."

—Napoleon Bonaparte

"Leadership is the process of persuasion or example by which an individual (or leadership team) induces a group to pursue objectives held by the leader or shared by the leader and his or her followers."

—John W. Gardner

"Leadership over human beings is exercised when persons with certain motives and purposes mobilize, in competition or conflict with others, institutional, political, psychological and other resources so as to arouse, engage and satisfy the motives of followers."

—James MacGregor Burns

"Leaders are people who perceive what is needed and what is right and know how to mobilize people and resources to accomplish mutual goals."

—Thomas E. Cronin

"Leaders are individuals who significantly influence the thoughts, behaviors, and/or feelings of others."

—Howard Gardner

"Leaders are pioneers. They are people who venture into unexplored territory. They guide us to new and often unfamiliar destinations. People who take the lead are the foot soldiers in the campaigns for change. . . . The unique reason for having leaders—their differentiating function—is to move us forward. Leaders get us going someplace."

—James M. Kouzes and Barry Z. Posner

"Leaders . . . are responsible for building organizations where people continually expand their capacity to understand complexity, clarify vision, and improve shared mental models—that is, they are responsible for learning."

—Peter M. Senge

may also be shared with a board chairman or a committee. In larger nonprofits there may be dozens of people in top leadership roles. For example, Goodwill Industries is a national organization with national leadership, but each city in which it operates features a semiautonomous organization that is led by its own board of directors and president. Below that city level there may be other leaders responsible for individual plants or thrift shops.

Apart from the top leadership there are usually others who exercise leadership in most nonprofit organizations. For example, think of any medium-sized church or human services organization. A few paid staff members might be leading the key departments and programs, and many unpaid volunteers might be leading fundraising efforts, planning, or teams of volunteer service providers. These leaders are also trying to mobilize resources to move their areas of responsibility, which are parts of the larger entity, in the right direction.

Leadership should never be confused with the *management* or *administration* of a nonprofit organization. The main responsibility of a manager is to operate and maintain the organization efficiently, ensuring that it provides useful services to clients or the community at the lowest possible cost. The leader, though always cognizant of current operations, is more concerned with building the organization for the future—that is, securing new resources, developing new capacities, positioning the organization to take advantage of emerging opportunities, and adapting to change.

Leading and managing are quite different functions. They require two separate mind-sets and two different sets of skills. Because managers are chiefly responsible for processes and operations, they are mostly interested in what needs to be done and how it can be accomplished. In contrast, the leader is concerned with strategies and direction, with where the organization should be headed and what it can and should be doing in the future. This means that the manager's attention tends to be present oriented, with one eye on costs and the other on performance. The leader cares about these things as well, but most of his attention tends to be broader and longer term, with one eye on the challenges that lie just over the horizon and the other on the growth potential of the organization.

The manager, in order to schedule the staff and volunteers, allocate the budget, and control the delivery of services, prefers a stable and relatively predictable environment. That makes the management job easier. Managers work within current constraints. They depend on structures and systems to routinize and simplify complex tasks. They hate unexpected disruptions that interfere with providing services to the community.

Leaders, conversely, prefer flexibility and change to predictability and control. They embrace complexity and uncertainty because they know that change often provides new opportunities for service and may suggest innovative directions for future growth and development. They search for ways to shatter constraints. There's nothing routine about leadership.

In addition, managers tend to be problem solvers, forever seeking better ways to deploy their resources to get the job done. They tend to be analytical thinkers, basing their judgments on performance evaluations, client surveys, financial reports, and other organizational data to diagnose problems and deal with them.

Leaders are more intuitive and divergent in their thinking. Harold J. Leavitt (1986) calls them *pathfinders* as opposed to problem solvers. In their search for new directions their interests transcend organizational boundaries to include many external relationships. For example, most leaders need to interact with or influence government officials, potential funding sources, other nonprofit organizations, and the media. They are forever networking and searching the world outside their organizations to find new allies or opportunities that can help them shape their institutions and position them for the longer term.

Finally, the successes of managers and leaders can be evaluated on different scales. Managers are deemed successful when they operate the organization efficiently, delivering services on time and within budget. Leaders are deemed successful when they enable their organizations to grow in their ability to serve the community, whether that be by discovering new community needs to satisfy, by expanding the resource base, by entrepreneuring new approaches to service delivery, or by energizing or transforming the organization itself. In an often-quoted phrase, "managers do things right, while leaders do the right thing" (Bennis and Nanus, 1997, p. 20).

Clearly, nonprofit organizations need both good leadership and good management if they are to succeed. Either one alone is necessary but not sufficient. Every year thousands of worthy nonprofit organizations fail for lack of one or the other.

Anyone who has ever tried to speak about leadership and management at executive seminars is sure to be challenged on the practical significance of the differences between these two roles. "In my organization," someone will say, "we're expected to do both jobs at the same time." That's like asking bears to dance—they'll do it as best they can, but they're still bears, and their interests and aptitudes aren't for ballet.

Because the skills, interests, and thinking patterns of leaders and managers are so different, it's as unlikely that you will find a single person equally skilled in both roles as it is that you will find a great basketball player equally talented in baseball, or vice versa. Indeed, many great leaders, like Nelson Mandela, Martin Luther King Jr., and Bill Gates, had no managerial experience at all when they assumed positions of leadership. Even when their organizations were relatively small, they were wise enough to concentrate on leadership and trust others with the management responsibilities.

There are times when a manager is called upon to lead, and some managers are able to rise to the occasion. However, when a person is hired specifically to be a leader, such as the CEO of a nonprofit organization, he should be allowed to lead. It has been our observation that whenever a leader is asked to handle managerial responsibilities as well, the short-term demands of management tend to crowd out attempts to lead the organization in a new direction. A few are able to do it, but most find that effective leadership itself is more than a full-time job.

Clearly, if leadership is important to an organization, leaders must have the time and scope to be leaders and must be able to count on others for most of the managerial tasks. This is true in all organizations but especially in the distinctive context of nonprofits.

The Distinctive Character of Nonprofit Leadership

Every year scores of new books on leadership cram the shelves of bookstores and libraries. All but a few of them are written for leaders in business or government. Although nonprofit organizations share some characteristics with their corporate or government brethren, they are in many ways quite different and present their own distinctive leadership challenges.

The purpose of nonprofit organizations is to improve people's lives or to address society's larger issues. Although businesses seek to increase the need for their services in order to grow, many nonprofits would be only too pleased to reduce or eliminate the need for their services. People voluntarily contribute their time and money to such organizations as an expression of their idealism and desire to serve the common good. This has several implications for leadership:

• Unlike work in the public and private sectors, much of the work in nonprofits gets done by people who are unpaid activists giving of themselves to achieve social purposes. Often these volunteers are busy people with full-time jobs and family commitments that may have little to do with the purpose of the nonprofit. They aren't looking for another job, but they are looking for a way to express the best that is in them in service to their community. Even paid staff members often consider their salaries secondary to the psychic income they derive from helping others less fortunate than themselves. Both the unpaid volunteers and the paid staff hope to experience personal fulfillment through their participation; they want to be able to feel better about themselves. Leading these kinds of people requires much more reliance on inspiration, passion, coaxing, persuasion, and peer pressure than upon authority, financial incentives, or fancy job titles, though in some cases these do have a role to play.

• The success of a nonprofit organization is measured not in profits or fulfillment of legislative intent but in terms of social good. This is a more value-laden and less clearly defined criterion than those other organizations must meet, leaving considerable room for nonprofit leaders to exercise judgment, intuition, and innovation in seeking promising new directions.

• With the high ideals and aspirations expressed in their charters and their dedication to community service, nonprofits can often attract some of the most talented and successful people in the community to serve on their boards of directors. These individuals may be leaders in their own right, with strong egos and even stronger opinions on what should be done. They have the responsibility for oversight and trusteeship, which at times puts them at odds with the leadership. However, they also can be enormously helpful to the leader in many ways, such as fundraising, networking, or suggesting new strategic directions. Thus working with the board—some might say *using* the board correctly or even *leading* the board—is a much more critical part of the leader's job in nonprofits than in other types of organization. Moreover, given the number of unpaid board members and volunteers in most nonprofits, the sheer number of people to be led is far larger in nonprofit organizations than in businesses or government agencies with similar-sized budgets.

Beyond their social charter, nonprofits are distinctive in terms of the many constituencies they serve. As an example, consider a teen-runaway shelter. Its clients are likely to include some of the least able and most needy members of society, such as drug addicts, prostitutes, high school dropouts, criminals, teenage mothers, and kids who have been abused or abandoned. Each case presents a unique challenge and requires special treatment. These youths are served not as customers, who pay for a service and if satisfied will return again and again, but as people in need, who if well served will go on to become self-sufficient, productive members of society.

Nonprofits are also distinctive in the many overlapping interests they have with other organizations. To continue the example of the teen-runaway shelter, it would be impossible to operate such a service without public sector partners in the fields of health care, education, criminal justice, and social services. Similarly, private sector partners are needed to supply jobs and housing, and other nonprofits like food banks, legal aid organizations, and thrift shops are needed to provide essential goods and services. Thus many nonprofit leaders need strong diplomatic and political skills in order to assemble a well-synchronized public and private sector team to serve such clients.

Most other nonprofits have similarly diverse constituencies and fuzzy boundaries. Some, like museums, also receive support from a wide variety of sources—foundation grants, donations, entrance fees, product sales, endowments, and so forth. So the leader of such an organization must be comfortable with complexity. Unlike business leaders, who can prosper as long as their products are right for their markets, nonprofit leaders cannot be successful unless they become masters at building close working relationships with all kinds of individuals and many other organizations.

All organizations operate under financial constraints, of course, but nonprofits always seem to be closer to the margin than businesses and public sector agencies. Service needs and aspirations always seem to far outpace their shoestring budgets. Frequently, there is considerable uncertainty about where needed funds will come from or whether they'll arrive on time. This uncertainty about financing has increased recently as governments at all levels trim back their social services budgets. This puts an even larger burden on nonprofit leaders to be resourceful, innovative, and cooperative.

All organizations face changes and challenges from forces outside their control, but many nonprofit organizations seem to be peculiarly sensitive to change. To test this thesis, pick any nonprofit corporation and, looking at Table 1.1, identify the changes in the outside world that directly affect an essential aspect of that organization and then place a check in each appropriate box. To illustrate, if you were thinking about changes of importance to BRIDGE Housing, the demographic changes would include an increase in poor elderly couples, single mothers, and latchkey kids; the technological trends would include new building materials and designs; the economic developments would include more people working from their homes and wage pressure from global competition; the political trends would include government support for low-income housing; and so on. Nearly all of these trends have profound implications for the clients, staff, and operations of BRIDGE Housing and the organization's ability to supply housing to needy families.

Table 1.1. The Effects of Change on Nonprofit Organizations.

Major trends	Effects on Clients	Effects on Staff	Effects on Operations	Social Impact
Demographic changes				
Technological developments				
Economic forces				
Social values				
Political changes Federal State and local				
Philanthropic sector				
Private sector				
Community developments				

For all these reasons, then, nonprofit leadership has its own distinctive flavor. In a recent survey we asked a small sample of nonprofit leaders what issues actually commanded most of their time and attention. The results are shown in Exhibit 1.2.

Exhibit 1.2. Issues of Concern to Nonprofit Leaders.

1. Increasing the number of donors, increasing the size of endowments and the funds available for annual operations, or managing these assets while still maintaining a high level of service.

2. Positioning the organization, setting its direction, and developing a strategy to achieve the greatest long-term effectiveness, including choosing the "right" community needs to address.

3. Measuring effectiveness, especially the tangible long-term benefits to the community of the organization's activities.

4. Establishing an appropriate board of directors—one that encompasses the community's diversity and needs—and employing board members effectively to achieve the organization's mission.

5. Forming alliances and coalitions with other organizations and constituencies in the public, private, and nonprofit sectors and managing the resulting shared responsibilities.

6. Providing active community leadership in building consensus, addressing social problems, and promoting philanthropy and volunteerism.

7. Hiring, developing, and motivating effective leaders, managers, and professional staff.

8. Raising the program quality or improving the level of leadership, management, and community impact of programs.

9. Designing or ensuring the proper internal infrastructure—that is, effective organizations and processes, including the proper use of information technology—to ensure the cost effectiveness of operations.

10. Maintaining excellent relations with important outside constituencies—including relations with potential donors, the media, local governments, and so on—to ensure visibility and a favorable climate of public opinion.

11. Adapting to frequent changes in the tax law, community needs and expectations, and other social, political, and economic factors.

It is clear from this list that the nonprofit leader must be able to

- Reconcile the conflicting demands of clients, public and private sector partners, donors, volunteers, and others and align their energies in pursuit of socially useful services.

- Inspire trust, confidence, and optimism among those who care about a social issue and are willing to volunteer time or money to help address it.

- Ensure that the organization is financially sound, ethically above reproach, and fully accountable to the community it serves.

- Position the organization for the future in the face of the severe challenges of limited resources and frequent changes in the external environment; accomplish this through flexibility, innovative strategies, and rapid adaptation to threats and opportunities.

- Develop leaders on the board, in other parts of the organization, among the volunteers, and in the community to carry on the work of the organization.

Roles of Nonprofit Leaders

When Don Terner was asked what he'd be willing to do to improve the stock of affordable housing in San Francisco, his response was always the same—"whatever it takes." That's how the best leaders think, and surely there is much improvisation and experimentation in the way any true leader approaches a challenging social goal. However, if you probe deeply enough, you'll find a pattern and a logic to what they do. We have found a particular model useful in understanding the roles leaders play in nonprofit organizations, and why these roles are so essential (Nanus, 1992, p. 12).

Let's start with the notion that a leader's attention may at any time be focused in one or more of the following four directions:

1. *Inside* the organization, where the leader interacts with the board, staff, and volunteers to inspire, encourage, enthuse, and empower them.

2. *Outside* the organization, where the leader seeks assistance or support from donors, grantmakers, potential allies, the media, or other leaders in the business or public sectors.

3. On *present* operations, where the leader is concerned about the quality of services to clients and the community and also organizational structures, information systems, and other aspects of organizational effectiveness.

4. On *future* possibilities, where the leader anticipates trends and developments that are likely to have important implications for the future direction of the organization.

Great leaders of nonprofit organizations routinely look in all four directions and could hardly afford to do otherwise. When these directions are plotted on a single graph, as shown in Figure 1.1, six distinct roles of leadership are suggested.

Roles 1 and 2: leader as visionary and strategist. Because the leader is the person responsible for moving the organization in the right direction, the role of the leader as direction setter is crucial. Working with others in the organization, the leader scans the realm of future possibilities in the outside world, seeking clues to a more desirable destination for the organization. The leader points the way to a new tomorrow by clearly stating a vision, preferably one so compelling that others will be inspired to follow. Great leaders have great visions, and great visions, when they are widely shared, are the principal engines of organizational growth and progress. Chapter Four will show how leaders develop such a vision. Chapter Five

Figure 1.1. Roles of Nonprofit Leaders.

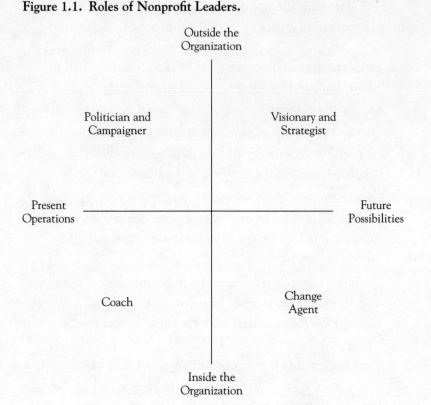

then discusses how leaders design the proper strategy for achieving the vision and mission.

Roles 3 and 4: leader as politician and campaigner. Politicians (in the best sense of the word) are spokespersons, advocates, and negotiators for the benefit of their constituents. They are passionate about the purposes of the organization and constantly speak out about it. Charles de Gaulle explained it best when he said, "I spoke. I had to. It is action that puts fervor to work. But it is words that create it." An effective leader is a super networker, a builder of relationships whose purpose ultimately is to provide useful resources, information, and support back to the organization or to the important constituencies it serves. This is explored in Chapter Eight. In addition, effective leaders, like politicians, are proficient campaigners, but in this case the campaign is directed at securing financial resources, not votes. Chapter Nine shows how the most successful nonprofit leaders are also superb fundraisers and campaigners for economic support.

Role 5: leader as coach. Leaders are inherently team builders. They create and nurture a family of people who share a similar passion and sense of responsibility for addressing social concerns. They build trust, which is the cement that holds an organization together. They create hope and confidence. They set the tone of the organization. They are cheerleaders, empowering and inspiring individuals and helping them learn, grow, and realize their full human potential as they serve the organization's clients and the community. Chapter Seven shows how nonprofit leaders accomplish these tasks.

Role 6: leader as change agent. Leaders position the organization for the future. They make critical choices or influence the decisions of others about which services are most needed and which target client groups should get the most attention. Often this involves introducing a new program or creating strategic alliances with public or private sector partners. Sometimes it involves restructuring the organization or reconfiguring some aspect of service delivery. Occasionally, it involves major entrepreneurship and innovation, when nothing less than a transformation in the nature of the organization is needed. This change agent role is discussed more fully in Chapter Six.

Many books on leadership are devoted to the relationship between leaders and followers, which we have labeled the coaching role. Others concentrate entirely on the management of change, as if that were all the leader needed to do to be successful. These are important, of course, but we have found that leaders cannot be effective in nonprofit organizations unless they master *all* six of these roles—as visionary, strategist, politician, campaigner, coach, and change agent—and that's why we've devoted an entire chapter to each of them.

Of course, at any given time one or another of these roles may be dominant. Think again about Don Terner at BRIDGE Housing. At first, having just received an anonymous grant, he spent most of his time as a visionary, developing BRIDGE Housing's sense of direction and strategy with his new board of directors and forming the organization. At the time when he was putting together the big investment pool for low-income housing with banks and public employee pension funds, his major roles were as politician and change agent. At still other times, he concentrated on hiring, inspiring, and coaching his new staff. However, even when one or another role occupied most of his attention, he could ill afford to totally ignore any of the others. Don Terner knew this and was a superb practitioner of all six leadership roles.

These diverse leadership roles are what make it possible for nonprofit organizations to succeed despite the distinctive challenges facing them that we discussed earlier. Volunteers and others not on the payroll can be led without major financial incentives because their leaders are not pushing, directing, or prodding them, as they might try to do in many firms and bureaucracies. Instead, as coaches, their leaders are seeking to inspire, encourage, energize, and focus their passion and social concerns in the most productive ways. Even board members, with all their experience and stature, are willing to be led in this fashion—not as docile sheep but as active team players helping the organization succeed.

For nonprofits that are habitually underfunded, the leader as politician and campaigner can form networks of mutual support, thereby tapping the collective resources of others in the private and public sectors. The complexity that comes from dealing with multiple constituencies and organizations with overlapping interests is made more manageable by leaders who can explain what the organization stands for, what it is trying to accomplish, and where it is headed.

Finally, leaders help the organization face uncertainty in the outside world by developing a clear vision and strategy, thereby removing at least the uncertainty about the organization's intentions and priorities. Leaders deal with turbulence by anticipating change and acting as change agent to position the organization to benefit from it if at all possible or adapt to it when necessary.

Leaders like Don Terner excel at all those roles. But what can we say about the personal qualities needed by nonprofit leaders to be successful in assuming these roles?

The Qualities of Successful Leaders

In our experience, successful nonprofit leaders come in all shapes and sizes, from every ethnic group and both genders. Many of them are articulate, assertive, well groomed, systematic, and courageous, but we've known others who had fewer of these qualities and still succeeded.

For decades researchers have been trying to understand what qualities contribute most to leadership effectiveness. After an exhaustive review of dozens of studies conducted among business leaders over a period of several decades, one scholar concluded that relevant personality traits for leaders were a high energy level, an ability to tolerate stress, self-confidence and self-control, emotional maturity, and integrity (Yukl, 1994, p. 280).

John Gardner (1990, pp. 48–53) also reviewed the literature and came up with a longer list of desired attributes—physical vitality and stamina; intelligence and judgment in action; willingness to accept responsibilities; task competence; understanding of followers and constituents and their needs; skill in dealing with people; need to achieve; capacity to motivate; courage, resolution, and steadiness; capacity to win and hold trust; confidence; ascendance, dominance, and assertiveness; and adaptability or flexibility of approach.

Others have longer or shorter lists. Our experience doesn't contradict any of these conclusions, but we find one study of leadership characteristics particularly helpful when thinking about leaders in the nonprofit sector. In a series of surveys begun in the early 1980s, Kouzes and Posner (1993, p. 12) asked fifteen thousand executives to select from a list of twenty qualities those that they most admired in a leader or expected in someone whose direction they would willingly follow. The twenty qualities had been distilled from four hundred interviews and an earlier study sponsored by the American Management Association of 1,500 managers who had identified some 225 characteristics they felt were relevant to successful leadership.

The results were remarkably consistent. Four characteristics always topped the list—being honest, forward looking, inspiring, and competent. These qualities handily beat out such other intuitively appealing leadership characteristics as intelligence, caring, loyalty, determination, dependability, and maturity. We think these results are especially compelling in the case of nonprofit leaders, for the following reasons:

Being honest. Unless leaders are trusted and believed, they will not be followed or supported. Nonprofit organizations depend heavily on gifts of time and money from volunteers, board members, and other donors, gifts that would quickly disappear if the leader were not completely trustworthy. So much depends upon the leader's integrity that even a hint of unethical behavior severely damages the organization, as United Way and others have learned to their great sorrow.

Moreover, many nonprofit organizations are themselves an institutionalized form of public trust. They may be entrusted with the care of children or helpless invalids, with the protection of valuable cultural treasures like great art objects, with the preservation of historical buildings or the survival of endangered species. Their work affects human lives in countless ways. They must earn their trust every day, with scrupulously honest behavior, or suffer the greatest public humiliation and condemnation. The media are ever on the alert for signs of shady dealings precisely because nonprofit leaders are expected to be role models of ethical behavior and the slightest deviation is newsworthy. Honesty is not simply the best policy for nonprofit leaders, it is the only policy, or they will no longer be leaders.

Being forward looking. People work for nonprofits or donate money because they hope that by doing so they can improve themselves, their communities, or society in important ways. Their passion and idealism is intrinsically tied to a notion of a better future. That's why they seek leaders who are forward looking, who can show them the way to a brighter tomorrow. That's why nonprofit leaders need to seek and accept responsibility for the organization's future. And that's why their roles as visionaries and change agents are so crucial to their effectiveness as leaders. As George Bernard Shaw said, we become wise not by remembering the past but by taking responsibility for the future.

Being inspiring. People in nonprofit organizations want to make a difference in their community. They want to be where the action is. They're attracted to a leader like Don Terner who displays a passion for the possibilities of his organization, who sets a good example, and who can inspire others with his enthusiasm and sense of optimism. As Ralph Waldo Emerson said, "Not he is great who can alter matter, but he who can alter my state of mind." People respond well to a leader who appeals to their better nature, inspiring them to do good works in the service of others. That's why they're willing to volunteer their time and donate their money. Perhaps nowhere is this more evident than in the many examples of great religious leaders who have had the ability to inspire their followers to exceptional acts of charity, devotion, and even self-sacrifice in service to humanity.

Being competent. People in nonprofit organizations expect their leaders to be effective, to get things done. They're impressed when a leader shows skill at fundraising or displays an ability to reach out to the public and business sectors to form powerful new partnerships. They'll follow someone they think can make them more effective or from whom they think they can learn and grow. Good leaders know their own strengths and weaknesses and are perpetual learners. People will follow leaders who show self-confidence and take the initiative, trying always to shape events and not merely react to them. Competent leaders attract volunteers and contributions, and they attract other leaders to their cause.

Our experience confirms the Kouzes and Posner studies in that we believe these four qualities—being honest, forward looking, inspiring, and competent—are the characteristics most likely to be found among successful nonprofit leaders. Other qualities frequently mentioned in the leadership literature are drive, determination, persistence, creativity, flexibility, charisma, decisiveness, and inclusiveness. We don't doubt that these are all useful in some situations, as are the ones identified in Yukl's and Gardner's studies, mentioned earlier, but the four qualities identified by Kouzes and Posner seem to be the most compelling in the context of leading nonprofit organizations.

Earning the Right to Lead

How does one learn to lead a nonprofit organization? Obviously, no one is born knowing how to do it. Some parents may be good role models, but that doesn't guarantee that their children will inherit their leadership qualities or skills or even that they'll want to do so. Moreover, unlike most professions, nonprofit leadership offers no clear educational path for men and women to gain the necessary qualifications.

Nor do leaders seem to have any common base of experience. To illustrate, here are the professional backgrounds of a few of the successful leaders of large and small nonprofit organizations that we've encountered over the past decade—Navy admiral, priest, housewife, former cabinet official, businessman, publicist, pilot, professor, rheumatologist, radio announcer, computer scientist, diplomat, attorney, nurse, high school teacher, and engineer. In none of these cases did the person set out deliberately to be the leader of a nonprofit organization.

So without formal education in leadership or a common experience base, where do nonprofit leaders come from? Like all leaders, they develop themselves. They're self-taught. Read the autobiographies of famous leaders like U.S. presidents, business tycoons, popes, and military commanders, and you'll find the same pattern repeated over and over again. Effective leaders pulled themselves up by their proverbial bootstraps. They actively sought leadership responsibilities. They paid their dues and earned the right to lead.

It's the same with nonprofit leaders, with one vital addition. The most successful nonprofit leaders, like Donald Terner, are motivated by a driving passion for some cause. Often they describe this consuming desire as the very purpose of their lives. Many of them would strongly identify with the simple words of the poem "What I Live For," penned over a hundred years ago by George Linnaeus Banks:

> For the cause that lacks assistance,
> For the wrong that needs resistance,
> For the future in the distance,
> And the good that I can do.

Some leaders find their passion in helping others who are victims of disease, poverty, or an array of other afflictions. Others view themselves as victims—of crime, congestion, pollution, a decline in societal values, a spiritual void, and so forth—and their efforts to lead nonprofit organizations that deal with these problems are a way of changing their own self-image from one of victim and complainer to one of community activist.

Thus driven they form a nonprofit organization or aspire to lead one because they truly believe that by doing so they'll be able to make a real difference. They see their leadership not as an end in itself but as a means to an end—that is, changing the world in some socially significant way.

Nonprofit leadership is available to any honest person with reasonable intelligence and drive, but there's a lot to learn. Some important lessons will be covered in this book, but there is much more that can be learned only through a variety of firsthand experiences. It may take years of hard work, and if the leaders we've met are representative, those who aspire to such positions will have to be prepared for many setbacks along the way. In fact, that's one of the key ways they learn.

Apart from learning from books and experiences, leaders learn by self-reflection, as they assess their own strengths and weaknesses to determine what works for them and what doesn't. They also learn from mentors, starting with their parents and friends and later progressing to respected teachers, coaches, and finally the role modeling of other successful leaders. Most of all, they learn by personal experimentation, often putting themselves in challenging situations that require tenacity, courage, and personal growth.

In fact leaders seem to be learning about leadership all their lives, often starting at a very young age. But even after they've learned all they can and mastered all the necessary skills, they still have to prove themselves on the job. They have to demonstrate that they deserve to be leaders, that people will follow them, and especially that they can get results. That's the ultimate test and the subject to which we now turn. What are the results that matter in judging the success of nonprofit organizations and their leaders?

2

The Greater Good

*A good thing which prevents us from enjoying a
greater good is in truth an evil.*

Baruch Spinoza

John van Hengel, like many of his friends and neighbors in
Phoenix, Arizona, in the mid-1960s, would occasionally volunteer to feed homeless people in a soup kitchen at St. Mary's Mission. In those days, soup kitchens were supported by small charitable contributions of food and money. As often as not the donations fell short of the real needs in the community. Sometimes van Hengel would take other volunteers out to local citrus orchards to pick fruit left on the trees after the regular harvest. When there was more fruit than St. Mary's Mission could use, he'd drive his car around to other soup kitchens in the area to share the surplus.

One day in 1967, van Hengel met a woman who told him she was able to feed her ten children most days just by going through the food discarded by her local supermarket. She said she thought of it as her bank, prompting van Hengel to conceive the idea of a *food bank*. He convinced the Franciscans of St. Mary's Church to let him use an abandoned bakery they had received in a will as a warehouse. He asked grocers in the area to drop off their damaged but still edible products—day-old bread, overripe produce, damaged packaged goods, and the like—instead of sending them to the city dump. Then he notified charities all over Phoenix that they could pick up free food at St. Mary's Food Bank, the first such bank in the country.

The idea had an immediate impact. Over 250,000 pounds of food were distributed to thirty-six charities in that first year. The word spread to other communities. Groups started visiting van Hengel's facilities for advice and assistance in starting their own food banks. In 1976, he received a $50,000 federal grant to assist in developing food banks elsewhere in the nation. He began to approach national food manufacturers, asking them to contribute food products that they'd otherwise discard, and receive tax benefits in return. In 1979, Second Harvest was incorporated to become the clearinghouse for large donations, with John van Hengel as its first director. In that year, Second Harvest distributed 2.5 million pounds of food to local agencies and food banks.

John van Hengel retired from Second Harvest in 1983, but the program continued to thrive under new leadership. By the mid-1980s, most cities had food banks. Second Harvest then shifted its attention to improving its efficiency and professionalism and to finding new sources of food for distribution to the needy. For example, after Operation Desert Storm in Iraq, it persuaded the military to donate over $300 million of surplus rations to the organization.

Today Second Harvest supplies nearly two hundred food banks across the nation, through which some fifty thousand local nonprofit organizations provide food for the needy. It distributes over a billion pounds of free food a year and feeds some twenty-six million people annually, including eleven million children. It is so efficient in locating and distributing free food that it is able to promise cash donors that for each dollar they contribute over $50 worth of free food will go to the needy.

The story of Second Harvest is a remarkable one, because of both the exceptional leadership it enjoyed at a pivotal time in its history and its outstanding accomplishments. Note that at the very beginning, St. Mary's soup kitchen was already providing a valuable social good in Phoenix. It was efficiently feeding the poorest, most vulnerable people in the community. It could easily have continued to serve its constituencies in the same fashion, perhaps with minor expansions in its services, just as other soup kitchens across the nation were doing. But John van Hengel saw a way to move the organization to a much higher level—that is, to provide a far greater good—by collecting large amounts of food from businesses and expanding the feeding program first to thousands and then to millions of deprived people all over the nation. And that made all the difference!

Not every nonprofit organization has the potential to completely transform its field as Second Harvest did. However, there's always the possibility of providing a greater good, which we define as moving the organization a few steps up to a new higher level of excellence, service, and benefit for society.

This greater good can be achieved in many ways. For example, it might involve expanding the service area, forming a new public-private partnership, finding and servicing an unaddressed social need, or renewing an otherwise lethargic and dispirited organization.

Raising the bar significantly on performance is never easy. Reaching for the greater good creates new challenges and risks for everyone attempting it. There will always be skeptics who will argue that the organization is already doing the best it can with its limited resources. That's why leadership is so crucial. Indeed, a major premise of this book is that *the primary mission of leadership in nonprofit organizations is to focus laserlike attention throughout the organization on the greater good that it is capable of providing and then to marshal the energy and resources to make that greater good happen.*

The remainder of this book will show what leadership skills and practical tools are needed to accomplish this mission. But first, to clarify what we mean by the greater good, we reexamine the evolving role of the nonprofit organization in the twenty-first century and introduce some measures that leaders can use to assess their progress.

The Societal Context of Nonprofit Organizations

At its most basic level every nation consists of three overlapping sectors—economic, political, and social. These three spheres coexist in a common environment that supports them all, as shown in Figure 2.1. Each sector has its own activities and responsibilities but also works in close partnership with the other two sectors where they have common interests. Also, each sector has its characteristic institutions that are designed for specific purposes and, once in place, act to constrain and direct human activity. Nonprofit organizations are largely a part of the social sector of the nation, where

Figure 2.1. The Three Main Sectors of Society.

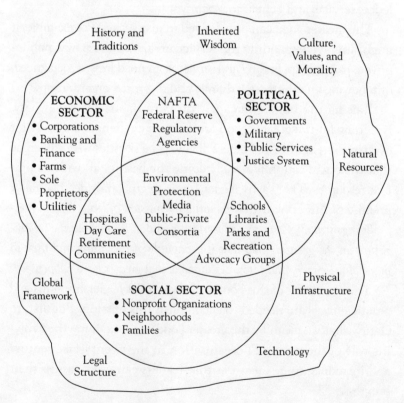

they act to improve the lives of individuals, families, neighborhoods, and communities.

In an ideal world all citizens would recognize that they receive enormous benefits from each sector and, just as important, have major obligations and responsibilities to each. The economic benefit of earning a living, for example, implies an obligation to serve all legitimate employer interests while doing so. The political benefit of protection from harm triggers a reciprocal responsibility to support police and firefighters and to serve on juries. And the social benefits of living in a community carry with them the obligation to help strengthen the institutions that support the community, many of which are nonprofit organizations.

Yet we all know that Americans feel their economic obligations most strongly and their social obligations much less. Why is this so? In an ideal world these three sectors would be well balanced, but recently, the economic sector has come to dominate the other two. To many people this is only as it should be. They point out that the economic sector has been responsible for the greatest human progress in the past century. Undeniably, the robust economy resulting from the industrial and information revolutions has led to massive improvements in the quality of life for the average family. The result has been not just greater financial security but also great strides in public health, literacy, and the general welfare.

However, as the twenty-first century begins some are beginning to fear that the economic sector has become too dominant in American lives. Consider some of its less appealing effects on the other two sectors:

Political effects. Governments are losing the power to assist their own citizens as corporations determine where jobs are located and which resources will be exploited, determine how citizens are educated and health care is administered, and through their lobbying and campaign contributions, even determine who shall have political power and what laws they may pass.

Furthermore, by cultivating a culture of excessive individualism and self-indulgence, the economic sector may subtly undermine democratic institutions. The more alone we are, the more powerless we feel, because a large, complex world can be changed only by collective action. Yet unions are far weaker than they once were, and political parties, which should be the vehicle for collective action, have become little more than money machines and poll takers. Fewer citizens each year even bother to vote.

Social effects. The toll levied by the economic sector on the social sector may be even worse. Although unparalleled in its ability to create wealth, the market economy creates losers as well as winners. The economic sector rewards its winners well but takes little or no responsibility for the losers—that is, those unable to compete in the global marketplace because they are unskilled, too old or too young, handicapped, unintelligent, sick, undereducated, or simply unlucky enough to be displaced by technology advances, mergers, or the movement of jobs overseas. Homeless people, alcoholics, child abusers, muggers, unwed mothers, and gangs in the inner city may all be reflections of the same phenomenon—economic losers reacting to their frustrating and seemingly hopeless personal prospects.

An overwhelmingly dominant economic sector creates other social problems as well. With both parents having to earn a living, millions of children are being given insufficient attention, and family life has become stressful for both them and their parents. Frequent plant closings and layoffs put family incomes at risk and cause neighborhoods to self-destruct. According to some critics the economic sector also undermines community values and culture through advertising and entertainment that stresses materialism, greed, promiscuity, the use of violence, the taking of drugs, and other socially harmful values.

These are not minor problems nor are they easily dismissed. If left unattended they will not only detract from the quality of life of

U.S. citizens but may ultimately destroy the very economic engine that produced them. Thus it is not surprising that there is a growing recognition that a U.S. system so substantially dominated by its economic sector is seriously out of balance.

More people are realizing this every day. Many are finding they can fill their homes with fine products and take expensive vacations and yet still experience a sense of rootlessness, a poverty of relationships, and a spiritual void. They are making individual accommodations to the all-powerful economic machine. They refuse business travel, leave the office early, work out of their homes, or use flextime to spend more time with their families and become more active in their communities.

Thus, as the twenty-first century begins, we are starting to see the first, still-faint signals of a significant social movement to rebalance the system. Though it is not generally recognized, a very real sense of duty to family and community, so central to human existence until just a few centuries ago, is being rekindled in the United States. According to INDEPENDENT SECTOR, a nationwide coalition of over eight hundred volunteer organizations, from 1977 to 1994, the growth in the nonprofit sector was 3.7 percent per year, substantially faster than the 2.1 percent annual growth in the business sector and 2.3 percent in government. In 1993 alone, an estimated 89.2 million Americans, or 47.7 percent of the adults eighteen years of age and older, volunteered an average of 4.2 hours per week, donating a total of some 19.5 billion hours (Hodgkinson and others, 1996, p. 69).

These figures suggest a large and growing commitment to the social sector. Millions of ordinary citizens are spending more time with their families and donating more of their time and treasure to strengthening community institutions. In the process they are reshaping their communities and leaving an important legacy for their children and the nation. And nonprofit organizations are in the vanguard of this movement.

The Role of Nonprofit Organizations

Nonprofit organizations are the primary instrumentality of the social sector—the characteristic organization where resources and purposeful activities are concentrated—just as businesses are the primary instrumentality of the economic sector and government agencies are at the core of the political sector. In this light, nonprofits are far more than the common stereotype of charities whose purpose is to assuage the guilt of the rich by providing a meager lifeline for the needy. Instead, the abundant benefits that nonprofits provide have become indispensable to U.S. society, as in these examples:

- Nonprofits design and deliver an astonishing array of critical services, some involved with life-and-death decisions for individuals, others affecting the quality of life of entire communities. These services range from conserving the past and ensuring the health and continuity of the current population to helping society change and adapt to new circumstances. They encompass services to individuals as well as neighborhoods, communities, and the larger society. Figure 2.2 offers some more specific examples of this vast array of services.

- Everyone benefits from the social services of nonprofit organizations, not just the specific people who receive them. For example, the Boy Scouts, YMCAs, and sports leagues might help boys grow into responsible citizens, but in the process they also decrease the likelihood of crime and delinquency that plague us all. The lives of alcoholics, drug addicts, and drunk drivers might be salvaged by Alcoholics Anonymous, free clinics, and Mothers Against Drunk Driving but so are the lives that these unfortunates would have threatened if they were left on the streets.

- In the absence of nonprofit organizations, social needs would grow, producing stresses that could overwhelm all three sectors if left untended. The alternative would be a much larger govern-

Figure 2.2. Examples of Nonprofit Organizations.

Serving the
Individual

Concert and   Food   Alcoholics
Ballet Groups   Kitchens   Anonymous

Homeless
Shelters   Free
Clinics

Day Care   Schools
Centers
YMCA

Churches and   Halfway
Synagogues   Houses   Girl Scouts

Preservation   **Social**
and Continuity   ACLU   **Change**
Second
Red   Harvest
Cross
MADD
Sierra
Club
Children's
Museums   Defense Fund

Worldwatch   United
Institute   Way
NAACP
Smithsonian   **Serving the**
Community

ment sector or a form of welfare state capitalism that stifles the private sector, as has been the case in many other countries lacking a viable nonprofit tradition. Either way, the costs to manage social issues would be much higher than those incurred by nonprofits supported by volunteers and charitable contributions. Just think, for example, of how expensive it would be to get a billion pounds of food to hungry people each year if Second Harvest weren't there to do it.

• All the people who work in the economic and political sectors are brought up in families and communities, places in which a variety of nonprofits are active in developing the *human resources* upon which those other sectors completely depend for their viability.

Churches and synagogues help instill morality and trust in young people. Scouting organizations and Little Leagues help develop physical skills, teamwork, and a sense of responsibility. Museums provide historical and cultural perspective. Community hospitals and nonprofit clinics help maintain the health of children. When the private sector hires a worker, it gets not just a set of physical and intellectual skills but a whole person with a variety of experiences and capable of self-control, initiative, cooperation, judgment, communication, and many other qualities that have often been developed through the person's active participation in one or more nonprofit organizations.

• Nonprofits contribute directly to civic culture and community building and can be powerful partners in the entire civic enterprise. They often serve a vital purpose in brokering agreements with the other two sectors to solve societal problems, as in the case of environmental protection (consider, for example, the work of the Nature Conservancy), low-income housing (consider Habitat for Humanity), and emergency services (consider the Red Cross). These special public-private-nonprofit arrangements frequently can accomplish what no single sector or institution can do on its own.

• Nonprofits are often better positioned than the other sectors to experiment and create new models for service delivery, leading those other sectors into important new areas of national transformation. They marshal common action for the common good, serving as the nexus for political action in such areas as public health, environmental protection, civil rights, and family issues. Some nonprofits are *think tanks*, like the Brookings Institution and the Worldwatch Institute, which analyze trends and sound alerts to spur the other sectors to action. Others, like the Ford and Rockefeller Foundations, in addition to directly funding human services, also conduct innovative experiments and demonstration projects that when successful, are adopted and extended by governments and businesses. In this sense, nonprofits are important laboratories and incubators for social change.

- Nonprofits serve as a major counterbalance to excessive individualism and materialism in society. They allow people to express the best that is in them, to give something back to their community, and to do good works that help others. In the process of doing so, people develop leadership skills and a sense of self-esteem. Indeed, nonprofits have historically empowered millions of citizens who would otherwise have led modest or invisible lives, such as the janitor who serves as a deacon of his church, the housewife who heads the local Parent Teacher Association, the coal miner who leads a Boy Scout troop, and the bookkeeper who chairs the fundraising for her community hospital.

These are vital contributions that nonprofit organizations make to a healthy society, not luxuries or "mere" altruism. Although they employ millions of people, nonprofit organizations already have an influence on human life, as well as on the economy and the public sector, far out of proportion to their numbers.

With all these benefits, one would expect that nonprofit organizations would be widely admired for their contributions. Yet they certainly don't enjoy the attention, respect, and recognition accorded to corporations and government agencies in our culture. A typical daily newspaper, for example, is crammed full of business and political developments, whereas nonprofit activities, if they appear at all, are in small clippings on the back pages. Business leaders and politicians are celebrities and role models, but few nonprofit leaders are well recognized. Most universities have a business school and many teach public administration, but only a handful have programs in nonprofit management.

Most nonprofit organizations toil on bravely despite this lack of attention. Still, it is a national disgrace that many worthy nonprofits are forced to operate from hand to mouth, often cast in the role of beggars jostling to seek alms from the affluent, whose attention is focused elsewhere. This situation is bound to change, especially as the quality of nonprofit leadership improves.

Nonprofit organizations are already an essential part of the nation's institutional infrastructure. They are destined to become much stronger contributors and more influential partners of corporations and government agencies in the future as their many contributions to the social good become more widely understood and highly valued.

What Are Social Goods?

The primary purpose of nonprofit organizations—their raison d'être—is to maximize the social goods they produce for both society and the people who participate in them. Social goods are the end, the fundamental purpose or mission, for which nonprofit organizations exist and the basis of their legitimacy. In this section we look more closely at this idea of social goods.

Nonprofit organizations exist to improve the lives of individuals and communities. All of us live in a variety of communities, some of which may be determined by family relationships, by neighborhood, by work, by a common faith or profession, or simply by mutual interests. Each community consists of many individuals working together to accomplish things that are good or useful but that no one of them can accomplish alone. In contemporary society these communities often overlap, and some may stretch over great distances, tied together by telephone, fax machines, and the Internet.

Social goods are the educational, health, cultural, and other benefits that accrue to society through the activities of these communities and their institutions, most of which are nonprofit organizations. This is a concept like friendship and love; it may be difficult to define, but it is easy to recognize. For example, there would likely be little disagreement that the following are social goods:

- Reduction of hunger, homelessness, and the worst effects of poverty
- Cures for dread diseases; health care for the indigent and handicapped; rehabilitation for the addicted, abused, and neglected

- Increased hope for the future, especially through attention to the needs of children

- Full flowering of human potential in arts, crafts, sports, and culture

- Decreased social tensions from racism and delinquency

- Preservation of the commons—air, water, parklands, natural environments, cultural traditions, great works of art, music, and dance

- Promotion of civic virtues, including mutual respect, generosity, neighborhood beautification, and cooperation in times of emergency

All these social goods and many more determine the quality of life for the larger society of which we are all a part. Furthermore, it is through our individual participation in various communities that most of us are able to find meaning in our own lives. As we act out our various roles and participate in community life, especially in nonprofit institutions, we learn what is worth doing and what we have passion for. We find out what we're good at and what further skills we need to develop. We discover what relationships matter to us and what contributions we can make to them. We learn who we are, what we want to do, and how we should invest our own lives to make a difference.

That's the ultimate social good produced in communities—millions of independent citizens self-actualizing and expressing their humanity while contributing to the greater good of their communities and the larger society of which they are a part.

And that is why the end to which nonprofit organizations are directed is the maximization of the social goods they produce for both society and the people who participate in them. It follows, then, that *contribution to the social good is the single most important measure of success of nonprofit organizations*.

Beyond social goods, however, there are two other measures that also are important, and they are the principal means by which social goods are achieved—namely, building organizational capital and generating social energy.

Organizational Capital

In discussions of economic matters the term *capital* is used to mean the physical and financial assets that can be put to work to produce goods and services. The term *human capital* refers to the knowledge, skills, and other assets that workers bring to a productive enterprise. Recently, the term *intellectual capital* has been used to describe the patents and copyrights, software, trade secrets, and other properties that may be hard to measure in an accounting sense but that also constitute valuable assets that can be turned to productive use.

Notice that in all these cases, the word capital means organizational assets that have productive potential. Nonprofit organizations need an analogous term—*organizational capital*—to describe assets that embody the potential for producing social goods. Organizational capital resides in the institutions around which communities coalesce, especially the nonprofit organizations responsible for so many of the social goods. Some of the forms organizational capital takes in nonprofit organizations are the following:

- Experienced and competent management, leadership, and staff

- Trained volunteers and loyal donors ready, able, and committed to supporting nonprofit efforts

- Well-staffed facilities (for example, halfway houses, runaway shelters, churches and synagogues, theaters, clinics) for the delivery of social goods

- Repositories of supplies and equipment (for example, food banks, blood banks, stores of medicines or clothing) that can be dispensed to needy individuals

- Organizational structures, information systems, and networks of like-minded individuals and nonprofits

- Special collections (for example, in museums, libraries, and data banks)

- Favorable organizational images or reputations that engender trust and attract volunteers in the community

Thus, in addition to the quantity and quality of social goods they deliver, nonprofit organizations can be measured by the extent to which they increase the stock and improve the quality of organizational capital in the community.

Social Energy

Social energy is the energy that is generated when a nonprofit organization marshals common action for the common good. Some of this social energy is generated inside the organization itself, and some of it is generated in the outside world.

Internally, nonprofit organizations are powered by the energies of professional staffs and volunteers working together to improve their communities. Some nonprofit organizations are among the most exciting places to work in the United States. They are filled with idealistic, high-minded individuals who care deeply about helping others. When their enthusiasm is amplified and channeled into productive directions by effective leaders, these individuals are capable of extraordinary achievements—changing lives, helping people realize their full potential, creating hope where none existed before. One need only observe a local Red Cross chapter responding to an emergency or a community theater group in rehearsal to see this type of social energy in action.

Externally, nonprofit organizations create social energy when they challenge other institutions in the public and private sectors to be more and do more to address social concerns. For example, the main purpose of Second Harvest is providing food for the needy, but by its very actions it also calls public attention to the issue of hunger in America. Its success can be measured not just in the tons of food it delivers each year to the needy but in the grassroots support it engenders for government assistance to reduce poverty.

Often nonprofit organizations serve as collection points for citizen's passions (a pure form of social energy) about issues of social injustice or widespread concerns that the nation is moving in the wrong direction. For example, think about the passions that animated the civil rights marchers under the leadership of Martin Luther King Jr. and the social goods that followed: desegregation in the south, greater access for minorities to college education, and improved job opportunities.

The public sector usually follows the social sector, addressing problems only after a substantial constituency has been mobilized for their solution by nonprofit organizations. Such a constituency may be triggered by a major exposé (for example, *Silent Spring*, by Rachel Carson, or *Unsafe at Any Speed*, by Ralph Nader) or by a few passionate individuals, but it is unlikely to rise to significance as a social movement until a nonprofit organization is formed to organize the activists and protesters, set priorities and strategies, and promote the issue in the media.

In just this fashion, social energy has been the driving force that made possible nearly every major advance in U.S. society—for example, the American Revolution itself, the freeing of the slaves, women's right to vote, Social Security, food and drug regulation, and Medicare. It is the continuing force behind liberal causes such as the environmental movement and gun control and conservative causes like the antiabortion movement and school prayer. All this social energy is generated and deployed by nonprofit organizations—sometimes directly through social action, sometimes indirectly as a by-product of the community services provided.

How does social energy work? We think a strong analogy can be made to electrical energy. Electricity is generated in various ways and transmitted through circuitry that includes resistors, filters, amplifiers, and transformers until it reaches a place such as a television set or microwave oven where it can do useful work. Similarly, social energy is generated in a nonprofit organization and flows through networks of human relationships, during which time it too encounters resistance, filtering, amplification, and transformation, until finally it is applied in a place where it can produce a social good. Just as electrical circuits must be carefully designed and maintained if electricity is to be used efficiently and well, so must the network of human relationships be designed and maintained if social energy is to be effectively deployed.

Social energy gets generated in many different ways, of course. However, it generally flows from a strong, widely shared mandate backed up with a certain amount of organization and resources. Though this may seem a bit whimsical (and we make no claims for its mathematical accuracy), we like to think of the generation of social energy as being analogous to another familiar equation for energy: $E = mc^2$ where

E = social energy

m = strength of the mandate

c = organizational capital that is invested in addressing the mandate

In this formulation the strength of the mandate depends upon a widely shared perception of the need for a particular change in the social order and of the power of the proposed solution or strategy to accomplish the necessary change. The organizational capital that is invested in creating social energy may include a dedicated group of activists, financial resources, volunteers, or any of the other assets of nonprofit organizations that have been mentioned here. Squaring the term for organizational capital indicates that investing organizational capital has a self-amplifying effect. For example, when the Red Cross applies its human and financial resources to helping victims of natural disasters, its very use of those resources stimulates more volunteers and money to come forth to address the need.

So, although social goods are the main measure of success for nonprofit organizations, increasing organizational capital and developing social energy are the principal means for achieving social goods, and they can be measured as well. They are related to each other and to the leadership of a nonprofit organization as shown in Figure 2.3.

The actual measures that are used to determine success or progress in a nonprofit will vary with the particular organization, but some possible measures are suggested for several familiar types of organizations in Table 2.1. Because these are the key measures of success of nonprofit organizations, they also are important indica-

Figure 2.3. Assessing Nonprofit Success.

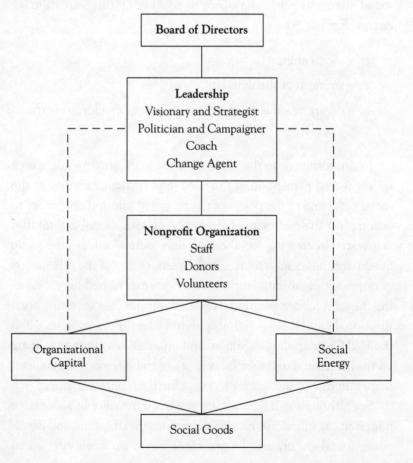

Table 2.1. Possible Measures of Success for Nonprofit Organizations.

	Social Goods (Producing)	Organizational Capital (Increasing)	Social Energy (Developing)
Second Harvest	Pounds of food delivered to the needy	Number of new corporations signed up to contribute food	Pressure on Congress for new laws to reduce hunger
Local Red Cross chapter	Number of disaster victims fed and sheltered	Units of blood stored in blood banks	Hours of volunteer help in disaster relief efforts
Church or synagogue	Number of children attending religious instruction	Number and quality of new programs	Number of volunteers for charitable activities
Museum of art	Attendance at regular and special exhibits	Number and quality of new acquisitions	Strength of arts outreach into local school system
Rape treatment center	Number of rape victims treated	Network of mental health professionals	Number of school programs on rape reports and prevention

tors of leadership success (see Chapter Ten). After all, the whole purpose of leadership in a nonprofit organization is to enhance its long-term effectiveness.

So now we can state more precisely what is meant by the term *leadership effectiveness*—it means producing a greater social good, usually by increasing organizational capital or creating and harnessing social energy. That's why Figure 2.3 illustrates organizational capital, social energy, and the social good feeding back to the leader. All the things that a leader does—setting direction, inspiring people, making organizational changes, and all the rest—are simply means to these ends.

The Emerging Character of Nonprofit Organizations

Nonprofit organizations have always played a role in the United States but especially so in the twentieth century. In just the recent past the number, size, and influence of nonprofit organizations have greatly increased. There are now over a million of them in the United States alone. According to INDEPENDENT SECTOR, nonprofit organizations spent about $570 million in 1994, and their ten million paid employees and five and a half million volunteers (calculated as full-time employee equivalents) represented about 10.6 percent of the total labor force (Hodgkinson and others, 1996, p. 4).

Nor is this strictly an American phenomenon. *The Economist* ("The Nonprofit Sector," 1998, p. 68) points out that in the Netherlands, Ireland, Israel, and Belgium, the percentage of the workforce employed in the nonprofit sector is now even larger than in the United States. In Britain, nonprofit employment grew by 30 percent from 1990 to 1995, much faster than the entire economy. There are also substantial nonprofit sectors in Australia, France, Germany, Spain, and other countries.

There are many changes on the horizon for nonprofit organizations. Recently, governments at all levels have systematically decreased budget expenditures for welfare programs. This has created enormous pressures on the other sectors. A heavier caseload is being thrown on nonprofit organizations for relieving poverty, job training, and providing basic necessities such as food, shelter, and health care for the needy.

In response nonprofits have had to become more efficient. Many have had to pool their efforts to find new sources of support and better ways to serve their clients. An increasing number of strategic alliances have strengthened some nonprofit organizations but have also blurred the boundaries between them and made them more complex to lead. Similarly, the boundaries between nonprofits and other sectors have become fuzzier due to overlapping interests and many public-private-nonprofit partnerships, such as those for job training and placement.

In another recent development a few highly publicized scandals, such as those involving the United Way and the New Era Foundation, have put the work of nonprofit organizations in a fishbowl (see Chapter Ten). They are now subject to much greater public scrutiny and accountability. Journalists like those at the *Philadelphia Inquirer* win Pulitzer Prizes for their exposés of questionable practices. In response board members have had to exercise a higher level of diligence over the affairs of nonprofits. Some nonprofit leaders have had to work hard to overcome a loss of public trust and have had to pay much more attention to effective community relations.

Heavier caseloads and public accountability have combined to push nonprofits to become more like for-profit corporations in their drive for efficiency and demonstrable performance. They strive for professionalization using many of the same management techniques as the private sector—strategic planning, marketing, financial analysis, public relations, computerized databases, and the like. In fact nonprofits are becoming so businesslike that a few business schools now offer degrees in nonprofit management, and special educational programs in this field are proliferating. Yet the differences between nonprofits and other organizations are profound, as discussed in Chapter One.

Meanwhile Americans are reassessing the entire role of the social sector in their lives. Thought leaders and influential books are examining the social fabric of the nation and finding serious issues. A noteworthy example is the so-called communitarian movement that has emerged in the last few years (Etzioni, 1993). The communitarian movement seeks to strengthen community institutions by emphasizing *we-ism* over *me-ism* in societal relationships—that is, the importance of collective social effort and the obligations of all citizens to assist in what we have called the development of social goods.

As we peer ahead, we see even more dramatic changes in store for nonprofit organizations:

- Information and communication technologies are dramatically reshaping education, health care, recreation, and most other activities and events through which people relate to each other in communities. This is likely to have profound impacts on what nonprofits do and on the way many of them deliver their services.

- A new generation of philanthropists, having accumulated vast wealth from high technology, finance, international trade, and other ventures, might soon be investing that wealth in their communities, supporting existing nonprofit organizations and spawning their own generation of new ones. For example, the financier George Soros has contributed millions of dollars to create a nonprofit organizational infrastructure in Europe.

- There is a growing uncertainty about whether certain social problems can be resolved at all. They may get worse before they get better, and perhaps the best the nation can hope for is to contain them and prevent certain situations from deteriorating too badly. How will the elderly be cared for when Social Security and Medicare funds are challenged by their increasing numbers? How will children grow up to compete in a sophisticated global economy when they start out with dysfunctional neighborhoods, weak family structures, inadequate school systems, and a witch's brew of other problems? Can the war against drugs be won?

In light of these changes and the uncertainty they engender, it is not surprising that the leaders of nonprofit organizations are experiencing a great deal of turbulence and confusion. Conflicting forces and pressures are pulling and pushing their organizations in every direction. They know that they can no longer get by with business as usual, and they are constantly being challenged to find new, more effective ways to deliver services. At the same time, they're well aware that the need for services is growing while the human and financial resources they need for performing those services are not keeping pace. And those who are most passionately committed to their causes believe in their hearts that the future viability of the nation may well depend on how well their clients and their communities are able to function in the twenty-first century.

That's reality . . . and as Lily Tomlin once pointed out, "Reality is a leading cause of stress for those who are in touch with it!"

These tough circumstances require nonprofits to have extraordinary leadership just to survive. Exceptional leaders are needed who will be able to find new sources of support, do more with less, and sustain hope among their staffs, volunteers, and client communities. That's a tall order and may portend a new kind of nonprofit leadership.

The Common Thrust of Nonprofit Leadership

Excellence in leadership is never easily attained, as is immediately obvious from the many books on leadership in the private and public sectors. It is especially difficult to achieve in the context of nonprofit organizations, where many of those who must be led (for example, volunteers, board members, and other community leaders) are not on the payroll of the leader's organization and where measures of success are often elusive and controversial. Yet, as John Gardner points out, "skill in the building and rebuilding of community is not just another of the innumerable requirements of contemporary leadership. It is one of the highest and most essential skills a leader can command" (1990, p. 112).

Without great improvements in leadership it is unlikely that nonprofit organizations will be able to meet the new challenges they face, and the cost of their failure could very well be measured in a lower quality of life for everyone. These challenges suggest the need for a new kind of nonprofit leader, who is able to achieve these goals:

- Build an organization that is responsive to present and emerging community needs, capable of delivering high-quality services, firmly integrated into its community, and highly innovative in its approach to both operations and outreach.

- Build and sustain mutually beneficial relationships, based on trust, integrity, and credibility, with a multiplicity of constituencies, including the staff, donors, volunteers, the client community, the board of directors, and the general public.

- Promote agreement on a shared vision, mission, and set of values that provide meaning to all the constituencies and guide the evolution of the organization.

- Design effective policies and strategies for change and ensure that the necessary changes are implemented in order to move the nonprofit organization in the desired direction.

- Ensure that the organization is an exciting and vital place to work so staff and volunteers can collaborate creatively and enthusiastically, perpetually growing, learning, and deepening their understanding of how to help their community.

- Develop and grow as leaders themselves, and support the development of others in order to expand the pool of potential and seasoned nonprofit leaders.

This may sound like a daunting challenge, and it is. But John van Hengel did it at Second Harvest, and there must be thousands and perhaps millions of potential John van Hengels in this nation. The lesson of Second Harvest and other nonprofit success stories is a simple one. Leaders of nonprofit organizations need to *build the organization* (that is, create organizational capital) *through strengthening relationships* (that is, generating and channeling social energy) *to make a real difference* (that is, produce social goods). The remaining chapters of this book elaborate on these themes and what leaders need to do to excel at them.

3

Getting Started as a Leader

*If you would have the kindness to begin at the begin-
ning, I should be vastly obliged; all these stories that
begin in the middle simply fog my wits.*
Count Anthony Hamilton (1646–1720)

B onnie Pitman, the new director of the thriving Bay Area Discovery Museum (BADM), a children's museum in Sausalito,
California, had large shoes to fill. The founding director of the
museum, Diane Frankel, had departed to accept a presidential
appointment as director of the Institute of Museum and Library Services. The museum, which opened its doors in 1987, had been very
successful under Frankel's leadership, attracting thousands of children and their parents each year with participatory exhibits and
hand-on experiences.

By the time Pitman came aboard, BADM was offering many
popular educational programs in art, media, and science, featuring
the San Francisco Bay Area and its shoreline. It had an impressive
board of directors and volunteer cadre. Funds had been raised for a
new museum location at a former military installation, Fort Baker,
nestled along the shoreline near the Golden Gate Bridge. The Bay
Area Discovery Museum was growing and its prospects were bright.

Even before accepting her new position, Bonnie Pitman was a
well-known museum leader herself, having served as deputy director

of the University of California Art Museum and as director of the Seattle Art Museum. She knew she needed to put her own imprimatur on BADM, building on Frankel's success and laying the foundation for her own vision and legacy.

Pitman quickly learned that her predecessor had developed and nurtured a large network of relationships in the local community, all supporting the museum in one way or another. Frankel had courted politicians because the BADM facility is on National Park Service land. She'd been in close touch with district superintendents and principals because school outreach was a critical part of BADM's rationale and a strong selling point to funders. She had also established strong ties with the environmental community and the media.

To retain and build upon these valuable contacts, Pitman immediately set out to meet the key players and learn about their expectations. One foundation funder reported that no sooner had he read about Bonnie Pitman's appointment than a call from the new CEO to set up a meeting was waiting for him. She wanted to send a message that past relationships would be continued and would be highly valued. She also knew that people are more likely to share their views when changes in leadership occur. They know that there might be changes in priorities, strategies, or practices, and they welcome the opportunity to give their input to a new director.

Pitman met at all hours of the day and night with staff, volunteers, funders, and community leaders. She introduced herself, shared her excitement and passion for the new assignment, and gathered valuable feedback. Her approach was typically along these lines: "I couldn't have asked for a better professional opportunity. I feel so fortunate to pick up where Diane Frankel left off. She gave me an incredible head start. I know that with your help we can build BADM into one of the leading children's museums in the country. This would be a good time to assess how we're doing and for you to let me know where you think we can be better. I'm ready to roll up my sleeves and address every challenge faced by our staff and board."

To establish her own credibility, Pitman kept careful track of what she committed herself to do in these early discussions and quickly acted on these commitments. She knew that follow-through was essential to developing trust. Besides, she received many good suggestions that influenced her initial thinking about such areas of museum policy as admissions, memberships, fundraising, and programs.

Pitman succeeded in maintaining the momentum at BADM. She mounted a successful capital campaign to finance additional program space, new exhibits, a café and training areas, and new programs. With support from the board and staff, she negotiated with the U.S. military to obtain additional surplus lands at Fort Baker for expansion. This eventually led to the restoration of ten historic buildings, dating from the early years of this century. As a result of all these efforts, during fiscal year 1997–98 almost 180,000 people visited the museum, and its outreach programs benefited thousands of students from hundreds of schools and community groups throughout the Bay Area.

Pitman was perceived by the search committee that hired her as having the right stuff to succeed her celebrated precursor. Her actions upon taking charge reassured the board that they had made the right choice in hiring her. The board's confidence and support then enabled her to lead the BADM to a new level of accomplishment.

Taking Stock

A person who rises to leadership in a nonprofit organization, or one who, like Bonnie Pitman, is hired from the outside, invariably finds himself in a strange position. Just before assuming office, he's a recognized expert in some area and a leader in his field. The day he assumes the new leadership position, he suddenly feels like a student again, with much to learn in a very short time.

The start of new leadership is a time of transition. It is a period of learning and orientation during which the incoming leader is indulged in his naive questions, allowed a few minor mistakes, and permitted to get grounded. If he inherits a mess or is faced with critical challenges early in his tenure, the honeymoon period may be disturbingly short. Ordinarily, however, a new leader has ample time to meet people and review the condition of the organization. As Bonnie Pitman demonstrated, if this time is well spent, a strong foundation can be built that will serve the leader well throughout his tenure.

The first task of any nonprofit leader is to deliberately take stock of his new position, finding out what exists, assessing the condition of the organization, and exploring what might be possible in the future. Specifically, he needs to evaluate the strengths and weaknesses of the organization in four distinct areas, as illustrated in Figure 3.1 and discussed further in the following paragraphs.

Figure 3.1. Taking Stock of a New Leadership Assignment.

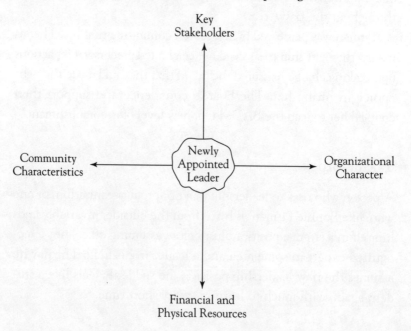

1. *Key stakeholders* include the members of the board of directors and its relevant committees, staff, volunteers, and important donors and supporters in the community. The leader needs to find out who these persons are, what they value about the organization, and how their needs and expectations are being met.

2. *Community characteristics* include the recipients of the organization's services, other public and private entities that serve similar clientele, and relevant trends in the community and the economy at the local, state, and federal levels. The new leader needs to understand who is being served, how well their needs are being met, and how the organization fits into the larger context of the community.

3. *Organizational character* includes the current structure of the organization, its culture and values, the strategies and policies that govern its operations, and the distinctive qualities of its services to clients and the community. The leader needs to find out how the organization works and how effectively it is fulfilling its mission.

4. *Financial and physical resources* include the sources and uses of the organization's funds, its budget, its facilities and equipment, and the information systems used to deliver services and monitor performance. The leader needs to know what resources are available and how effectively they are being used.

In all four areas, the new leader is trying to understand how the organization evolved, what strengths are available to build upon, and what possibilities there might be for significant improvements in the future. This understanding is essential for a new leader, especially if, as Rothschild (1993) suggests, he needs to decide early in his tenure whether his role should be primarily that of a risk taker, a caretaker, a surgeon, or an undertaker for his organization.

Of all these concerns, establishing a good working relationship with the board may be the most critical. A study by INDEPENDENT

SECTOR concluded that "the relationship between a nonprofit's board and its chief staff officer is so important that it can make or break an organization. A good working alliance can be a prime factor in success. Conversely, strong unresolved differences are probably the greatest single reason for mediocre or unsatisfactory performance" (Knauft, Berger, and Gray, 1991, p. 137).

Each nonprofit board of directors has its own expectations regarding its executive director. At one end of the spectrum are boards that exercise strong leadership, reserving to themselves all the important policy decisions and treating the executive director as a hired hand charged with implementing the board's directives. At the other end are boards that look to the CEO for leadership, expecting him to make policy, set direction and then tell the board how it can be most helpful and supportive. Between these two extremes are boards that try to share leadership responsibilities with the CEO in varying degrees.

No matter what pattern of interaction the board prefers, it always retains the ultimate legal and fiduciary responsibility and the power to veto even the best-laid plans, policies, and budgets of the CEO. Board members also control the leader's salary and could replace him just as easily as they hired him if they ever concluded that his actions were inconsistent with their expectations or their responsibilities as trustees.

So although the board and the CEO are truly interdependent, and neither can succeed without the other, they are not equal in power. Moreover, the board represents continuity whereas new leaders may come and go. This puts the burden squarely on the shoulders of every new leader to determine how best to develop mutual trust and cooperation with the board during his tenure.

Immediately upon assuming office, most incoming CEOs will engage in a series of one-on-one meetings with the board chairman and the chairs of major committees. The CEO listens carefully to the interests, priorities, and expectations of each board member. He asks board members to share their hopes for the future of the organization and discusses what worked best in their relationships with prior leaders. He develops an understanding of the board's pre-ferred operating style, including how it uses committees, how it sets agendas and reaches agreements, how long it takes to deliberate on issues, and what information board members need to receive between meetings.

These inputs will prove invaluable in deciding how best to work with the board in the future. But taking stock of the organization and beginning to establish good relationships with the board are just the first steps. The incoming CEO also has to start building effective working relationships with the staff and other key constituencies.

Valuing the Legacy

The honeymoon period is an excellent time for a new leader to acknowledge the contributions of his predecessor's work, even as he begins to form his own agenda. Sometimes people need a period of healing to deal with their lingering feelings about the loss of a pop-ular predecessor. For example, Bonnie Pitman understood the need to assuage the feelings of loss and anxiety among those close to her popular predecessor. Her heavy meeting schedule attested to the high priority she put on getting off to a good start with the board, the staff, and other stakeholders.

Except in a start-up situation an incoming CEO always inherits a legacy from the prior leader—people, policies, resources, practices, and traditions—that serves as a foundation on which to build. This legacy reflects the organization's past successes and is the basis for its current reputation and legitimacy. Acknowledging and using this legacy is important for building trust and confidence.

People both inside and outside the organization will desire change in varying degrees, but virtually no one is likely to want to see the organization turned upside down overnight. An example of a newly appointed CEO who didn't understand this simple fact illus-trates what is at stake here. His interviews with the board had left him with no doubt that the organization was in trouble and needed a wholesale makeover. Well-intentioned, and harboring no ill-will toward his predecessor, he quickly took steps to transform the agency, dismantling programs that had been in place for a long time and citing his "mandate" from the board to take such actions.

Although most board members supported this approach at first, a few became concerned at the speed with which the changes were being implemented. Staff members protested that major alterations were being rushed through without a systematic review of current activities and without a carefully formulated implementation plan. Many were upset that the leader did not consult more often with the staff and volunteers. The rumor mill soon filled with criticism of the new CEO's political naivete. Clients and others in the community also were not prepared for an overnight transformation, and their concerns were communicated back to the board members.

This leader's precipitous actions turned out to be a fatal mistake. His failure to confer with others deprived him of the opportunity to build trust and credibility. His actions showed no appreciation for the effective parts of the programs he had dismantled and little sensitivity to the views of those who had a vested interest in them. Morale plummeted. The story had a predictably unhappy ending. An emergency meeting of the board was called, and embarrassed board members negotiated a quick resignation for the CEO.

Experienced nonprofit leaders like Bonnie Pitman move more deliberately. They know how important first impressions are. Recognizing the accomplishments of a prior leader is a way of graciously closing the past as a prelude to entering a new era. Doing so also generates pride and goodwill in those who contributed to the legacy.

Furthermore, the legacy usually contains much that is well worth preserving, such as relationships with key donors, programs that have proven effective over time, and experienced staff and volunteers. Acknowledging the strong parts of the legacy and promising to perpetuate them is the way a new leader begins to build trust and credibility. After all, the carryover staff and board members are the very same people the new CEO will have to motivate and energize if the organization is to move forward under his leadership. A few of the practical ways leaders honor their legacies are listed in Exhibit 3.1.

**Exhibit 3.1. Ways of Acknowledging and Honoring
a Predecessor's Legacy.**

- Express gratitude to the predecessor and acknowledge his or her contributions in public statements, at orientation and get-acquainted meetings, and in conversations with staff, board members, volunteers, and key supporters.

- Organize a testimonial dinner or public reception for the departing leader.

- Create opportunities in the annual report or other publications to celebrate the legacy.

- Establish a *portrait wall* in the offices, with pictures and dates of service of former CEOs.

- Name a portion of a facility or a program in the former CEO's honor, or establish a prize or endowment in his or her name.

- Offer to use the outgoing CEO as a consultant.

- Keep the former CEO on the mailing list, and invite him or her to future events, both public and within the organization.

Good leaders are good askers as well as great listeners. Soon after being appointed, they can learn about their predecessor's legacy quickly simply by asking questions such as the following:

Mission

What is the mission of the organization and how committed are people to it?

Does the mission continue to be timely and relevant? When was it last examined?

What suggestions exist for its modification or redirection?

Does the mission appear to have support in the community?

Social Good

How does the organization serve its clients and the larger community?

What have been the organization's greatest accomplishments, how did they come about, and what were the results?

Have there been any disappointments and why did they occur?

Organizational Capital

How broad and deep is the leadership and management pool?

What has been the organization's experience with its volunteers and donors?

What is the legacy in terms of fundraising capability and facilities management?

What is the organization's image and reputation in the community, and where might it be improved?

What unfilled needs are there for new organizational capital?

Social Energy

What are the trends in volunteerism?

How much time and energy is dedicated to advocacy?

Who are the strategic allies of the organization, and what would strengthen these relationships?

Are people's talents and energies well used?

How do staff members interact with clients and the public?

Is teamwork valued or is the emphasis on individual accomplishment?

Performance

How does the organization measure its performance, and what has the trend been in these measures?

Which programs or activities have been outstanding, and what contributed to their success?

Where has the most progress been made?

Is there a performance review system for the staff, and is it respected or ignored?

What are the expectations of board members regarding the CEO and the staff, and are they reasonable or excessive?

Work Environment

What is it like to work in the organization?

Is the atmosphere friendly and collegial or conflictual and competitive?

What are the bedrock values and attitudes that people seem to share?

Did the prior leader value flexibility in work styles and participation in decision making?

Perhaps the most sensitive part of any leader's legacy is the proprietary feeling that many in the organization have for their work. Over the years they worked with the prior leader, they will have developed a sense of responsibility for and even ownership of what the organization does and the way it serves the community. Everyone from board members and staff to clients and supporters is likely to experience such sentiments to a greater or lesser degree. It is this sense of ownership that causes resistance when a new leader tries to change the organization. Yet connecting with these feelings and sensitivities can also help the new leader gain acceptance and can foster a sense of optimism about the future of the organization.

One novice CEO learned about the power of this sense of ownership when he made the error of privately criticizing his organization to outsiders. He was upset about several problems that weren't apparent until after his appointment. Although his concerns were legitimate, he erred in expressing them to outsiders. Word quickly got back to the board and staff and undermined the development of trust and credibility in his leadership. It took a long time to repair the damage of those ill-chosen remarks.

Apart from their proprietary feelings, staff members may have developed a comfortable pattern of interaction with their former leaders that they view as normal and expect will be continued. For example, if the predecessor was open and receptive to new ideas, staff members and volunteers are likely to feel they deserve a voice in the decision-making process. They would expect their new leader to continue to seek their advice and welcome their inputs and would feel disenfranchised otherwise.

This pattern of interaction is just one facet of the leadership style that is a significant part of the legacy of the former leader. Exhibit 3.2 identifies nine basic leadership styles resulting from a ten-year study of over five thousand leaders (Lipman-Blumen, 1996). Moreover, some nonprofit leaders may employ more than one style, developing their own distinctive patterns of leadership. It is incumbent on a new leader to determine exactly what the leadership style or pattern of the previous leader was, how he communicated with his staff, and to what extent staff members were involved in decision making.

Trust can develop only when there is clarity about such matters. For example, did the CEO meet regularly with the entire staff or only with department heads? Was there an open door policy, or did

---

Exhibit 3.2. Basic Leadership Styles Identified by Lipman-Blumen.

1. *Intrinsic:* the leader concentrates on his or her vision or task and measures progress strictly in those terms.

2. *Competitive:* the leader is driven by a passion to outdo competitors.

3. *Power:* the leader is driven by a need to control events and people.

4. *Collaborative:* the leader favors teamwork and collegiality.

5. *Contributory:* the leader is driven by a need to help others achieve their goals.

6. *Vicarious:* the leader encourages or mentors others.

7. *Personal:* the leader uses charm, wit, prestige, and other personal attributes to attract followers and persuade them to act.

8. *Social:* the leader networks extensively to form alliances (not what you know, but whom).

9. *Entrusting:* the leader selects capable people and entrusts them with his or her goals and visions.

Source: Adapted from Lipman-Blumen, 1996.

staff members have to go through channels to take up matters with the CEO? Did staff and volunteers participate on working committees of the organization?

In all these inquiries the new leader is learning about the legacy while listening carefully and trying to establish rapport with his new staff colleagues. These discussions often have to do with working conditions, communications, and expectations for performance and rewards. Trust can be built up in small increments by sharing staff concerns that may at first appear to be of minor importance to an incoming leader but may have high priority with key staff members or volunteers.

This section has been emphasizing what an incoming nonprofit leader can do to honor and leverage the legacy of his predecessor. However, what happens when the predecessor does not make a graceful exit but instead hangs around, perhaps retaining a seat on the board and making life difficult for the new leader? This is not a healthy situation for the organization, but unfortunately, it does happen occasionally.

This situation calls for the new leader to exercise tact and diplomacy with his predecessor but at the same time to try to reach a clear understanding with the board regarding his own agenda and his degrees of freedom in pursuing it. He needs to establish his credibility as a leader and build his own relationships as quickly as possible. Of course, if the prior leader becomes too great an obstacle to progress, the organization will suffer, and eventually either the old or the new leader will have to leave.

Establishing a Base in the Community

Bonnie Pitman's experiences in community building are instructive. Apart from developing a good working relationship with the board of the Bay Area Discovery Museum and retaining the loyalties of the staff she inherited, she met with key outside stakeholders and began the process of cultivating new advocates and supporters in the community. She expressed her appreciation for the support of the museum's dedicated volunteers. She met with existing and potential donors to reaffirm the mission of the museum and assure them of a good return on their contributions. She made herself known to the educators and parents who bring children to the museum by accepting speaking engagements in the community and making herself available for interviews by local reporters.

An incoming CEO needs to help the community understand the purposes of the organization and the roles it plays with all of its constituents—donors, civic supporters, and clients. Stakeholders who are not kept informed of the attitudes and priorities of a new leader are likely to become resentful. The resulting misunderstanding may hamper the organization and be costly to correct. Whenever possible, these communications should take place in personal conversations rather than in written form.

One nonprofit leader was overly guided by the organization chart, neglecting to seek out those who did not report to him directly. He quickly acquired a reputation for being cold and unresponsive, as his attempt to maintain *channels* and *reporting lines* kept him from reaching out to the community. Not surprisingly, his remoteness undercut his effectiveness as a leader.

He should have followed the example of another executive director who was hardly ever to be found in her office and rarely was observed writing memos. Instead, she was always "out there," talking to clients in the meeting rooms or visiting in the community. As a former junior high school principal, she had learned early in her career the practical importance of building and sustaining a community of interest.

Some of the most valuable sources of information and feedback throughout a leader's tenure are peers in his field, especially the leaders of similar organizations with whom he can establish regular and ongoing contacts. A new leader has an opportunity to ask other community leaders for their candid assessment of his organization.

Most colleagues will recognize the importance of giving a fair and honest answer, and their help can be crucial in forming the proper perspective.

The use of leadership peer groups is fairly common in nonprofit organizations. Leaders may get together regularly to share information or discuss common problems. A more or less formal leadership peer group becomes a valuable support mechanism—people with whom a leader can talk when the going gets tough, and objective and candid advice is needed. A peer group of this kind is also handy when the board wants comparative data, such as salary ranges for professional staff in other community organizations.

If a formal peer group doesn't already exist, a new CEO should consider forming one. For example, he could start a community leadership council (CLC), a small group of perhaps twelve to fifteen senior leaders of similarly sized nonprofit organizations who agree to meet for a few hours or a day each month. Several purposes might be served by these meetings:

- Providing a safe and confidential setting for leaders to explore common leadership issues, such as fundraising, motivating volunteers, strategic planning, and maintaining good relations with governing boards.

- Establishing a supportive educational climate, including bringing in guest speakers for discussions of topics both professionally and personally important, such as new nonprofit leadership ideas, dealing with stress, career planning, and retirement.

- Building personal relationships among the members and a sense of mutual obligation and trust, so that each comes to view the CLC as his or her own unofficial advisory board and feels comfortable calling on the others for informal advice on leadership issues as they arise.

- Allowing leaders to explore common problems and
  trends in the community and the roles leaders and their
  organizations might play in shaping the future. Joint
  projects and collaborations between the group members' nonprofits could result from such deliberations.

In addition to their peer groups many nonprofit leaders seek to
form relationships with influential business and government leaders in the community (see Chapter Eight). Together these contacts
form a valuable informal network that can be tapped at any time
for mutual assistance, information, and ideas.

Establishing Values and Expectations

From the very first day a new leader arrives on the job he is closely
scrutinized by the staff and board to determine what sort of a person he is and what his expectations are of others in the organization. Leaders are role models, whether they wish to be so or not.
People look to them for guidance on what is legitimate to do and
value, and individuals often model their own behavior on that of
the leader. They listen to what is being said, observe the leader's
actions, and are quick to recognize any inconsistencies between
words and deeds.

Thus the early words and actions of a new leader make a strong
impact on the staff, donors, volunteers, and other stakeholders. This
gives the leader an excellent opportunity to establish some ground
rules about the values that he believes should guide the behavior of
the organization.

One example is the leader's attitude toward service. Imagine a
new leader making the following statement soon after taking office:
"I believe we should serve all our constituencies with empathy, compassion, and caring. We want to make a difference in their lives,
and we'll measure our own success by the amount of social good

we are able to do. To that end we're committed to listening to our clients and responding to their needs. We should be constantly learning and growing in our ability to serve."

Such a statement places a high value on client service, on compassion, and on learning and conveys a desire for openness and willingness to change in pursuit of that end. If the leader then follows up on the statement with actions that reinforce these values, such as creating an advisory group of service recipients, people in the organization will understand that the statement is meant to be taken seriously.

The new leader may also want to send out some strong signals regarding the importance of fairness and teamwork in the organization. For example, when Roger Jacobi was hired as president of the Interlochen Center for the Arts in Michigan, he took two actions that immediately endeared him to the faculty. He made it a condition of his appointment that a report prepared by the faculty on management and finances, which had been approved but subsequently ignored by the board, be released and implemented. He also arranged for full compensation for a faculty member who had been fired by his predecessor after what many felt was an unfair process. These moves were tangible evidence that the new leader cared deeply about collegiality and would treat the faculty fairly (Knauft, Berger, and Gray, 1991, p. 81).

Another important value is integrity. The leader has the opportunity early on to establish high standards of personal and organizational integrity. People should know that the new leader expects them to act honestly and honorably, sharing responsibility for the reputation of the organization and observing not just the letter but the intent of all laws that apply. Here again, action speaks louder than words, and the leader's early decisions and behaviors will reinforce or undermine the stated values.

Other values that the leader may wish to promote and reward from the beginning are professionalism, attention to quality and excellence, focus on the mission, creativity and initiative, mutual respect and teamwork, commitment to the dignity of every person, and personal growth.

Practicing Forward-Looking Leadership

As the new leader starts to take charge of the organization, it is critical that he convey a sense of optimism, enthusiasm, and hope for the future. In Chapter One, we cited research that found that most managers expect their leaders to be forward looking. One of the defining characteristics of nonprofit leaders is that they are in the business of building bridges to the future for their organizations. Indeed, one might say they are in charge of creating the future for their organizations.

The reason nonprofit leaders need an orientation toward the future is readily apparent. Many people donate their time and money to nonprofits or invest their working lives there precisely because this action offers a way to change the future. They hope their involvement in such an undertaking will help improve the lives of the people in their community and leave the world a little better off. For some, doing social good to heal the earth and make the world a better place for their grandchildren is a deeply religious commitment. Others find their own lives are enriched when they act through nonprofits to preserve and improve the future.

Because the people to be led in nonprofit organizations are themselves inherently future oriented, they look to their leaders to show them how to be most effective in improving their communities. The leaders must respond to these needs if they are to have any hope of being followed.

Leaders need to establish early on in their tenure that it is their intention to act not as passive caretakers of the organization nor as frantic reactors to every little change in society. Rather they are setting out deliberately and soundly to build their organizations for the future so that these organizations will be able to provide what we called in the last chapter a greater good—a much higher level of performance and far more benefits for the clients and communities they serve.

Moreover, nonprofit leaders need to convey to all their constituencies—board members, staff, volunteers, donors, clients, and the general public—that they are confident and optimistic about the organization's ability to make a much stronger contribution in the future. That's the way leaders sustain hope and develop enthusiasm in the organization.

As important as it is to express these intentions clearly and frequently from the beginning, it takes more than just words to rekindle hope and enthusiasm in an organization. It takes a strong vision, an effective strategy, and decisive actions. That's what the next three chapters are all about.

Part II

Building the Organization

4

Leader as Visionary
Dreaming the Dream

*If one advances confidently in the direction of his
dreams, and endeavors to lead the life which he has
imagined, he will meet with a success unexpected in
common hours.*

Henry David Thoreau

By the early 1980s, John Mroz had already established a national
reputation in international diplomacy and negotiation. He had
been teaching at the Foreign Service Institute, consulting to governments and international organizations, and serving as executive
vice president and director of Middle East studies at the New York–
based International Peace Academy.

One day Mroz was at a conference on foreign affairs having a
casual conversation with a man sitting next to him. They were discussing the dangerously escalating arms race between the United
States and the Soviet Union, when Mroz was asked this question:
"If money were not a problem, what would you do to make the
world a safer and better place for our grandchildren?" He responded
that even though the two governments seemed to be locked into a
hostile confrontation, he thought there might be some opportunities for progress if discreet, unofficial talks could be held to explore
various options. He shared his dream of an independent nonprofit
organization located in Eastern Europe that could work unofficially

with Soviet-bloc governments at all levels to defuse tensions and perhaps nudge these governments toward permitting more open societies. He already knew several Eastern-bloc officials who might welcome such help and some experts in both the United States and Eastern Europe who might join such an effort.

As Mroz revealed his vision the person with whom he was speaking became enthused by its promise and Mroz's obvious passion for it. Shortly afterward, his new friend offered Mroz a small initial grant to launch the project. The Institute for East West Studies (IEWS) opened its first office in New York City in 1981, with John Mroz as president. He quickly assembled an international board of directors, composed mainly of U.S. philanthropists and Soviet-bloc officials.

In the ensuing years Mroz received several foundation grants and opened small offices in Prague, Budapest, Warsaw, and other Central European cities. The institute was able to serve as an honest broker and facilitator for policymakers on several important economic and political issues in Central Europe, especially those requiring cross-border, multilevel collaboration. For example, from 1982 to 1986, the institute sponsored secret bilateral NATO and Warsaw Pact talks on arms control issues, paving the way for an arms control agreement and pioneering the development of "confidence building measures" credited with accelerating the end of the Cold War.

By 1989, the Soviet Union had collapsed and the formerly captive nations, like Poland and Czechoslovakia, had become newly independent. It was time for a new vision for IEWS. Mroz repositioned the institute so that it could act as a catalyst in those nations' transition from communism to a market economy and could serve as a trans-Atlantic bridge, helping private and public organizations form partnerships.

The institute was the first Western organization to address the need for efficient capital markets in the countries of the former Soviet Union, offering expert advice and assistance on bankruptcy and pension reform and the creation of viable commercial banks.

It also helped create the Carpathian Euro-Region, designed to reduce security threats, promote economic prosperity, and engender civil society in a region that encompasses the least developed areas of five countries sharing borders in the Carpathian Mountains.

By 1997, conditions in the former Soviet Union had changed once again. The boundaries for Eastern and Western Europe were shifting as Poland, Hungary, and the Czech Republic sought admission into NATO and the European Union. Issues of democratization and privatization had become paramount in the former Soviet Union. Russian power was no longer projected across the globe, and in fact Russia had become an ally of the United States in resisting some common threats like nuclear proliferation, terrorism, drugs, organized crime, and environmental degradation.

At IEWS, John Mroz sensed that it was time for a new vision, his third in sixteen years, that would guide the institute into the twenty-first century. He also wanted this new vision to serve as the rallying point for a bold campaign to raise $50 million for the institute's endowment, far beyond anything yet attempted by IEWS. In November 1997, the new vision was rolled out and soon attracted funding commitments from board members and foundations.

Here's a relatively small nonprofit organization with large aspirations. It operates in a part of the world that is experiencing a hurricane of changes, on the scale of the earlier Russian and French Revolutions. All is in flux in the economic transition from communism to free markets, the political transformation from state socialism to democracy, and similar upheavals in the social, military, institutional, international, and other domains.

In such tumultuous conditions, opportunities and dangers lurk everywhere for an organization like IEWS. Without a vision, a leader would have little hope of leveraging the limited resources of the institute to achieve a meaningful impact. John Mroz realized that from the beginning. So do thousands of other leaders who find that a well-articulated vision is the most powerful tool they have for leading a nonprofit organization.

Why Does Vision Matter?

As the old saw goes, "If you don't know where you're going, you might end up someplace else." Nonprofit leaders like John Mroz use their visions to point the way. That's not new, though it may not be widely recognized. Visions have been important from the very earliest days of nonprofit organizations. After all, only the most compelling dreams—clearly stated, challenging, and meaningful—have the power to inspire donors and volunteers to risk their money and time to launch great universities, community hospitals, museums, and other organizations whose sole purpose is to benefit others rather than enrich themselves.

Simply stated, a *vision* is a realistic, credible, attractive, and inspiring future for the organization. One nonprofit leader with whom we spoke defined vision as the answer to this question, "If our fondest dreams were to be realized, what would this organization look like or be doing in twenty years?" Like a travel poster, a vision doesn't show you how to get somewhere, but it does present a clear and exciting image of what the world might be like when you arrive. And like a good travel poster, the vision creates wants. It paints a future that in every way that truly matters can be seen as greater and more meaningful than the present for everyone who elects to make the journey.

Walt Disney understood vision. He knew that dreams are wishes the heart makes and that if you can dream it, you can make it happen. Some years after Walt Disney died, a tourist to Disneyland remarked to her companion that it was too bad Disney didn't live to see it. The friend replied, "He did see it. That's why it's here!" Disney knew that vision is the first step into the future.

The relevance of vision to leadership is not difficult to discern. It is axiomatic that people lead by acquiring allies and followers. They do this by addressing people's hidden concerns. Between all nonprofit leaders and potential followers a typically unspoken but ongoing dialogue about these concerns exists, and it goes something like this:

"Follow me," says the leader, "and together we can really make a difference. We'll be able to do great things to help people and improve our community."

"Not so fast," reply the donors, staff, volunteers, and board members. "First you need to tell us where you're trying to take us. Show us what you'd like this organization to become or be able to excel at and why you think it is important for us to move in that direction."

"And then you'll follow me?" asks the leader.

"Maybe, but only if the vision and your passion for it excites us and only if you can persuade us that by moving in that direction we can make a strong contribution and realize our own deepest needs for a sense of accomplishment, meaning, and recognition in our own lives."

"And if I can do all that, then you'll follow me?" the leader asks.

"Not exactly. If you do all that, and we find the vision truly compelling and in accord with our own values, we'll commit to it and make it our own. We'll do everything we can to work with you to make it happen. Then we'll see ourselves not as your followers but as colleagues and allies, working together on the same team with you in a common cause."

That commitment is exactly what the best leaders hope for, because what they really seek is not followers per se but results. Martin Luther King Jr.'s dream was full civil rights for black people. Getting hundreds of thousands of people to march with him to Washington was a part of his strategy but not the end in itself. King knew that the reason people followed him into Washington was because, as he said repeatedly, "I have a dream!"

Leaders want to make a difference, and many of them are far less concerned about who gets the credit. Effective leaders know that nothing else will unite and enthuse people in a nonprofit organization so much as a shared vision. It gives people a sense of common ownership that enables them to cooperate with and support each other in pursuit of their common destiny. And it is only when people are united and enthused that great accomplishments become possible.

A shared vision authorizes and legitimizes the activities of all who commit to it and act accordingly. As Victor Hugo said, "there is nothing like a dream to create the future." It empowers people, encouraging them to exercise initiative to advance the common effort. As they do so, the vision also enables them to prioritize their efforts and improve their ability to serve the needs of clients and donors.

A shared vision is a major source of hope and self-esteem for people in the organization. Look into the eyes of anyone investing sweat equity to build a house as part of a Habitat for Humanity project, and you'll see what we mean. Once people understand the big picture, they can see the value of their own contributions. They feel pride in being part of an organization with an important social purpose. For many people a shared vision gives meaning to their lives and makes them want to go the extra mile to help the organization achieve that vision.

These motivational effects on followers more than justify any effort to develop a new vision, but there are other important payoffs of a shared vision for the leader and the organization:

- A shared vision provides focus, guiding decisions and actions and enabling managers to filter the many issues competing for their time and attention. Nearly all nonprofits have vast opportunities to serve but are very limited in their resources, so there is no hope of being all things to all people. That makes the focusing and filtering function very valuable.

- A shared vision stimulates new ways of thinking. When Girl Scouts CEO Frances Hesselbein announced her new vision for the future of the scouts, all sorts of initiatives were unleashed throughout the organization. A challenging but highly desirable image of the future justifies change and experimentation. It encourages people to learn, try new approaches, and take risks. This applies from the smallest soup kitchen to the largest nonprofit.

• A shared vision can be the front end of a strategic planning process or the launching pad for a major effort to renew or revitalize an organization. It guides the setting of priorities and the creation of new agendas. It also influences program design and evaluation and the measurement of progress. In many cases it triggers a search for new alliances and partnerships, occasionally leading to a complete transformation of the organization.

• A shared vision can be used (as it was in IEWS) to spark the launching of a major fundraising campaign. Donors need to know what the organization stands for and where it is heading. They are much more willing to be generous when they can see how their funds will contribute to achieving important results in the future. That's why an architect's model of a proposed new building is so powerful as a fundraising tool; it is a vivid image of a dream that has the potential to be made real once the resources become available to move ahead.

• A shared vision serves as a wake-up call for the board and the staff to reexamine the organizational culture and operations in the light of the new sense of direction. More appropriate measures of effectiveness might be suggested. New policies, staffing, or revised organizational designs might result.

These are all reasons why vision is so important to a nonprofit organization. It follows that one of the main responsibilities of the leader is to ensure that an organizational vision exists, is thoroughly understood, and is widely shared throughout the organization.

Many leaders mistakenly think that if they have a good mission statement, that's enough. We disagree. An organization with a mission but no vision is like a well-intentioned wanderer without a destination: she may have some fine experiences, and even do some good things, but she's just as likely to dissipate her resources or get lost.

A *mission* is a statement of purpose, a brief delineation of the organization's reason for being. For a hospital, it would be to cure the sick; for a museum, to collect and display great art; for a church, to tend to spiritual needs or save souls.

Clearly, every organization needs to know what business it is in and why, but that's not enough. For example, although all universities have a similar mission—to educate the young, do research, and provide public service—they all have different visions. MIT aspires to be the world leader in technical education and research, the University of Southern California seeks to be a truly international university renowned for its professional schools, the University of Texas wants to be the best public university, and so forth. It is the vision that distinguishes them, determines each university's unique character, and animates each university's spirit.

When a new leader joins an existing nonprofit organization, the mission is usually well understood. It is often embodied in the organization's charter and repeated in every annual report. The vision, however, may be more ambiguous, lost somewhere in the varied perspectives of board members or the different agendas of the senior staff. So one of the first things a new leader needs to do is to bring these views together and distill out of them a single vision that can serve the entire organization. Later in this chapter we give a case study that shows how this can be done.

Varieties of Vision Statements

Given that every nonprofit organization needs a vision, the next obvious question is, What kind of a vision? After all, any organization has hundreds of vision possibilities. It could move in the direction of providing the highest level of service quality, like Cal Tech, which tries to hire only future Nobel Prize winners for its faculty. Or it can move toward serving the greatest number of needy people, like a food kitchen that aspires to feed every hungry person in its community. It can focus on some unique aspect of its service, like a museum that strives to build an outstanding collection of American Indian art. Or it can aim its service at some underserved or special constituency.

Picking through potential visions the leader seeks the most appropriate one for her particular nonprofit organization, the one that will inspire commitment and enthusiasm. The right vision will reflect the distinctive character and culture of the organization and will leverage its history and network of connections. This vision will incorporate high ideals, pointing to how the organization can achieve greatness or excellence in its field. It will be ambitious, setting challenging expectations and stretching everyone associated with the organization. It will be easily understood and capable of being expressed in a few short sentences.

To further illustrate the difference between vision and mission and to show the varieties of visions available, we constructed the following vision and mission statements for various kinds of nonprofit organizations:

Visions Based on Services Provided

1. An urban policy think tank

   Mission: to do leading edge research and consultation on issues affecting the economic development and quality of life in central cities

   Vision: to become the outstanding national center in urban design, with acknowledged excellence in mass transit, low-income housing, and community development

2. An aquarium

   Mission: to collect and display ocean creatures and educate people about the central importance of ocean resources to society

   Vision: to build a new ocean sciences research facility in collaboration with the local university and become a major center for the study of fisheries and sea life preservation

Visions Based on Clientele Served

1. A small private university in a resort area

   Mission: to educate our students, conduct leading-edge research, and provide outreach services for our local community

   Vision: to become one of the leading universities in the nation in serving the needs of the biggest industry in our region—tourism and hotel management

2. A community theater

   Mission: to provide performing opportunities for local talent while presenting good modern and classical plays to our community

   Vision: to become so well recognized for our outstanding programs in the schools and at senior citizens centers that we attract major grants to form a permanent repertory company in our area

Visions Based on Organizational Arrangements

1. A home for battered women

   Mission: to provide temporary shelter and a range of counseling services for women and their children trying to escape from abusive homes

   Vision: to develop two new shelter facilities in other areas of our city that will triple our current capability for serving our clients

2. A volunteer fire department

   Mission: to prevent fires in our community when possible and put them out when necessary, using trained, unpaid volunteers who live in the community

   Vision: to organize and become a key part of a regional network of emergency response organizations, including hospitals, police departments, and other fire departments within a three-hundred-mile radius

Visions Based on Processes

1. A private elementary school

   Mission: to provide a high-quality education for children from kindergarten to sixth grade

   Vision: to become the statewide leader in the use of information technologies to introduce young children to math, science, and reading

2. A community hospital

   Mission: to cure the sick and provide a high level of health care to prevent and detect illnesses

   Vision: to become the leading trauma center in the region, with special expertise and equipment for the treatment of burns, fractures, and strokes

On rare occasions a new leader will find a perfectly adequate vision statement in place upon arrival. The vision may even have been developed by the board as the basis for the CEO search process. However, because this doesn't happen very often, an incoming leader usually needs to develop a new vision to reflect her own passions and intentions. Sometimes she needs to do so simply to get the organization moving again.

When a leader finds confusion about priorities, lethargy, a lack of pride, or a tendency to play it safe, she knows a new vision is called for. Similarly, if she believes the organization is out of tune with trends in the community or is not moving ahead purposefully, chances are it either has no vision or has a vision that is no longer effective. In all these cases vision becomes a major challenge for the new leader, and it cannot be delegated to anyone else.

Furthermore, as the case of John Mroz suggests, a leader may find it necessary to develop a new vision statement several times during her tenure. Frequent changes in the social and political climate or new strategic alliances may trigger the need for a new vision. Board and staff members come and go, bringing new ambitions and perspectives.

All these changes raise questions about old visions. They may cause confusion about what really matters. The organization may be pulled in every direction by well-meaning constituencies, dissipating energy and resources until a new vision is created that can reunite its people.

Developing a New Vision Statement

Leaders sometimes speak as if their visions came to them like a lightning strike in the dark that suddenly illuminates an entire landscape. Sometimes visions do arrive dramatically, but more often a new vision is the result of a deliberate process of imagination and creativity and the product of long hours of analysis and consultation.

In practice, vision statements are developed in many ways, not all of them equally effective. Some nonprofit leaders prefer to develop a vision themselves, perhaps seeking advice from a few trusted board or staff members. Some boards choose to develop a vision statement and then seek a leader who they believe has the desire and the necessary skills to make it happen. Some nonprofit leaders decide to wait for the vision to emerge out of the experiences of the organization as it tries to fulfill its mission.

An earlier book by one of the authors (Nanus, 1992) describes the four-phased approach to developing a vision statement shown in Exhibit 4.1. It has worked successfully in a variety of organizations, large and small. This approach works because it is logical and systematic and because it employs a principle well known in photography—to sharpen an image, illuminate the subject from many directions. This multifaceted process is also relatively inexpensive to use.

Although a leader can work through this process alone, we strongly advise her to use a team approach or a vision retreat to help her think through these issues. A *vision retreat* is a meeting of from ten to twenty key people led by a facilitator who systematically guides the group through the visioning process. Participants might

Exhibit 4.1. Four Phases for Developing a New Vision Statement.

Phase 1: The Vision Audit

Fundamental questions are raised about the nature and purpose of the organization, its values and culture, its strengths and weaknesses, the benefits it provides to society and client groups, the strategies being used to improve performance, and the ways improvement is being measured.

Phase 2: The Vision Scope

The major constituencies of the organization are identified and examined, threats and opportunities are evaluated, and the boundaries of a new vision statement are specified.

Phase 3: The Vision Context

A wide range of future developments that may affect the choice of a new direction are identified and evaluated, including changes in the needs and wants of various client groups, and forces affecting the future economic, social, political, and institutional climate of the organization.

Phase 4: The Vision Choice

Alternative vision statements are formulated and compared using a set of criteria developed from the earlier analysis, a new vision statement is developed, and the strategic implications of the new statement are considered.

Source: Adapted from Nanus, 1992.

include the president and other key executives, board members, volunteers, and even major donors, clients, or trusted outside advisers—people who have a stake in the future of the organization or special insight into its future possibilities.

Among the reasons for using a group process are the following:

- It encompasses a broad range of perspectives and that reduces the likelihood of overlooking important considerations in the search for a new vision. Each individual's ideas are tested, elaborated, and refined by the arguments of others, and the process often leads to new insights that might escape the attention of a leader trying to develop a vision alone or with only a few advisers.

- It involves others in the search for a shared vision and this frequently leads to a sense of group ownership, making it much easier to gain others' commitment to the vision and the actions that follow from it.

- It draws the participants closer together in their attitudes and beliefs about the nature of the organization, fosters mutual respect and trust, and leaves people with a sense of pride in their joint accomplishment. Thus it helps in team building.

- It broadens the participants' understanding of the challenges and opportunities that await the organization in the future. Dealing with alternative future assumptions is a creative, mind-stretching exercise in itself. It puts people in touch with tomorrow. This may have benefits far beyond the exercise itself, as the participants apply their new insights to their own decisions and actions after the retreat.

To illustrate these benefits of a group visioning exercise more specifically, the next section describes the visioning exercise carried out by John Mroz at the Institute for East West Studies.

A Case Study of Visioning

On September 21, 1997, twenty members of the IEWS staff, representing the leadership of all IEWS offices, met in Prague for a three-day visioning exercise. One of the authors was the meeting facilitator. John Mroz opened the meeting by stressing that he was seeking bold, creative new ideas about how the institute should evolve over the next ten to fifteen years.

Prior to the meeting the facilitator had developed an agenda based on the four phases listed in Exhibit 4.1. On the first day the group was to discuss the mission, values, institutional framework, measures of success, strengths and weaknesses, stakeholders, and current strategy of the institute. On the second day the participants were to explore the boundaries of a new vision statement and identify developments that might occur in the institute's future external environment (social, geopolitical, economic, and so on) and have a bearing on the choice of a new vision. The third day was to be devoted to identifying and exploring possible new vision statements for the institute.

Prior to the vision retreat the institute's mission statement described IEWS as "a transnational nonprofit organization [whose purpose is to help] . . . challenge, bridge and transform the security, economic, political and social situation in Central Europe and Eurasia." In the opening discussion at the vision retreat some of the participants expressed concerns about this conception. For example, some thought the mission should go further and also aim for the propagation of certain values (for example, capitalism and regional integration), whereas others wanted the mission to distinguish IEWS from other think tanks by stressing its action orientation, its brokering, outreach, and rapid response capabilities. The group agreed that the mission statement might need to be reformulated after further work on the vision statement and discussions with the board and potential donors.

The group next identified a wide range of benefits and values currently provided by IEWS to its clients. Included were access to other influential people, resources, and ideas; action facilitation (for example, confidence building, nontraditional problem solving); substantive expertise; independent policy analysis and advice; and training.

The participants recognized that many other institutions attempt to serve the same clientele as IEWS, although in different ways and with differing objectives. Some have strengths that complement or compete with those of the institute. However, the participants felt that IEWS had certain strengths relative to all these other organizations—its innovativeness and flexibility, its neutrality and inclusiveness, its independence and willingness to take risks, its network of leaders who have confidence and trust in the institute, and its ability to operate across cultures, across disciplines, and at many levels, both public and private. They agreed that the benefits provided by the institute, its track record, and its unique position among other institutions were strengths that should be leveraged in any new mission and vision statements.

The participants then identified the measures of success they thought would be most important for IEWS over the next ten to fifteen years. Twenty-six such measures were listed and discussed, and a voting procedure narrowed the list to the most important ones. These included measures of impact (for example, the extent of cross-border cooperation engendered by IEWS); measures of IEWS' influence or prestige or its recognition among others; measures of long-range institutional survivability; measures of IEWS' ability to remain on the cutting edge (in thought leadership, for example); and measures of constituent satisfaction.

The discussion next turned to the IEWS culture and its strengths and weaknesses. The culture was characterized by collegiality, shared values, diversity, responsiveness, flexibility, and willingness to take risks. The group determined that the institute's strengths lie in its powerful board and loyal donor base; the capabilities of its staff and network; and its tradition of being activist and unconventional in its approach to regional problems. They also acknowledged some weaknesses, including a small donor pool, inadequate distribution of project results, and a variety of staff limitations.

In the discussion that followed the participants revisited the strategic plan they had developed several months earlier and concluded that the institute needed to be more focused and more innovative. They were especially concerned that in the next decade many of the traditional activities of the institute might be carried out by stronger local institutions, so that extrapolation of IEWS' past experiences might be misleading.

That completed the vision audit phase of the visioning process. The participants ended their first day of discussions by initiating the vision scope phase. They identified twenty-three key IEWS stakeholders and selected the five most important ones—potential donors, policymakers, collaborators, business leaders, and thought leaders.

At the start of the second day the group was divided into five teams to discuss the needs and expectations of the five critical stakeholders and the threats and opportunities each of them might pose in the future. This was followed by a discussion of the kind of vision statement the participants wanted. They decided that a ten- to fifteen-year time horizon was about right, and that the vision must provide a sound basis for a permanent role for the institute. They were unwilling to place geographical boundaries on the vision, signaling their openness to the possibility of offering IEWS services not only in Central Europe but elsewhere in the world. They wanted the institute to remain nonpartisan, and they wanted to create a vision statement that would inspire their colleagues and form the basis for many new alliances and joint ventures.

For much of the second day of the vision retreat the participants were engaged in exploring the implications of high-impact, long-term trends. They identified those developments that had a reasonable chance of occurring by the year 2012 and that if they did occur would have a significant impact on the institute's vision and operations. This was the third phase of the visioning process—the vision context.

Hundreds of different developments were identified in seven major categories—future needs and wants, stakeholder trends, economic developments, geopolitical trends, social trends, technological developments, and other relevant changes (for example, human, financial, and institutional). By the end of the day, they had prioritized their list and identified the most crucial developments that needed to be considered in drafting a vision statement.

On the third day the participants first tried to develop an institutional map that located IEWS in relation to its competitors and allies. One participant summed up the mapping exercise by pointing out that there seemed to be an emerging consensus that the institute was moving toward bottom-up rather than top-down activities, toward issue-driven rather than client-driven projects, and toward global or at least extraregional programs.

The remainder of the meeting was devoted to identifying attractive vision possibilities for the institute. A list of vision themes was generated, and the top vision candidates were selected by asking the participants to vote three separate times—first for the options most likely to advance the institute's mission, then for the options most likely to contribute to the long-term survivability of IEWS, and finally, for the options the participants personally were most enthusiastic about. This voting procedure reduced the list to five major choices, which were then discussed in some detail. For example, these were two of the vision possibilities:

• IEWS could evolve into a Central European *institute for entrepreneurship* that could develop and help finance thousands of new entrepreneurs in the region, thereby creating employment, prosperity, and models of free enterprise that could be widely replicated.

• IEWS could become a new sort of *institution incubator*, creating and launching a series of new transgovernmental institutions for the twenty-first century. They would be self-supporting public-private consortia, each designed to manage a single significant policy issue (for example, terrorism, environmental problems) that requires transborder, multidisciplinary, and multisector cooperation.

After the meeting in Prague the facilitator prepared a report summarizing the findings and describing three scenarios of the world facing IEWS in the year 2012—a *business as usual* scenario, which represented a continuation of trends of the prior decade; a *global market-driven* scenario, which focused attention on the consequences of globalization and the universal desire of nations to become effective global competitors; and a *geopolitically driven* scenario, which envisioned the emergence of new security threats and danger zones throughout the world. These scenarios were intended to help in further deliberations on the vision.

One month later, in New York City, John Mroz met with some of his senior executives and board members to reflect on the results of the Prague meeting and to synthesize a new vision for IEWS. Basing his thinking on this discussion, Mroz developed a new vision statement for his organization. The vision went through several drafts before being submitted to the full board of directors for ratification in November.

IEWS' vision for 2012 was "to become a new kind of international public policy institution that anticipates and preempts twenty-first century threats to civil society, economic prosperity and security by promoting civic entrepreneurship." The last term was the key. By civic entrepreneurship John Mroz meant working with various allies and partners to instill an entrepreneurial culture and skills in Central Europe, developing innovative responses to transnational problems, and creating new nongovernmental institutions that link public policy and demonstration projects with both public and private funding.

This new vision represented a significant shift for the institute. For instance, it required IEWS to move beyond the postcommunist transition and to focus on longer-term issues of socioeconomic development. It also meant an expansion of IEWS activities throughout the region, developing new capabilities for institution building and leadership development, and developing sources of investment capital for entrepreneurial ventures. All this would take new resources, so Mroz used his new vision as the leading edge of a major fundraising campaign designed to add tens of millions of dollars to the IEWS endowment.

This example is instructive for several reasons. It shows that vision can be developed in a systematic, efficient fashion. It shows how a nonprofit leader can involve the staff and board of directors in the visioning process and secure their commitment to a major change in direction. And it demonstrates how an effective nonprofit leader can use vision as a tool for organizational renewal and transformation.

From Vision to Action

The leadership may be enthusiastic about the vision, but it has no potency until it is widely embraced in the organization. There is a sort of Mount Everest principle at work here. The mountain was always there, of course, but once someone had climbed it and was able to describe what he saw, others became aware of what was possible and suddenly hundreds of mountain climbers felt they had to go there as well.

There are hundreds of ways to translate vision into action. For example, here are some of the approaches that leaders in nonprofit organizations use to ensure that their visions have the desired impact:

• Show passion and commitment to the vision. Express it simply but dramatically to set the tone. Show how it opens up new opportunities for the organization and everyone in it and how it can make a real difference in society. Trumpet it prominently in publications and press releases. Gain endorsement of the vision by opinion leaders inside and outside the organization.

• Action speaks louder than words. Behave consistently with the vision. Create a sense of urgency for progress toward the vision. Show how leadership decisions move the vision forward. Use the vision as the basis for strategies. Promote incremental change, using each success as an opportunity to reinforce the vision.

• Engage others in advancing the vision. Bring all the stakeholders into the tent. Encourage people to assume responsibilities and take risks consistent with the vision. Solicit ideas from others, both inside and outside the organization. Celebrate progress, such as grants received to implement parts of the vision or new programs successfully launched. Show appreciation for vision champions, those who take the initiative to advance the vision.

• Provide the necessary support. Secure funding targeted at important parts of the vision. Hire people or recruit volunteers who share the passion for the vision and can bring useful skills to bear in achieving it. Invest in training and pilot projects. Design policies, plans, and practices that support the vision. Help lower-level leaders develop their own visions and strategies consistent with the larger vision.

• Measure progress toward achieving the vision. Evaluate the levels of synergy and innovation in the organization in pursuit of the vision. Determine whether the rate of progress is satisfactory and whether performance is improving on the key measures of effectiveness. Track the external environment to see if it is changing in ways that affect the relevance of the vision.

In the final analysis a vision will inspire, renew, or transform an organization only if it can be translated into action. As Will Rogers once said, it isn't enough to be on the right track; if you're not moving, you can still get hit by a train. One of the best ways to get an organization moving is to develop an effective long-range strategy based on the vision. That's the subject to which we now turn our attention.

5

Leader as Strategist
Finding the Way

If I had eight hours to chop down a tree, I'd spend six sharpening my ax.

Abraham Lincoln

Regis College was ninety-five years old in 1972 when Father David M. Clarke became its twenty-second president. At the time the small Jesuit liberal arts college located in Denver, Colorado, was failing. Fewer students applied each year. The college consistently lost money. Its physical plant was deteriorating. It seemed only a matter of time before the trustees would have to decide whether to close the college.

David Clarke knew that Regis was at a severe disadvantage compared to other colleges in attracting its traditional eighteen- to twenty-two-year-old students. It couldn't begin to match the flexibility and range of courses offered at the excellent state universities in Colorado, and its tuition was much higher. Clarke convinced the trustees that Regis could not continue on its historical path, and he offered a new vision.

He pointed to the burgeoning high-technology and financial services industries around the Denver area and noted that their need for sophisticated professional employees was increasing. Without compromising its values and philosophy, he suggested, Regis College could become a leading center in Colorado for nontraditional adult and midcareer education that would help satisfy some of those needs.

The trustees agreed, and the Regis Career Education Program, an accelerated undergraduate program for adult learners, was established in Denver and Colorado Springs. An M.B.A. program was also launched, using adjunct faculty from the many high-technology companies in the region.

These early experiments were so successful that in 1981, the board of trustees established the National Commission on the Future of Regis College, under Clarke, to develop a long-term strategy. Nine task forces were formed to study and analyze major issues. The task forces drew on the wisdom of over 170 corporate, civic, educational, and religious leaders from all over the country. The result was a detailed strategy with over 250 recommendations, including a $15 million capital campaign, reorganization of the college, and a plan for opening new campuses closer to the centers of the adult learner populations Regis wanted to serve.

Over the next decade Clarke implemented the strategy and Regis College flourished. Regis developed a relevant curriculum and employed experienced faculty who were attractive to adult learners. Ten new campus locations were established around Colorado so that most students would be able to reach their classes within twenty minutes. Books and course materials were brought to the students. Branches were established within or very close to the facilities of large employers like IBM and Coors.

The program offerings also expanded. The School of Professional Studies was launched, including master's degree programs in community leadership, business administration, computer information systems, and nonprofit management. And the School for Health Care Professions was opened to prepare students for careers in nursing, physical therapy, and health care administration.

Clarke was named chancellor in 1992, to make way for a new president. Under his twenty years of leadership, Regis College (now called Regis University) had experienced a complete turnaround.

The student body had gone from about a thousand students to over eight thousand. Older buildings had been refurbished and well-designed new ones had been constructed to house a variety of new programs. Unlike other small colleges that went bankrupt over the same time period, Regis consistently ran a budget surplus. It enjoyed substantial financial support from the business community in Colorado. And in all this time its core values remained essentially intact. For example, all students, even hard-driving corporate managers, were required to take the same religion and philosophy courses that had been taught for years to Regis's undergraduate liberal arts students.

Another measure of David Clarke's success was his legacy. A year after he stepped down, on August 12, 1993, Regis University flashed across television screens worldwide as Pope John Paul II and President Bill Clinton met there as part of the International Youth Forum. A couple of years later *U.S. News and World Report* ranked Regis in its top tier of western colleges. In fact Regis had become so successful that it was able to franchise its operations to other colleges for a fee. It offered an educational strategy, a complete package of courses and teaching materials, and a team of Regis faculty members to help with the implementation. By 1997, eighteen colleges and universities nationwide had become partner schools.

David Clarke had dramatically transformed a ninety-five-year-old college and repositioned it for the demands of a new clientele and a new age. A clear vision and a well-considered strategy had combined to make this transformation possible. Effective leaders know that both are needed to get a nonprofit organization moving again.

Strategy and Vision

If a mission is a statement of why an organization exists and a vision is a statement of where it's headed, then a strategy is a statement of how it intends to get there. In other words, strategy is the overall framework governing the decisions and actions to be taken by a nonprofit organization to realize its vision and mission. Examples of strategic decisions include introducing new services, expanding the service area, opening a new facility, and offering services to a new set of constituents. Such decisions need to fit into an overall pattern or framework to ensure that the resulting actions are consistent with each other and supportive of the organization's vision and mission.

All leaders need strategies. Business leaders have strategies for differentiating their organizations from competitors, introducing new products, and growing the business. Candidates for public office have campaign strategies as well as strategies for dealing with major issues like crime, education, and economic development.

Nonprofit leaders have strategies too. They use them as a framework for actions that will position the organization to be most effective in meeting present and future challenges. Strategies embody the organization's shared goals and expectations. They communicate to all the stakeholders that the organization is not drifting but has taken charge of its own destiny. Strategies make the basis for action explicit, open to feedback and subject to improvement over time. They also form the basis for relationships, both internal and external, because leaders can't foster collaboration unless people know where they're headed and how they're getting there.

Research supports the importance of strategies for leadership success. According to a survey by the Foundation of the American Society of Association Executives (1989), two of the characteristics that distinguish "very successful" from "less successful" nonprofit executives are the former's leadership in policy matters and their focus on long-range strategic objectives.

Unfortunately, sometimes the strategies of nonprofit leaders are poorly defined, misunderstood, or no longer effective. For example, many churches and synagogues have seen their congregations dwindle over time as those attracted by the religious services they offer get older, lose interest, or move away. The traditional strategies of their leaders are no longer working, and even heroic efforts to sustain an outdated strategy are unlikely to have significant payoffs. Even as their traditional membership is declining, however, other churches and synagogues are thriving with new strategies developed by their leaders. Some of these new strategies involve a deepened spiritual covenant with members of the congregation, and others target the needs of specific populations, such as singles, young married couples with small children, or active seniors.

Every strategy must be designed to advance the mission of the organization, but the best strategies also flow directly from a well-formulated vision statement. Strategies can be developed without a vision, of course, but that can be a serious mistake. We know of nonprofits that go through an annual strategic planning exercise that amounts to little more than simply extrapolating past performance into the future. "Let's plan to increase our caseloads by 10 percent a year," they might say, or, "let's try to increase the contributions in our next fundraising campaign."

Although such an approach may be consistent with the mission, it is also a formula for perpetuating the status quo, not for moving to a greater good. It is not future oriented and rarely takes account of trends in the environment. It doesn't tell the organization how to move in new and more productive directions. It doesn't help the organization set priorities for goals and actions, so people have no guidance on where to look for new opportunities or which new capabilities need to be developed. It is simply a thinly disguised statement of business as usual.

In contrast, when strategies are designed to support a clear, shared vision of the future, they tend to be far more powerful as guides to action. The visioning process itself, as described in the previous chapter, will often generate attractive new strategic options. Strategies tend to be more innovative when they are driven by a vision of the future and decision makers are released from the constraints of habits and current practices. This approach allows strategic opportunities to be prioritized, because they can be evaluated in terms of how they contribute to the attainment of the vision. Strategies and agendas are more likely to be mutually supportive when they all contribute to moving the organization in a common direction.

Thus strategies are most effective when they serve as the bridge between vision and action. They should be used to coordinate and commit the board, leadership, staff, and volunteers to a common set of goals and objectives. They should make effective use of resources, concentrating them in programs where they can do the most good for clients and for the community. They should position the organization so that it can respond quickly to take advantage of changes in the external environment. And they should provide the benchmarks against which performance in the organization can be measured over the long term.

Strategic Thrust and Strategic Issues

At Regis, David Clarke's vision was for the college to become a leading center in Colorado for nontraditional adult and midcareer education. There were many ways to move in that direction. Regis could have chosen to be faculty driven, seeking strategies that would make the most effective use of existing faculty resources in serving adult learners. Alternatively, Regis could have chosen to be facilities driven, seeking to maximize the use of its underutilized campus by contracting programs that attract adult learners, like elderhostels and corporate training programs. Or it could have become program driven or technology driven.

As it happened, Clarke convinced his board that Regis needed to be client driven. He reasoned that adult learners were different. They were usually employed, had families, and had little time for additional education unless it directly helped them in their careers and offered classes that were easy to attend. Only if its educational programs were tailored directly to the needs of adult learners, Clarke argued, would Regis College ever be able to attract enough high-quality students to make its programs economically viable and educationally sound.

As a result he needed a set of strategies tailored to client needs. He needed a faculty hiring strategy that sought experienced practitioners who were more practically and professionally oriented than the traditional Regis faculty. He needed a facilities development strategy that moved the instruction sites closer to where the students worked. He needed a strategy for building alliances with other organizations, especially for linking the Regis programs with the needs of employers in the region. And he needed other strategies detailing what types of programs Regis would offer, how academic standards would be maintained, and how the programs would be funded.

Any of the different strategic thrusts we have mentioned (faculty driven, facilities driven, client driven, program driven, and so on) would have been consistent with Clarke's overall vision, but each would have led to far different strategies and potential outcomes for the institution. So the first task of a leader who is building a bridge from vision to strategy is to work with his board of directors to select the most appropriate strategic thrust—that is, the one that in the long run holds the most promise of fulfilling the vision and achieving the greatest social good.

Once the overall strategic thrust is determined, many issues become obvious. Strategic issues are the controversial matters that must be resolved in developing a strategy. Usually, they involve choices that will shape the organization for years to come. They are the big issues, involving large sums of money, producing major changes in the character or operations of the organization, and ultimately, requiring the full commitment of the board. For example, once Regis College decided to make its strategic thrust client driven, it might have had to resolve these strategic issues relating to its adult learners:

Program Issues

Which degree programs will best serve adult learners?

What balance will there be between the undergraduate and graduate programs?

Which subjects will be emphasized?

Educational Issues

What emphasis will be given to broad educational goals compared to narrower professional goals, and what will be the balance between theory and practice?

To what extent will the traditional Jesuit philosophy and values be reflected in the curriculum?

Faculty Issues

What faculty mix will be most effective (for example, full- or part-time instructors; traditional Ph.D.'s or experienced practitioners)?

How, if at all, will new, practitioner-oriented faculty relate to traditional, tenured faculty?

Student Issues

What types of adult students will the college recruit?

What will a student have to accomplish in order to graduate?

Delivery Issues

What types of new facilities and equipment will be needed?

Where will the new facilities be located?

How will information technology be used?

Institutional Issues

What strategic alliances will the college try to develop to strengthen its programs?

How will the programs be funded?

Clearly, this is only a sampling; many more strategic issues would have been identified in the actual situation. The choice of strategic issues to be addressed is one of the most critical and difficult responsibilities of any nonprofit leader. Here is where judgment, vision, and experience combine to form a strategic agenda. Just as the president of the United States lays out his strategic agenda in the annual State of the Union Address to the nation, so must every nonprofit leader identify those strategic issues whose solution is critical to the realization of the vision and the long-term success of the organization.

Thus far we have been discussing the first three steps of a strategy process—developing a vision, deciding on a strategic thrust, and identifying the strategic issues to be resolved. The remaining steps are described in the next section.

The Strategy Process

The strategy process, sometimes called strategic planning, is the way the organization identifies and evaluates the strategic options flowing from its vision and mission; decides upon goals, objectives, and a plan of action; and implements them. Every nonprofit organization has its own approach to a strategy process, tailored to its own character and aspirations. Although we cannot hope to be comprehensive in our discussion of strategy processes in this short chapter, we can give the reader a flavor of the important considerations. For a more complete discussion, see Bryson (1995), Barry (1986), Koteen (1989), or Nutt and Backoff (1992).

Some nonprofit organizations use a strictly top-down process. The entire board or a planning committee of the board works with the CEO to develop strategies, either on a regular basis or, more commonly, on an ad hoc basis as issues and opportunities arise. For example, the board of one local theater association formulated a strategy for restoring an old opera house, including the development of an architectural plan, fundraising methods, and policies to govern the use of the restored building.

Other nonprofits use a strictly bottom-up approach, with strategies developed by each program manager or by committees of the professional staff on a regular planning cycle and submitted upward for approval. For example, the president of a museum might ask the curators of each department and their staffs to develop long-term strategies for the evolution of their respective collections.

Peter Drucker (1993) advocates a strategy process driven by an organizational self-assessment. His approach centers on asking fundamental questions about the mission, customers, value provided to the customers, definition of results, and possible ways to focus efforts for improvement.

Many organizations evolve strategy processes that work well for them. Often these processes contain elements of both the top-down and bottom-up approaches. For example, an INDEPENDENT SECTOR study (Knauft, Berger, and Gray, 1991, p. 47) describes the process used by the Baxter Community Center in Grand Rapids, Michigan. In 1988, Candy Fluman, a board member and respected hospital administrator, was asked to spearhead the strategy process. Her approach was data driven. She held interviews and meetings with staff and board members, reviewed a needs assessment of the area, collected demographic information, developed statistical profiles of each of Baxter's programs and surveyed similar organizations in the area. Then she conducted a half-day planning session with the staff to discuss Baxter's strengths and weaknesses and identify areas of opportunity. After gathering more data from clients and the community and holding discussions with the management, she analyzed all the information and prepared a list of recommendations for the board. Her suggestions were discussed and accepted. Finally, she prepared detailed strategic plans for implementing the recommendations.

Still other variations of strategic processes are used. Sometimes the different units of a large organization, such as various schools in a large private university, will use quite different strategy processes, each tailored to an individual unit's needs. In other cases a strategy process may be specifically designed to deal with an unexpected challenge, like the termination of a state subsidy program, a sharp increase in the client pool, or the resignation of key personnel.

Clarke chose to use a series of strategic task forces involving dozens of people over an extended period of time. Each task force was free to use its own approach and expertise to develop its recommendations for the Regis board. Task forces or focus groups are commonly used in nonprofit organizations because they bring many perspectives to bear on the search for new strategies, reducing the likelihood that important considerations will be overlooked. They also broaden participation in the strategy process, expanding the pool of people committed to the viability of the institution and spreading ownership of the results. Moreover, task forces are more likely than other planners to discover bold new approaches because their outside participants are not as tied to traditional ways of doing business as internal strategic planners typically are.

There are also commonalities in all these processes, and from them we have drawn the remaining steps of our strategy process. The three initial steps, as described earlier, are (1) developing a vision, (2) deciding on a strategic thrust, and (3) identifying the strategic issues to be resolved. We illustrate steps 4 through 10, those often involved in developing a strategy, with the example of an issue task force concerned, as the ones at Regis College were, with developing an adult education program strategy.

4. Select an appropriate time horizon. If the president or board has not already specified a time horizon, the task force needs to establish one of its own. It may reason that any new educational program would take from three to five years to implement, given the need to design curricula, hire a chairman and faculty, recruit students, and so forth. It would take at least two years after that for the first graduates to complete the program and a few years after that to measure the educational benefits from the program and ensure its financial viability. So the task force might conclude that a reasonable time horizon for a program strategy is seven to ten years.

5. Specify what needs to be included in the strategy. The task force may want to propose one or several new adult education programs (that is, courses of study leading to an undergraduate or graduate degree) and establish priorities for each of them. The strategy needs to include clear goals and objectives for each program, specify the market that it targets, and evaluate the costs and benefits for the college, the students, and the region. The strategy may also include several alternative approaches to launching each program, such as starting from scratch, building on current faculty strength, or forming alliances with one or more other organizations.

6. Assess client and stakeholder needs. The task force must determine the needs of adult students in the region for various kinds of degree programs. The task force may conduct a survey of potential students or poll regional employers about their educational needs. It may analyze current adult student participation in other programs in the region and in other parts of the country. The object is to determine not just what programs are needed but what it would take in terms of cost, location, course coverage, and other factors to attract students to these programs.

7. Evaluate long-term trends affecting the strategy. With a seven- to ten-year time horizon, the task force needs to develop some forecasts about the future of the region. For example, it needs population and employment projections, as well as forecasts of state and federal funding for adult education programs. It also needs to assess the present and future capabilities of competing institutions, such as community colleges and distance learning offered by national universities, and trends in adult education such as the use of computers in adult programs.

8. Identify strategic factors, problems, and opportunities. A strategic factor is an element of a strategy so important that it is pivotal in determining the strategy's success or failure. In this case, strategic factors include the ability of the program to attract highly qualified adult students and the demand by employers for program

graduates. The task force should also identify program-related problems, like the proper mix of required and elective courses for adult learners and such opportunities as contracting with existing institutions for portions of a program. It should also identify internal problems and opportunities by analyzing the college's strengths and weaknesses in regard to establishing new programs.

9. Create and evaluate strategic alternatives. By this point the task force may be able to narrow the program alternatives to three or four—say, graduate degrees in business administration, human resource management, computer science, and public health. The task force needs to specify each alternative in sufficient detail that it can evaluate the program's costs, benefits, and potential contributions for the college, the students, and the community, as well as the ability of the college to launch the program successfully. The result of this evaluation may be the selection of strategy for a single program or for multiple programs with phased introductions.

10. Devise an implementation plan. No strategy recommendation is complete without a clear statement of goals and objectives and specific ways to measure milestones if the strategy is implemented. The plan also includes some suggested policies to govern the program and spells out the implications for budgets, marketing, and operations. The plan may even include a job description for the person to be appointed to head the program.

This strategy process (summarized in Exhibit 5.1) is logical and systematic. It is inherently both top-down (steps 1 to 3) and bottom-up, in that steps 4 to 10 can involve many people both inside and outside the organization, as in the Regis College example. It can be used to develop overall strategies for a nonprofit organization, to launch a new initiative, or to redirect an ongoing program. Its purpose is to generate an effective strategy to guide the evolution of the organization toward the realization of its vision. But what is an effective strategy?

Exhibit 5.1. Summary of a Ten-Step Strategy Process.

1. Develop and clearly state the vision and mission of the organization.

2. Decide upon the strategic thrust.

3. Identify the strategic issues to be resolved.

4. Select an appropriate time horizon.

5. Specify what needs to be included in the strategy.

6. Assess client needs and the needs of other key stakeholders.

7. Evaluate long-term trends affecting the strategy.

8. Identify strategic factors, problems, and opportunities.

9. Create and evaluate strategic alternatives.

10. Devise an implementation plan.

Properties of an Effective Strategy

A strategy can be judged for effectiveness only after it has been fully implemented. Enough time has to pass so that the organization can judge the value of the contributions the strategy made to the bottom line—that is, the social good. However, effective strategies have certain qualities that leaders can look for in advance to increase the likelihood of success.

Some of these qualities have already been discussed in the examples. An effective strategy makes the vision real by transforming that vision into a series of decisions and actions. It has clear goals, objectives, and policies, especially regarding the services to be provided and the client groups for whom they are intended. It reflects a single strategic thrust so that its different aspects have a common focus and are consistent with each other. It is future-oriented—that is, anticipatory and consistent with long-term trends. It is practical, feasible, and fully capable of being implemented.

In most cases, to be effective a strategy has to reflect the needs of the major stakeholders. That's why representatives of various constituencies are often brought into the strategy process. A good strategy usually is consistent with the organization's culture and values, building upon and often enhancing the core competency. It also sets high standards and creates a common perspective on the future of the organization.

An effective strategy has consequences. It serves as a guide to action, especially in such resource allocations as budgets and the assignment of organizational responsibilities. It identifies new opportunities. It helps the organization prepare for contingencies and enables it to react to unexpected changes.

What is contained in a strategy that fulfills these criteria? Because that depends on the context and the issues, we can illustrate it by following through on the Regis College case study. Without knowing the details of the actual strategy Regis developed, we can imagine what it might have contained. Here are some of these hypothetical elements:

1. The vision: Regis College aspires to become a leading center in Colorado for nontraditional adult and midcareer professional education as it also remains faithful to the values and philosophy of its founders.

2. The strategic thrust: Regis will be client driven, tailoring its programs directly to the needs of adult learners and their employers.

3. Program goals (broad statements of intentions) and objectives (more specific, often quantifiable targets):

   Example of a goal: Regis will create two new degree programs for qualified midcareer students, both offered on evenings and weekends: a master of business administration (M.B.A.) and a master of science in computer sciences (M.S.C.S.).

   Example of an objective: the first class of the M.B.A. program, two sections of approximately twenty students each, will be admitted in two years, and the M.S.C.S. program will open one year later.

4. Educational goals and objectives:

Example of a goal: both these degree programs should make full use of tested adult learning methods such as learning contracts, experience-based learning, team projects, and competency-based assessment.

Example of an objective: complete a detailed survey of employer needs for specific M.B.A. skills (for example, financial analysis, communications, information systems, and the like) in the next six months.

5. Financial goals and objectives:

Example of a goal: after the initial start-up phase, both the M.B.A. and the M.S.C.S. degrees should be fully self-supporting from tuition and fees.

Example of an objective: raise $500,000 from donors and potential employers in the coming year as seed money for the new programs.

6. Personnel goals and objectives:

Example of a goal: instructors in the new programs should be highly qualified part-time faculty who have advanced degrees in the disciplines they are teaching and considerable experience in their fields.

Example of an objective: conduct a nationwide search and appoint a full-time associate dean to head each program within nine months.

7. Organizational goals and objectives:

Example of a goal: include adult student representatives on faculty committees dealing with school policies and procedures.

Example of an objective: within three months establish an advisory board for each program, consisting of Regis faculty and senior professionals in the region.

8. Facilities goals and objectives:

Example of a goal: insofar as possible, instruction in both programs should take place in locations within twenty minutes of travel time from major concentrations of students.

Example of an objective: form agreements within six months with three major employers in the region to hold classes at night in their conference facilities.

9. Technology goals and objectives:

Example of a goal: students in both programs should have access to personal computers and be proficient in their basic operations.

Example of an objective: set up a World Wide Web site for each program within six months.

10. Student recruiting goals and objectives:

Example of a goal: all prospective students should have four-year undergraduate degrees, be able to demonstrate proficiency in English, and score at least at the seventieth percentile on standard admissions tests.

Example of an objective: prepare the admissions package for the M.B.A. program so that it is printed and ready for mailing within one year.

11. Policy guidance: for example, part-time faculty teaching in these two programs shall be paid on a course-by-course basis, and after teaching six courses with acceptable student evaluations, faculty members shall be eligible for a 20 percent salary increase and promotion to adjunct status.

12. Measures of effectiveness: for example, the success of the two programs should be measured by the number of students seeking admission, the demand by employers for the graduates of each program, the programs' financial viability, and the programs' contributions to Regis College's reputation and academic standing in Colorado.

13. Implementation plan: this should contain the sequence of decisions and actions necessary to implement this strategy.

Note that the entire discussion thus far has been about the strategy itself and the strategy process, not about developing documents called strategic *plans*. This is an important distinction, especially from the leadership perspective. A leader's credibility and effectiveness depend heavily upon the power and quality of his vision and strategy. No amount of documentation will compensate for a poor strategy.

Unfortunately, far too many nonprofit organizations seem to be more concerned with producing an impressive planning document than with ensuring the quality of the strategic thinking that goes into it. We have seen many so-called strategic plans of nonprofit organizations that have little or no real value. Some of them are prepared annually by staff members without much board or CEO guidance and end up being little more than requests for additional funding support for current programs. Some of them summarize lowest common denominator agreements, reached after endless meetings among interested stakeholders. Some of them are designed more to impress donors than to guide actions in the organization.

These kinds of documents offer little hope of improving effectiveness, let alone of achieving excellence or moving the organization in the direction of a greater good. At their worst they are a testimonial to a real lack of leadership in the organization. It is no surprise that such documents typically end up on a shelf, unread, unused, and largely irrelevant.

Still, even though the strategy itself is what matters most, planning documents do serve a purpose. The proper place for documentation in the strategy process is after the hard thinking has been done. Then the resulting strategies can be laid out, along with the reasoning behind them and the steps needed to turn them into reality. The resulting plan serves as the record of the choices made and agreements reached between the board and the leadership. It has value as a guide to action, a reference point for future strategic deliberations, and a training document for new employees. An executive summary can be prepared for distribution to all the stakeholders.

The Leader's Role as Strategist

The English word *strategy* is derived from the old Greek word *strategos*, meaning the general of an army. Thus, from the very beginning, strategy was understood to be the essential art of the general or, by extension, an important responsibility of any leader. Although some of the fact finding and planning tasks in reaching a strategy can be delegated to others, it is up to the leader (either alone or with the assistance of a board committee) to ensure that an appropriate strategy for the organization is formulated and implemented.

Leaders are the ones who decide when a new strategy is needed. They may sense the need for a new strategy in many ways. In the case of Regis College, Clarke had unmistakable evidence that the college would fail if it continued doing business as usual. Sometimes, however, the clues are more subtle. There might be a steady drumbeat of complaints from clients about the diminishing quality of the services. Key board members might be losing confidence in the ability of the organization or its leadership to meet its challenges. The number of people volunteering to help the organization or to contribute funding might be declining, or the cost of servicing clients might be escalating. These are all examples of internal signals that the old strategy might no longer be working very well.

There are also other occasions that demand a new strategy. When the board of directors hires a new leader from the outside, it is very often hoping that the new leader will come up with a more effective strategy for the organization, and it may even build that requirement into the job description. Similarly, institutionalizing a new vision or mission statement almost always triggers the search for a new strategy. Sometimes, the need for a new strategy is sparked by a major change in the external environment, such as the passage of new legislation affecting the organization or the appearance of a generous new donor.

Whatever the stimulus for a new strategy, leaders are the ones who must initiate and champion the strategy process. Their involvement endows the strategy process with legitimacy. They create the necessary mandate and a common game plan. They decide who will be involved in the process and form the necessary committees. They create a sense of expectation about the results and a sense of priority and urgency for the process.

As suggested earlier in this chapter, leaders provide a great service for the strategy process when they spearhead the development of a mission, vision, and strategic thrust to guide it. These steps not only inform and focus the strategy process, but also set high standards and ensure that the resulting strategies will have some degree of coherence and consistency.

Once the strategy process has begun, the leader usually will be deeply involved to move it along and keep it on track. Occasionally, all the leader needs to do is to have an optimistic mien about the process and to be, as William Wordsworth said, "a man of confident tomorrows." The leader's sense of optimism and confidence in the process can infect others with the determination to carry the process to completion. More often, however, the leader will have to provide continuing guidance to the strategy committees, lest they become paralyzed by concerns about what might be acceptable to the CEO and the board. Even if other duties prevent the leader from participating in all the meetings, he still is likely to be needed on occasion to ensure that the views of all key stakeholders are properly sought and considered and that the inevitable conflicts that arise are resolved satisfactorily.

Sometimes the CEO doesn't have to carry the full burden of leadership during the strategy process. For example, in a collegial organization like Regis College, where faculty members collaborate regularly to resolve educational issues, it is likely that several of them would step forward to exercise leadership at critical stages of a strategy process. Some may be key idea generators or strong advocates of change. Others may have good process and political skills for guiding task forces toward consensus on issues. Such people are important allies of the leader and should be appreciated and publicly acknowledged for their contributions.

When the strategy process has been completed, it is up to the leader to ensure that the resulting strategy is fully implemented. The first step is to collect all the pieces of the strategy into a single coherent whole and to present that strategy to the board for its consideration and endorsement. The leader is the one responsible for getting everyone's agreement, ensuring that everyone fully understands and supports the strategy.

Next the strategy has to be communicated to all the stakeholders so they can coordinate their actions with it. For example, at Regis College, David Clarke would have had to discuss the strategy with the Regis Alumni Association and with local reporters, interested employers, and civic associations.

The leader appoints the people who will have responsibility for implementing the strategy. He usually takes the lead in locating financial resources, hiring senior personnel, and establishing the necessary organization. He may commission studies or launch pilot programs to test elements of the strategy and learn what works best.

Throughout the process, and for as long as the strategy is in effect, the leader serves as a role model, spokesperson, negotiator, and chief cheerleader. The leader must be ever vigilant to ensure that the strategy drives decision making and action throughout the organization. As the implementation process proceeds, he monitors progress, keeps the board informed, and celebrates accomplishments.

In short, strategy is the instrument with which the leader determines how to renew or transform the organization. We're reminded of the words of the English poet Samuel Taylor Coleridge, who said that, "often do the spirits of great events stride on before the events, and in today already walks tomorrow." The "spirits of great events" in a nonprofit organization are incorporated in its strategy, which serves as an indispensable guide to the leader as he performs his role as change agent, the subject of the next chapter.

Leader as Change Agent
Transforming the Organization

It is not the strongest of the species, nor the most
intelligent, that survives, but rather the one that is
most adaptable to change.

Charles Darwin

By 1991, when it was featured in a book sponsored by INDEPEN-DENT SECTOR (Knauft, Berger, and Gray, 1991, pp. 68–76), the Indian Health Board (IHB) of Minneapolis had become a model American Indian health center for the nation. With a staff of more than sixty and a $2 million budget, it handled over twenty thousand medical and dental patients annually and provided a wide array of other social services. It was not always so. Norine Smith was the person who more than anyone else made this happen.

Born and raised on Minnesota's Red Lake Indian Reservation, Smith was well aware of the primitive medical services available to most Native Americans. Plagued by alcoholism, poverty, poor nutrition, and inadequate housing, many suffered from chronic diseases, short life expectancy, and high infant mortality. Moreover, physicians and dentists were not anxious to serve this population because the patients often lacked medical insurance and were dispersed over large geographical areas with few nurses or health care facilities.

Norine Smith became a social activist for the cause of Indian health care in the 1960s, and in 1971, she and Charlie Deegan founded the Indian Health Board. Deegan became the IHB's first director, and Smith became its office manager. As office manager, she helped the IHB make the transition from an advocacy organization that helped Indians get proper medical services to a primary health care organization that ran its own small clinic, located in what was formerly a morgue.

In 1976, Charlie Deegan left the Indian Health Board and Norine Smith succeeded him as director. Several immediate problems confronted her. She felt that the IHB board of directors, which consisted of twenty-four members chosen to represent each Indian tribe in the area, was clumsy, uninformed, and ineffective. Through attrition and a redesign of the structure of the board, she reduced its size to nine board members and clarified its responsibilities. She wrote new personnel policies to eliminate sloppy work practices. Faced with an archaic accounting system, especially in patient billing where deficits were mounting up, she persuaded the president of one of Minnesota's largest public accounting firms to volunteer his firm's services to redesign the system.

Meantime the patient load kept increasing. By 1978, the IHB was outgrowing its space, but it also had a budget deficit. Smith convinced the board that it needed to take on the additional financial burden that larger quarters would entail. She arranged to get a community development block grant to renovate part of an old housing project into a medical clinic. However, the new location didn't work. The housing project was run by the American Indian Movement, which proved to be unsupportive of the IHB. A few years later Smith moved the IHB again, this time to a location near Fairview Deaconess Hospital. A consummate deal maker, she arranged a sixty-nine-year land lease from the hospital at a mere $100 annually in exchange for the promise of patient referrals to the hospital. By 1983, the IHB had moved into a brand-new clinic.

Major problems struck again two years later when Smith decided to computerize the accounting system to speed payments from the government for Medicaid and Medicare patients. The new system,

designed by an outside contractor, failed to operate correctly, resulting in losses of more than $300,000 in patient billings. A 1987 law-
suit against the contractor recovered some of the money spent for
equipment and software but left the IHB with a substantial deficit.

Soon after that, space problems rose again, as the IHB's burgeoning social and health care programs once again outgrew its
facilities. Ever entrepreneurial, Smith asked a volunteer to conduct
a space analysis and determine the needs, which were to be met by
a new capital campaign. This time the facility would be built in a
Minneapolis minipark, with the city providing land and building
maintenance.

Norine Smith, like many leaders of small and midsized nonprofits, faced what seemed to be an endless series of crises, each of
which threatened the very existence of her organization. She used
her passion and her entrepreneurial skills to steer her organization
through a series of changes to address these threats as she also expanded and improved the services the IHB could provide to its
clients. With each change, she brought her board along and made
new allies and friends.

At each step of the way Smith made risky decisions. Some of
these decisions did not turn out as expected, but eventually enough
of them succeeded to enable the Indian Health Board to become
the largest and most successful organization of its kind in the nation.
In the process Norine Smith also helped create a sense of community and common purpose among the thousands of people who were
helped by her persistence and determination.

The Nature of Organizational Change

The leader in a nonprofit organization is the chief change maker.
As Warren Bennis, a renowned scholar on the subject of leadership,
puts it, "a leader is, by definition, an innovator. He does things other
people haven't done or can't do. He does things in advance of other
people. He makes new things. He makes old things new. Having

learned from the past, he lives in the present, with one eye on the future. And each leader puts it together in a different way" (1989, p. 143).

To understand how the leader acts as change agent, we first need to understand the nature of organizational change. The condition of a nonprofit organization at any given time is the result of an unending struggle between continuity and change. Continuity characterizes the steady, ongoing services provided by an organization to its clients or to the larger community. Church services every Sunday morning and daily meals at a soup kitchen are examples. These activities are subject to some amount of routinization and control by managers and administrators. The main tasks of the leader in such a situation are to set high standards for service, see that the right people are put in charge and that they have the necessary resources to serve their clients, and act as a coach and mentor for those who need such assistance.

Change presents a totally different set of circumstances. It characterizes an organization in transition. There are at least four sources of change that are important in nonprofit organizations, and all four were experienced by the Indian Health Board:

- Change occurring in response to a shift in the client's or community's needs: for example, when AIDS became an issue in the Indian community, the IHB had to respond with a series of special programs for testing, counseling, and treating people in the community who might have become infected.

- Change resulting from political, economic, or social forces in the community: for example, the IHB had to respond whenever a new piece of legislation made funds available for certain kinds of health or educational programs.

- Change accompanying growth or a quest for greater efficiency of operations: for example, each time the IHB outgrew its facilities or tried to improve its accounting system, major changes became necessary in the way it was organized and operated.

- Change initiated by the organization to alter its external environment in a significant way: for example, changes occur whenever an organization reaches out to form new coalitions or to change the public's attitudes toward a particular social problem. The IHB formed many such partnerships. All advocacy groups, from the National Rifle Association to Greenpeace, have this kind of change as their main mission.

In all these kinds of change the leader serves as the main change agent—the person who often initiates the change and is responsible for promoting it and ensuring that it happens in a way that is beneficial for the organization, its clients, and the community. Indeed, James MacGregor Burns ends his monumental Pulitzer Prize–winning study of leadership with these words: "the ultimate test of practical leadership is the realization of intended, real change that meets people's enduring needs" (1978, p. 461).

Change is rarely achieved easily. It may sow confusion and uncertainty in an organization. Some people are genuinely threatened by change, especially if it disrupts activities they have mastered and found rewarding. They're uncomfortable because they cannot know at the outset whether they'll be able to measure up to the expectations that accompany the change. Many people fear that a proposed change will complicate their jobs and require more of them, which of course it often does. James O'Toole (1995, pp. 159–164), in a comprehensive work on the subject, lists no fewer than thirty-three reasons why people resist change.

The three universal prescriptions for overcoming resistance to change are the following:

- Honest and frequent communication throughout the organization about the change to explain its purposes, to reduce uncertainty, and to show how the change will contribute both to the greater good of the clients and the community and to the personal needs of the staff and volunteers

- Widespread, genuine participation in the change process so that people in the organization feel they have a voice in designing the change and can exercise some control in its implementation

- Effective training programs that enable people to learn why the change is necessary, what it will require of them, and what it means for them personally

These three approaches are very helpful in reducing resistance to major change and are widely used by nonprofit leaders. However, some irreducible level of resistance to change may still remain even after the most professional and conscientious use of these procedures. When this happens, the leader must proceed with caution.

We have observed many situations in which leaders have wasted much time and energy trying to eradicate every last vestige of resistance to change. Leaders can tie themselves up in endless meetings, trying to persuade people that a change is necessary, only to find that some people will never be persuaded. Also, there will always be people who, although agreeing that a certain change is needed, will have little interest in being involved in it themselves. A donor to the Indian Health Board, for example, might agree that AIDS education is important for the Indian community and yet prefer that his funds be used for other purposes.

We have found that the most successful leaders are not those who spend the bulk of their time fighting to overcome resistance to change but rather those who find ways to avoid it or minimize its effect. One way to do so is to find champions of the change, either inside the organization or hired from the outside, and put them in charge. A champion of change is an enthusiastic supporter who is personally committed to the change and has the skills and motivation to make it happen. The leader assigns the job to such people, supplies the necessary resources, and facilitates their actions.

A second way to avoid resistance to change is to establish pilot programs separate from the traditional activities so that those resistant to the change can continue doing what they do best. In time, if the change is right, the pilot program will grow and resistance to it will diminish in proportion to its demonstrated success.

The third and arguably the best way to minimize resistance to change is to take preventive action. Over time the leader creates an organizational climate that not only accepts change and the adjustments accompanying it as normal and exciting but actively seeks and welcomes change as the source of new opportunities to better serve the clients and the community. In essence the entire organization learns how to be entrepreneurial and comes to view itself as dynamic and innovative.

The Entrepreneurial Nonprofit Organization

An entrepreneurial organization is one that regularly launches and nurtures new nonprofit ventures and programs through a process of creative experimentation and prudent risk taking in pursuit of its mission and vision. One well-regarded study of sixty highly successful leaders of nonprofit organizations found that among the major attributes they shared were an entrepreneurial attitude, a vision, and an orientation to action and risk taking (National Assembly of National Voluntary Health and Social Welfare Organizations, 1989).

An entrepreneurial organization is open at every level to input from all its stakeholders (staff, volunteers, clients, donors, and so forth) about how its services can be improved, and it acts promptly and creatively to implement these changes. Staff members are encouraged to make many contacts in the outside world and to forge new relationships to achieve organizational ends. The organization encourages grassroots innovation and expects people to take prudent risks in pursuit of excellence. Ineffective practices are easily abandoned in favor of those that show promise of achieving a greater good. As a result of all these ongoing activities, change is considered a normal, welcome, and enjoyable part of the operation.

The Indian Health Board under Norine Smith is an example of an entrepreneurial nonprofit organization. So are most of the organizations described at the start of the previous chapters. Here are three more:

• A Houston minister, Kirbyjon Caldwell, took over the Windsor Village United Methodist Church in 1982 and built it from 25 members to over 10,000, with an average worship service attendance of 5,500 congregants. Along the way the entrepreneurial clergyman started 120 ministries, launched several nonprofit ventures that employ over 125 people in the fields of low-income housing and child welfare, and developed the 104,000-square-foot Power Center, a complex of business and nonprofit groups serving the black community, which employs hundreds more.

• Goodwill Industries has 186 member groups, each of which runs from one to thirty-two stores selling donated goods to support its social services programs. Each group is encouraged to be entrepreneurial. For example, a Goodwill store in Indianapolis features upscale clothes and accepts credit cards, another in Portland serves latte to shoppers, one in San Francisco runs gay-oriented ads, and some groups choose to have outlets that don't call themselves Goodwill at all but have names appropriate to used-clothing boutiques.

• June Holley started the Appalachian Center for Economic Networks to help local subsistence farmers move out of poverty. The organization operates an enormous commercial kitchen in which over one hundred farmers test products and network with each other. With donated marketing assistance and cut-rate financial loans, many of these poor farmers have gone on to start successful small businesses, creating hundreds of new jobs in an area notorious for its high unemployment.

How does an organization become more entrepreneurial? Every nonprofit organization is structured in some way, has evolved its own processes for communicating and resolving issues, and has a distinctive culture reflecting its values and beliefs. Together, the structure, processes, and culture make up the organizational climate, which is the distinctive way the organization pursues its mission. In an entrepreneurial organization the climate is carefully designed to support innovation, creativity, and entrepreneurship.

In a new organization, like the Appalachian Center for Economic Networks, the leader has great latitude to design the organizational climate from the outset. When a leader steps into an ongoing organization, as David Clarke did at the ninety-five-year-old Regis College (see Chapter Five), a strongly entrenched organizational climate already exists, but with persistence and board support, it can be redirected over time. At both the Appalachian Center and Regis College, both the organization and the leader could properly be characterized as entrepreneurial.

There are many steps a leader can take to create an entrepreneurial organizational climate, including the following:

Act entrepreneurially. Because leaders are seen by others as role models, it is important that they act as entrepreneurs themselves, constantly challenging the conventional wisdom and welcoming new ideas. They can put themselves at the leading edge of change by networking with the most creative people in their fields and taking the lead in public-private consortia to develop new programs. They can set goals for innovation, such as starting a new program each year. They can proudly feature new organizational initiatives in annual reports, newsletters, and public speeches and make sure that board members do likewise.

Organize for innovation. Leaders can fight bureaucratic impediments to innovation by, for example, minimizing the number of people needed to approve expenditures or authorize changes. They can create less hierarchical organizations, where more staff members are in contact with clients and have both the authority and the responsibility to exercise initiative in serving client needs. They can establish project teams with client representation to design new programs and pilot programs to test them. They can make the organization more future oriented by ensuring that their actions are consistent with the vision and with evolving trends in the outside world.

Create processes and programs that support entrepreneurial initiatives. Leaders can strive, as shown in the Appalachian Center example, to make it easy for people to experiment with new ideas. They can constantly measure client satisfaction and design processes that are flexible and responsive, allowing the staff and volunteers considerable latitude in the way they deliver services to clients. They can ensure that timely information is available to everyone in the organization, not just the management, and trust people to use it wisely.

Gear the incentive systems to entrepreneurship. Leaders can evaluate people on the creativity and innovation they bring to their jobs and on improvements in their areas of responsibility. They can recognize and reward those who make entrepreneurial contributions with salary increases, bonuses, and promotions. They can be tolerant of failure, knowing that if there aren't some failures, it is likely that people aren't trying hard enough to find new ways to do things.

Invest organizational capital in new ideas. Leaders can invest in those who champion innovation and take prudent risks, and allow them sufficient time to develop their ideas. They can support training to increase entrepreneurial skills. They can authorize many pilot projects to test new ideas. They can institutionalize suggestion systems and respond promptly to worthy proposals.

Promote creativity and organizational learning. Leaders can seek to hire bright, creative people with the curiosity and motivation to try new things. They can challenge people to be creative by questioning traditional approaches and using every opportunity in meetings to brainstorm new approaches. They can help the organization learn by pushing people to engage at all levels with others who share similar goals and are addressing similar issues.

This nation will be well served if leaders steer their nonprofit organizations toward becoming more entrepreneurial. In the end, that's what will lead nonprofit organizations to the greater good we have been advocating throughout this book. An entrepreneurial outlook will renew and transform organizations that, for all they have accomplished to date, may still have enormous unrealized potential.

Organizational Renewal and Transformation

All major changes involve serious choices between alternatives that will have very different outcomes for the organization. The leader is called upon to act as change agent by exercising her judgment and shaping the way the institution evolves. Some of these choices will gently redirect the organization, whereas others will more dramatically revitalize the organization or even lead to its complete transformation.

To understand the nature of organizational renewal and transformation, we need to review the life cycle of a typical nonprofit, which goes through four stages. In the start-up phase, a single individual or small group determines the need for a new organization, gathers the resources, entices people to serve on a board of directors, establishes a charter and a legal entity, and commences operation. With effective leadership, good management, and good luck, the organization then enters the second, or growth phase, where new resources are found in order to expand the size and scope of the organization. The first two stages are thus highly entrepreneurial.

The growth of the organization may be slow or fast, but eventually it reaches the third phase, known as maturity. A mature organization has enough experience to know what works and has established itself in the community. By this time its structure and procedures have been formalized. It delivers its services efficiently and well. Other organizations and clients have come to depend upon it. In many ways maturity is both the most successful and the most dangerous stage for a nonprofit organization, because from here it can move in one of three directions—decline, renewal, or transformation.

Decline is the fourth and final phase of an organization's life cycle, often ending with its demise or merger into some other entity. Decline happens when the activities of an otherwise successful organization become so inflexible in the pursuit of efficiency and continuity that the organization loses touch with the changing needs of its clients or the community. The organization then either slowly sinks into irrelevance or is made obsolete by more responsive groups. Boarded up church buildings and small private colleges no longer able to attract students are examples of nonprofits in decline.

Organizational Renewal

Instead of falling into decline, however, an organization can continually renew itself, thereby prolonging its maturity phase for a very long time. Many religious institutions, for example, have survived for centuries by holding fast to their basic beliefs as they also interpret and adapt their practices in response to new needs and circumstances. Today it is as inconceivable to imagine the Catholic

Church conducting an Inquisition or a Jewish synagogue endorsing animal sacrifice as it would have been for an ancient leader of one of these religions to imagine television ministries. Harvard University enjoys international prominence today not for the programs it established in 1636 under a Puritan minister but for the many leading-edge programs it introduced year after year since then in science, medicine, business, law, and other fields.

An organization can renew itself in any of several ways, depending on the nature of the challenges it faces. Certainly, the appointment of a new executive director or board chairman will often rekindle hope in a dispirited organization, but renewal need not await such an event. Anytime an organization gets stale or seems to be in a rut, an attentive leader can act promptly to deal with the problem and signal to the board and staff that better days are ahead.

Often relatively minor changes can contribute to organizational renewal. For example, if the organization is basically sound but is becoming lax about cost controls, all that might be needed to get it back on track is for the leader to highlight the problem and perhaps engage in some prudent cost cutting to slim the organization down or shape it up. If certain programs are losing their attractiveness to the clients or the community, they may have to be revised, or in some cases replaced, by more effective ones. The Indian Health Board was renewed and energized each time Norine Smith introduced a new program or upgraded its obsolete systems and facilities.

Sometimes more dramatic actions are needed to renew an organization and maintain its momentum. For example, soon after Faye Wattleton became president of Planned Parenthood Federation of America, she completely reorganized the staff to emphasize public affairs and closer relations to the 178 affiliate chapters across the country. She recruited top people for these jobs and created pay-for-performance compensation packages. She became far more visible on the lecture and television circuit than her predecessor and over time was able to triple the organization's budget through increases in donations.

Strategic planning is another way for leaders to revitalize a nonprofit organization, as discussed in the previous chapter. For example, Bryson (1995, p. 17) tells how a Protestant congregation originally founded in 1857 renewed itself in 1989 with a strategic plan designed to make the church more attractive to young families with children.

Organizational Transformation

Instead of moving into the fourth phase and declining or of prolonging the maturity stage through renewal, organizations have one other alternative. An organization can transform itself into a new entity, with an entirely new vision and mission and a dramatically different operating style. Here are three examples:

• In the last chapter, we showed how David Clarke transformed a small liberal arts college for undergraduates that was already beginning to decline into a thriving regional university serving midcareer professionals. This required a change in the fundamental nature of the organization and a new paradigm of service. No aspect of the structure, programs, operations, or management of the organization remained untouched. Transformation always entails a good deal of risk and uncertainty and may take many years to complete, but the results can be dramatic.

• The Rand Corporation in Santa Monica, California, started out as a nonprofit organization conducting leading-edge research and development on national defense issues. Because many of its projects involved computers, Rand soon had large numbers of programmers producing software for major air defense systems. Rather than have the programming work overwhelm the research, Rand spun it off into a new independent nonprofit called System Development Corporation. In time the spin-off grew so large and diversified into so many other areas of software development that its board eventually sold the entire operation to Burroughs Corporation and distributed the proceeds for charitable purposes. Meanwhile Rand itself went through several other transformations, so that today defense research is only a part of a much larger operation that includes a doctoral degree program in policy sciences and research on a variety of economic, demographic, educational, health, and other issues at the local, state, federal, and global levels.

• The National Audubon Society was founded in the nineteenth century for the study and protection of birds and their habitats. But a century later Audubon found this to be too narrow an interest, as other vigorous environmental organizations attracted supporters by concentrating on the larger ecosystem. In response Audubon transformed itself. It continued to respect its original mission as the friend and protector of birds, but it also embraced a wider sense of environmental consciousness. For example, it created excellent educational programs to help young people understand the role and importance of birds in the larger ecology. It also created a national headquarters in New York City that is a national model of environmental responsibility.

There are many other modes of organizational transformation, but the one that has received the most attention among nonprofits recently is the formation of strategic alliances.

Strategic Alliances

A strategic alliance is any form of coordination or collaboration between two or more nonprofit organizations who pool their strengths in order to achieve common goals. The alliance may range from loosely coordinated, as in a network or coalition, to fully integrated, as in the merger of two or more nonprofit organizations into a single entity. We can only introduce the subject here, but many comprehensive treatments are available: for example, Arsenault (1998), McLaughlin (1998), and Bartling (1998).

A network is a loosely affiliated group of individuals and organizations that address similar societal problems and join together to share information or resources. For example, regional networks might deal with problems of child abuse, community development, or the environment. Each nonprofit organization in the network retains its own identity and board of directors but meets from time to time with the others to pursue common interests, such as advocating the passage of a new ordinance, sharing technical information, or conducting workshops and seminars on areas of mutual interest.

A coalition or consortium is a more structured form of collaboration between nonprofit organizations, such as a group of organizations that aid the homeless or a regional arts association. The consortium might have its own budget, executive director, and board of directors. The individual member organizations retain their own identity but use the coalition to pursue certain projects they have in common: for example, to carry out joint fundraising efforts, to coordinate program offerings, to conduct community surveys and needs assessments, and to educate the public and legislators on critical issues.

A particularly successful example of a coalition is a group put together in 1988 by the city officials of Rock Hill, a small suburb of Charlotte, North Carolina. The steering committee consisted of the CEOs of seven institutions: the Rock Hill Economic Development Corporation, two private colleges, the school district, and three other public and private entities. The coalition set up six committees of about twenty leading citizens each to produce a plan (titled "Empowering the Vision") that would transform the community from a decaying textile town with high unemployment into a thriving modern city.

Although not relinquishing any of its own powers, each member organization of the coalition agreed to synchronize its decisions with those of the members for the greater good of the community. For example, when the Economic Development Corporation launched TechPark, an office and light manufacturing park, York Technical College opened a day-care center nearby to train day-care aides and to serve TechPark, and the city built a greenway linking TechPark to other community facilities. Within a few years the coalition had revitalized Rock Hill's downtown area, beautified the city, launched several arts festivals and a new art center, and attracted new employers and foundations to invest in the community.

Although networks and consortia don't necessarily cause their member organizations to transform themselves, they often do. Moreover, they can evolve over time from loose affiliations to close relationships between the member organizations. This can happen when confidence builds between the partners as they work together and get to know and trust each other.

Eventually, some organizations might pool their resources, merge, or transform themselves into a totally new entity that goes beyond what either partner attempted previously. A common example is when several local agencies combine to form a regional nonprofit organization. Alternatively, a funding agency like a community foundation might urge two nonprofit organizations to pool their resources or merge to achieve economies of scale or provide better service to their clients. For example, the Marin Community Foundation in California encouraged the merger of several youth programs into the Youth Leadership Institute and also helped consolidate several environmental organizations, each of which had been working on some aspect of San Francisco Bay.

In many fields, such as low-income housing and job training, government agencies favor the development of a particular form of consortium, the public-private partnership. This is an independent nonprofit organization specifically chartered to accept and administer public funds to achieve an integrated and comprehensive solution to a particular social problem. The partnership often includes representatives of public agencies, private corporations, and nonprofit organizations. It has its own board and executive director with specific fiscal and operational responsibilities.

Sometimes a profit-making corporation will sponsor or adopt a nonprofit organization to achieve a social purpose. For example,

American Honda Corporation developed Eagle Rock School in Colorado as a home for troubled teenagers. Under the leadership of Robert Burkhardt, the school has had an excellent record of turning these students around and helping them become useful members of society. Honda built the school for $17 million and still spends $25,000 annually on each student. The successful techniques developed there are shared with some two thousand teachers, principals, and scholars who visit the school each year to learn how to improve their own programs.

Strategic alliances may take many forms beyond the networks, coalitions, and public-private partnerships discussed here. Whatever the form, however, an important effect of strategic alliances is that they enable leaders of nonprofit organizations to leverage their influence in a community. Together these leaders can help each other see the big picture, identify service gaps and community needs, and share useful information.

Through a strategic alliance, leaders making efforts to address community issues can engage a wider spectrum of the community with diverse talents and resources. They can reach out to critical stakeholders, allowing them to build confidence in each other and have meaningful participation in decision making. They can command the attention of the media and help build grassroots support for community change.

The leaders of nonprofit organizations have a degree of flexibility that is frequently unavailable to their strategic partners in government agencies or public corporations. They can initiate programs free of the suspicion that they are doing so to realize profits or political gain. Moreover, nonprofits can seek support from foundations and public fundraising events, can run experiments to test risky ideas, and can enlist volunteers in the common cause.

Because of this flexibility, nonprofit leaders can often serve as the catalyst that enables a strategic alliance in the first place or that moves it along when the other partners encounter institutional constraints. They can act as deal makers and facilitators in the public interest. They can lubricate the processes through which corporate resources and public authority are marshaled to achieve a public good. Thus, through strategic alliances, nonprofit leaders can play a major role in shaping their communities.

The Leader's Role as Change Agent

Throughout this book, we have been highlighting nonprofit leaders who made a big difference in their communities. Like Norine Smith, they led their organizations through difficult transitions, ultimately passing on to their successors nonprofits that were stronger, better able to serve their constituencies, and considerably changed from what these individuals found when they assumed leadership.

Much of the time that's what leadership is all about—making the right changes at the right time to improve the organization's effectiveness. Effective leaders tend to be extremely sensitive to opportunities for change. One study of twenty successful university presidents found that these leaders seemed to have an almost uncanny ability to pounce on opportunities before others were even aware that they existed (Watkins, 1986, p. 20).

Being the principal agent of change requires that the leader be able to perform six tasks. We have already discussed two of them: namely, creating an entrepreneurial climate and developing strategic alliances. The other four tasks are to define reality, to get everyone into the act, to keep an eye on the prize, and to make timely decisions.

Define Reality

A prominent corporate leader maintains that a prime responsibility of a leader is to define reality (De Pree, 1989, p. 9). This is especially important when the leader is trying to effectuate change, because the greatest enemy of change is the tendency of boards and staffs to want to perpetuate the present, thereby implicitly denying a change is needed. It is up to the leader to identify the need for change and create a sense of urgency for it.

Think of the leaders of great societal movements for change, such as Martin Luther King Jr. fighting for civil rights or Betty Friedan campaigning for women's rights. In every case their most powerful weapon for arousing public sentiment was their ability to define the full dimensions of reality, with all its injustices, hardships, and failures. In this way they demonstrated the need for change and set in motion the forces for reforming the system.

Successful nonprofit leaders are able to foster a shared view of reality, the necessary first step in any change process. They understand the true needs and expectations in the community and are able to articulate the strengths and weaknesses of their constituencies in addressing these needs. They describe trends shaping the future context of the organization and suggest what has to be done to adapt to these trends. They explain the board's priorities and agendas to the staff, and the staff's needs to the board, and all of this to potential donors, volunteers, and other stakeholders.

Get Everyone into the Act

Nonprofit leaders are great believers in participation. Sometimes it seems as if they feel it is necessary for all constituencies to be involved in everything. Of course that's a formula for disaster. It explains why nonprofit boards sometimes get to be so large and often unwieldy, and why endless meetings seem to be needed to resolve even simple issues. If getting everyone into the act means that nothing gets done unless everyone agrees with it, then there's little hope for change.

Instead, the art of involving people in change processes is like that of directing an orchestra—that is, it requires knowing what role each person should play and how people can interact most effectively with each other to achieve what needs to be accomplished. Effective leaders select the team that will be responsible for implementing change and create a setting in which team members can work well together. They establish a common framework of values and expectations. They appoint to positions of team leadership those already strongly committed to the change. They make sure the change process moves along on schedule and express their concern when it does not.

In the end, getting everyone into the act means that all points of view are heard and all who can advance the change or make it more effective are given an opportunity to do so. It also means that the leader has lined up the necessary political and financial support from outside the organization (see Chapters Eight and Nine).

Keep an Eye on the Prize

Because a nonprofit organization has its own momentum, a proposed change will interact with ongoing activities in many ways, with results that cannot be wholly predictable. Effective leaders are ever on the alert for signs that the change process is losing its focus or is being marginalized by other activities in the organization.

By the questions they ask and the measures they monitor, leaders ensure that the change process stays on target and helps move the organization closer to achieving its mission and vision. They are always ready to step in to remove obstacles or reinforce the need for change.

A more delicate task for the leader is keeping the board fully informed and supportive of desired changes yet also preventing individual board members from micromanaging these changes. The board, which is a partner of the executive director in the leadership of the organization, must itself be led at times. As the president of one nonprofit organization told us, "I have to treat my board as if it were infallible, but malleable."

Make Timely Decisions

At critical points in every change process, decisions must be made that can be made only by the leader. Effective leaders seek all the information they can get and then, using their best judgment and intuition, make the critical decisions that shape the future of their organizations.

It is fashionable in management literature these days to downplay the role of leaders as decision makers in order to underscore the role of the board, the staff, and other stakeholders in the decision process. In this view, stakeholder participation, power sharing, team building, and the decision process are given more emphasis than the decision-making role of the leader or even the quality of the decision. Doubtless these aspects of decision making often influence leader's decisions. However, the effective leaders we know and have studied spend a significant portion of their own time analyzing alternatives and making and implementing decisions.

Leaders of nonprofit organizations recognize their obligation to establish priorities and choose among alternatives as an important part of their job description. Even when others are involved in analyzing or recommending a decision—as they often are and should be—the leader chooses whether to support or veto the recommendation and, if she does support it, determines how much organizational capital to invest in its realization.

Furthermore, it is the leader who bears ultimate responsibility for the success or failure of a decision. Her career and effectiveness depend in no small part on the quality of her judgments over time. Good judgment is an amalgam of good information, insightful analysis, foresight, and courage. A leader is not born with good judgment. It comes only from experience (and, as one wag has pointed out, experience comes from bad judgments). That's why track records are so vital when boards are selecting leaders.

Building the Community

Thus far we have been discussing the way leaders renew and transform their organizations. Another domain in which leaders act as change agents is the building of community. They do this in many ways, both directly and indirectly.

We have already shown how nonprofit leaders influence their communities directly by providing a variety of social goods and by acting as neutral, public-spirited, nonprofit partners in public-private consortia and strategic alliances. Similarly, they serve on the boards of other community agencies and have a voice and often considerable influence on the plans for the future of the community.

Indirectly, leaders build community by making their own organizations a haven for those who feel disenfranchised or otherwise powerless. Many individuals see themselves as victims of illness, pollution, crime, discrimination, or a variety of other social ills. Nonprofit leaders encourage these people to think of themselves as actors instead of victims, empowering them to serve as change agents in their communities. In the process they build community values, elevate the spirit, and contribute to a common quest for a higher quality of community life.

In the end the major decisions that move nonprofit organizations toward the greater good are those that create a new reality for both their clients and for the community they serve. When Norine Smith decided to pursue larger quarters for the Indian Health Board despite its budget deficits, she was not just boldly moving the organization to a higher level of performance but was also giving hope to the Indian community and helping community members to help themselves. In the process everything changed at the Indian Health Board as well—its values, its attractiveness to donors and volunteers, and most of all, its image of itself and what was possible. That's what we mean by identifying the leader as an agent of change.

Part III

Strengthening Relationships

7

Leader as Coach
Building the Team

*It is one of the most beautiful compensations of this
life that no man can sincerely try to help another
without helping himself.*

Ralph Waldo Emerson

Bill Strickland's life could be the script for a movie. *Strickland's Saga* would recount the archetypal journey of a native of Manchester, a multiethnic and low-income neighborhood in Pittsburgh, Pennsylvania, from student in an inner-city high school to president of two of the most successful nonprofit organizations in the nation and recipient of a $295,000 MacArthur genius grant.

Bill Strickland was a high school tenth grader when he was taken under the wing of art teacher Frank Ross. It was Ross who taught him the history and practice of ceramics and later helped him gain admission to the University of Pittsburgh in 1965. While a college student, Strickland periodically returned to Manchester to share what he had learned with street kids who were just what he had been a few years before. A local church lent him the use of an old row house, and Strickland opened a ceramics studio to teach poor students to make pottery. He raised $18,909 in contributions for two years, paying himself an annual salary of $2,000.

After graduating from college, Strickland learned to fly. He was a pilot for Braniff Airlines until it went out of business, flying commercial jets on weekends but spending his weekdays teaching ceramics in Manchester.

He first came to national attention on public television, talking about pottery on *Mister Rogers' Neighborhood* and escorting the children who watched the show through the Manchester Craftsmen's Guild, the name he had chosen for his ceramics studio.

At the guild, young people who were dropouts, in trouble with the law, or street kids alienated from their families were provided with first-rate mentors, top-of-the-line equipment, and an abundance of inspiration. Each year some three hundred Pittsburgh-area students came to the Manchester Craftsmen's Guild to study art, ceramics, drawing, photography, and digital graphics. Over the years about 80 percent of these students went on to college. In an atmosphere both sophisticated and nurturing, the faculty not only imparted useful skills but also motivated the students, reinforcing Strickland's philosophy that the arts can save lives and help bring about social change.

In 1972, Strickland also took over the Bidwell Training Center, a nonprofit vocational school for adults in the same Manchester neighborhood. In Pittsburgh, thousands of people had lost their manufacturing jobs as factories closed throughout the Rust Belt. These closures especially affected many blacks, women, and people with few educational credentials.

Bidwell offered training, hope, and results. Economically disadvantaged and dislocated workers could enroll in courses of study leading to such occupations as chemical laboratory technician, culinary arts worker, medical secretary, medical claims processor, pharmacy technician, and business travel counselor. Programs in adult literacy, information sciences, and GED preparation helped these populations meet their general educational needs. The Bidwell graduates had a high degree of success in finding places in the workforce at good wages.

Bidwell Training Center offered these programs in a 48,000-square-foot facility that included classrooms, a fully equipped kitchen, a 250-seat dining room, a culinary teaching amphitheater, a pharmacy, a chemical laboratory, an on-line computerized travel reservation system, and computer labs. The building was opened in 1986 after a $7 million capital campaign. The Manchester Craftsmen's Guild was also housed there, in a 14,000+-square-foot space that included a ceramic art studio, a photography studio and labs, a drawing studio and art gallery, digital audio and broadcast video recording studios, a library, and a 350-seat music hall.

Bidwell and Manchester are paradigms of entrepreneurial nonprofit organizations. Manchester now offers classes in the performing arts and hosts a world-class jazz festival. Performances are often broadcast on National Public Radio, and the 1997 Grammy for best large jazz ensemble went to a Manchester CD: *The Count Basie Orchestra Live at Manchester Craftsmen's Guild*.

Bidwell and Manchester also collaborate where feasible. For example, Bidwell trains food service workers employed by Manchester to feed hundreds of students a day in its restaurant. Strickland also launched a for-profit, minority-managed gourmet catering company. Recently, Bidwell moved into a second campus building with some 195,000 square feet of classroom and office space and 40,000 square feet of botanical gardens housed in nine stories, a $38 million expansion of the vocational training desperately needed by the inhabitants of Pittsburgh's inner city.

Of course Bill Strickland did not do all of this alone. Although he provided the vision, inspiration, and leadership, it took a large number of other people to operate the facilities and the numerous, ever expanding programs and course offerings of both the Manchester Craftsmen's Guild and Bidwell Training Center. He depended upon the energy and teamwork of many staff, board members, volunteers, donors, and community supporters, whom he was able to organize into efficiently functioning units.

From humble beginnings Strickland evolved into a consummate leader-coach, earning the trust, support, and loyalty of his staff. He did it by becoming an expert in performing the following tasks:

- *Building a staff team*

- *Igniting the passion* of everyone involved, including the unpaid board and volunteers

- *Designing the right kind of organization* and developing effective operating procedures

- *Creating an organizational culture* with common values, attitudes, and expectations

- *Developing a successful board-staff relationship*

- *Encouraging top performance* and ensuring that performance is carefully reviewed and good performance rewarded, understanding legal and employment issues such as respecting diversity and settling grievances, and facing the tough issues of accountability and responsibility

- *Fostering growth in the organization* so as to increase its capacity to make a difference in the community

These are responsibilities that all leaders share in performing their important roles as coach and as team builder.

Building a Staff Team

The premise of this book is that the central task of the leader is to help the organization reach a new, higher level of service to its clients and community. But that's like saying the task of a football coach is to win games. Both statements are true, but in both cases the work is actually accomplished not by the leader or the coach alone but by the team he develops for the purpose.

A strong team in a nonprofit organization is one in which team members have diverse skills and backgrounds but share common goals, are committed to a common cause, provide mutual support, and communicate well with one another. The fine art of team building requires selecting the right people with the right skills, positioning them so that they can make their greatest contributions, and fostering their sense of mutual responsibility for achieving the organization's mission and vision.

A new leader inherits the team of his predecessor but over time has an opportunity to reshape it to fit his own priorities. In a smaller nonprofit a change in just a half dozen positions might represent a wholesale turnover. In one medium-sized nonprofit, the new CEO inherited a staff of sixteen people, but with ordinary turnover and the growth of the organization, he had hired fully thirty-six of the people working on his expanded team of forty persons in only six years.

The leader-coach faces several issues in creating and organizing a team. First, he needs to establish a clear understanding with the board about his prerogative and authority with regard to staff changes. Of course it is never a good idea to replace well-functioning staff to make way for the CEO's own people. It is best to give people a chance to perform and to demonstrate their competence. Nevertheless the authority to make critical personnel decisions must be vested by the board in the leader to prevent future conflicts over hiring and firing.

Once this understanding is established the leader needs to assess the appropriateness of the existing organization for fulfilling its mission and vision.

Are the right people in the right jobs? Is the staff well structured, or does a reorganization seem called for? What additional skills and talents might be needed? How is the staff regarded in the community and among other nonprofit organizations, and who are the most respected staff members?

One especially important position is that of the chief deputy or second in charge. Every leader needs an assistant or alter ego to handle administrative matters and act for the leader when he is otherwise engaged. Some nonprofits, especially colleges and large advocacy organizations, split the leadership role; they have both an outside person (for example, a president or executive director), who handles mainly the political, fundraising, and direction-setting responsibilities, and an inside person (for example, an executive vice president, provost, or director of operations), who is responsible for running the organization day to day. In arts organizations of all sizes it is common to have both a general manager to focus on the administrative and financial side and an artistic director to lead the program effort.

Strong leaders want to build strong teams. They want people who can exercise initiative and leadership on their own, and who can operate more as colleagues and associates than as followers. This is what happened at Manchester Craftsmen's Guild and the Bidwell Training Center as they grew. Bill Strickland found himself relying on many colleagues to take responsibility and work closely with him for the success of the organization.

Strong leaders want the entire organization to have an integrity of its own and the ability to provide value to its clients and the community reliably and consistently. They also want the organization to develop its own distinctive competence and be recognized for its leadership in society. It takes strong teamwork to do that—and also a shared passion and commitment.

Igniting the Passion

A leader's passion for the possibilities of a nonprofit organization ignites the social energy needed to attain the vision. When it is widely shared, passion elevates the spirit of the board and staff members, helps them sustain optimism and hope for the future, and builds commitment and enthusiasm for the collective effort. Passion is most effective as an energizing force when the leader's words are accompanied by actions that exemplify and reinforce the spirit of the organization.

For example, one new leader of a venerable nonprofit think tank found that the fire had gone out of the organization and the staff seemed tired. Although the organization's studies and reports were still widely respected, the staff had lost confidence in the prior leader's ability to advance the organization's interests and influence. The new CEO expressed enthusiasm for the traditions and possibilities of the organization but also encouraged the board to see his presidency as a chance for a fresh start. When the board agreed to relocate the nonprofit to another part of the country, the new leader used the move as a symbolic declaration of the organization's reinvention. He knew that only those staffers who shared his passion for the organization's work would be willing to uproot themselves and relocate. He sparked excitement and dedication in his new staff and gave the organization a whole new sense of purpose and commitment.

The leader's vitality must be conveyed to others early on. This can occur both through collective interactions such as staff and board meetings and one-on-one conversations. To trigger enthusiasm in another person, the leader must marshal all his powers of vision, reason, and persuasion. People want to be inspired. They want to give their loyalty and support to their leader. But that support has to be earned; it is not automatically given.

Igniting the passion of colleagues and coworkers depends upon finding the right message. Many people will be encouraged by a new leader's vision. Others will respond to ambitious fundraising goals or new programs. Sometimes all that is needed is a stirring reminder of the organization's proudest achievements and a pledge to restore it to its former glory.

Leaders share their excitement and passion by forcefully describing the work ahead as a challenge to which they are committed and by inviting others to join them in meeting that challenge. They also take every opportunity to celebrate and cheer joint accomplishments and to reinforce people's feeling of being part of a team.

In the end what turns people on, what inspires and energizes them the most, is the opportunity to work with respected colleagues in pursuit of a worthwhile cause. People want to make a difference and to be where the action is. They will respond to a leader's passion and make it their own if they are shown how doing so will make them and the organization more effective and will help them grow and find meaning and excitement in their work.

Designing the Right Kind of Organization

Although nonprofit organizations vary greatly in size, structure, and complexity, they all exist for one overriding purpose, to make it possible for staff, board members, and volunteers to work together effectively to accomplish the organization's objectives. To achieve this cohesiveness, the leader must create the right kind of organization, one that is staffed by the right people, focuses on its mission and vision, and is appropriate for the circumstances in which the organization must operate.

Perhaps the dominant theme in designing organizations is the old adage that form follows function. Because the function of a nonprofit is to serve its clients and the community, most nonprofits organize themselves around the services they provide or the client groups receiving them. Beyond that, however, recent experiences suggest some other guidelines, as follows:

1. Organizations should be designed to foster collegiality, interdependence, and teamwork. Effective leaders work hard to clear away internal barriers to collaboration and to promote the emergence of many new leaders who can take the initiative in marshaling resources to serve the community better.

2. Organizations should be designed to be responsive to external developments. This means they should be open, flexible, and accessible. In fact, because many nonprofits today operate as part of public-private partnerships, many staff people owe their loyalties to several entities at once—their own organization, the public or corporate partner with whom the organization is teamed, and perhaps a third entity such as a quasi-independent board that manages the

partnership. These kinds of relationships can be quite complex but are manageable as long as everyone keeps the community service objective in mind.

3. Organizations should strive to develop a distinctive competence, something they can do better than anyone else. This might involve a unique service or service delivery system or a concentration on a particular underserved population. A recognized distinctive competence is a source of pride for everyone in the organization and a compelling argument when seeking funds from donors.

4. Organizations should strive to become what Peter Senge (1990) calls learning organizations: "organizations where people continually expand their capacity to create the results they truly desire, where new and expansive patterns of thinking are nurtured, where collective aspiration is set free, and where people are continually learning how to learn together" (p. 3). In practical terms this means there is a free flow of information in the organization, frequent feedback and consultation with all the stakeholders on major issues, and an openness to change (as described in the previous chapter).

5. Organizations should be designed to make full use of information and communications technologies, broadening their access to information from both inside and outside the organization. These technologies can also support new service delivery systems and enable people to work from their homes when that is appropriate. They make possible more fluid and responsive organizations than were feasible when information had to be compartmentalized and localized in individual departments or offices. Indeed, newer technologies like the Internet and remote conferencing may well revolutionize service delivery in such fields as health care, education, and counseling.

All these trends in the design of nonprofits suggests a movement from hierarchical structures toward organizational ecologies—loose assemblages of individuals, teams, public-private partnerships, and temporary alliances among various stakeholders, all contributing to the common effort and receiving sustenance from it. The leader in this conception is not so much the designer of the organization as the one who sets the tone and direction and shapes and fosters a shared organizational culture.

Creating an Organizational Culture

Passion provides the energy, and the organization provides the structure, but the culture—the shared beliefs, values, and basic assumptions that define "how we do business here"—determines how that energy and structure will be transformed into useful work. A major part of the leader's role as coach is to shape the organizational culture so that the resulting work contributes to the fulfillment of the mission and vision. Bill Strickland's success in Pittsburgh flowed from an organizational culture in which coworkers, board members, volunteers, and financial supporters all bought into the set of beliefs and values that he represented, the way of doing things that he had modeled from day one.

Upon assuming office the new leader needs to assess the existing organizational culture. For example, he'll want to determine how open and collaborative the organization is, how widely information is shared, which staff and board members have status and what the source is of their influence, and what the prevailing attitudes are toward various programs and client populations. With this understanding, and a clear sense of vision and strategy, the leader can identify the elements of the organizational culture that need to be strengthened and those that need to be changed.

According to a prominent scholar on organizational culture (Schein, 1992), leaders have five powerful tools with which they can shape the culture:

1. What the leader actually pays attention to, including what he asks about, measures, praises, or criticizes

2. How the leader reacts to crises, especially how he apportions responsibility and what he seeks to preserve

3. How the leader behaves as a role model, exemplifying certain values in his speeches and actions and demonstrating such qualities as empathy, loyalty, and self-sacrifice

4. Whom the leader chooses to reward, recognize, or promote, and especially what characteristics or behaviors seemed to elicit those rewards

5. Whom the leader hires and fires, which provides tangible evidence of the skills and attitudes he values and expects will contribute to the success of the organization

The nonprofit leader who is sensitive and responsive to the organization's culture will not act precipitously to change it, even if such change is on his eventual agenda, but will instead take a practical point of view and carefully lay the groundwork for significant alterations (see Exhibit 7.1). He will do his best to surface and

Exhibit 7.1. Initial Steps in Team Building.

- Show interest in people's ideas, but don't rush into commitments. People want to be heard, but they don't necessarily expect immediate action.

- Devise assignments that give colleagues opportunities to demonstrate their abilities and their potential before you make decisions about reassignments or fix roles and functions on the team.

- Select both short-term and longer-term goals for the first six months to a year of your tenure, and emphasize the importance of the team effort in achieving these goals.

- Plan a retreat, perhaps with an outside facilitator or presenter, to address and offer assistance with ongoing organizational issues of culture, communication, morale, and decision making.

- Seize every opportunity to express appreciation and give recognition to team units such as committees, task forces, and departments. Too often, only the head of the unit gets recognition; successful leaders reach out to all levels.

deal with issues that may have been simmering and causing discontent. He will open the organization to broad participation and seek continual feedback on proposed actions and policies.

This approach would have been a big help to one leader who left a major downtown law firm to head a small legal services agency. She was accustomed to lawyers using time sheets to track their work, but the legal services staff did not bill to clients and therefore had never kept such records. The new leader thought time sheets would be a good idea because they would help her demonstrate to foundation funders that they were getting their money's worth.

The staff grumbled but tried the idea out. After only a few days, however, the new leader was faced with a front office revolt. She quickly got rid of the hated time sheets because they simply were not appropriate in the culture of that organization. She could have avoided considerable pain had she moved more slowly and sought feedback from the staff in advance.

How does the leader know when the organizational culture is effective in uniting the organization? The best evidence is mutual support, loyalty, and trust; these form the cement that binds an organization together and provides a solid foundation for the leader's acceptance and legitimacy.

Developing a Successful Board-Staff Relationship

Few other topics in nonprofit organizations have as much of a life of their own as that of speculation about the governing body, the board of directors or trustees of the organization. The board has the legal and financial power—its members are the fiduciaries—and it makes such major policy decisions as hiring the CEO, approving the mission and vision, and investing in new facilities and equipment.

Usually recruited as volunteers from the community, board members almost universally serve nonprofits without remuneration. Many of them have other jobs, and they may be occupied with a nonprofit organization's affairs only periodically, depending upon their interests, the responsibilities of being an officer, and the needs of the organization. Each board has its own governing style, and this too will invariably shape the board-staff relations. John Carver, in his widely read book *Boards That Make a Difference* (1990), describes five typical prescriptions for governing style (see Exhibit 7.2). Most boards use some combination of these styles or switch from one style to another as circumstances require.

The leader is responsible for creating strong, stable, and positive relationships between the board and staff. Here are some of the things effective leaders do to bring that about:

Keep the board well informed. Board members frequently complain about access to information. They are especially upset when they appear to be the last ones to learn about something in which

---

Exhibit 7.2. Styles of Board Governance.

- *Board as watchdog.* The board's emphasis is on oversight as board members continually monitor the leader and his team. As Carver writes about this style, "Tight control is seen as the road to accountability." Consequently, frequent approvals and close questioning of the staff are routine when the board is a strict fiduciary.

- *Board as cheerleader.* The board is supportive of the staff, trusts the leader, and stays out of most operational matters, acting instead mainly in an advisory role.

- *Board as manager.* The board engages staff as a sort of super manager or, at least, as a partner in management with the top leadership. This setup may cause confusion over lines of responsibility and function.

- *Board as planner.* The board sees itself as responsible mainly for developing long-range strategies, and the board and its committees may spend long hours to create a plan document.

- *Board as communicator.* Believing that "the path to better governance lies in better human relations," the board treats the staff as collegial professionals with something worthwhile to offer and not just as employees. This is the traditional style in universities and health care agencies.

Source: Adapted from Carver, 1990.

they have a material interest. Board members deserve to be kept in the loop and appreciate receiving a well-organized and cogent newsletter, briefing paper, or regular e-mail to keep them up-to-date. One CEO makes it a practice to send a one- or two-page "President's Report" to each board member weekly, summarizing recent developments, important upcoming dates, special accomplishments or milestones, and items from the press.

Give special attention to the board chair. The relationship between the CEO and the chair or president of the board is a most critical one in establishing solid and productive board-staff relations. As an intermediary between the board and the staff, the CEO has to represent each party to the other, and the board chair is the leader's primary resource for that exchange of information. One CEO might schedule a regular breakfast with the board chair; another might prefer to speak with the chair periodically throughout the week. Sensitive issues like personnel or labor disputes are shared in these meetings so that the board is officially on notice about what is happening. Also, trial balloons can be offered to the board chair, to test their acceptability to the larger board.

Move quickly to resolve conflicts. The CEO must move promptly and directly to resolve any disputes threatening working relationships within the board or between board and staff. Candor and directness usually provide a strong impetus toward dispute resolution.

Reward success and celebrate achievements. Calling staff accomplishments to the attention of the board (and vice versa) is one of the smoothest avenues to good board-staff and CEO-staff relations.

Encouraging Top Performance

An important part of the leader's role as coach is establishing high standards of performance and being actively involved in giving both the praise and the criticism that are warranted. Recognition may be provided in different ways—through public acknowledgment, increased responsibilities or visibility, promotion, or in a few cases, merit pay or bonuses. The nonprofit leader should take full advantage of every opportunity to commend, recognize, acknowledge, and reward outstanding performance. It is one of the keys to building a team that trusts and respects its leader. Exhibit 7.3 lists some practical things a leader can do to thank, recognize, and reward his staff and other team members.

One nonprofit leader created a novel way to thank employees. Called Caught in the Act! the program asked staff members to briefly write up actions they felt deserved commendation and put these notes in a box in the staff lunch room. At the monthly staff meeting a drawing was held to determine the winner of a modest prize, a book certificate. Each of the nonwinning entries was also read and applauded, so everyone nominated had a brief moment of public acknowledgment.

Caught in the Act! highlighted such ordinary but important events of the workplace as staying late to help with someone else's project or taking an unassigned turn answering the phones because the receptionist went home sick. By supporting this staff-maintained program the leader showed that she thought it important to be

---

Exhibit 7.3. Reward and Recognition for Top Performance.

- Begin a staff or board meeting by highlighting the achievement of an individual or team within the organization.

- Write a memo for the personnel file outlining performance that is outstanding or exceeds expectations, and include the item in the annual performance review.

- In the nonprofit's newsletter or other publications, report staff members' contributions to professional groups, including service on committees or as officers, presentation of papers or workshops at conferences, publications, and so forth.

- Take a top-performing staff colleague to lunch or give him or her a small gift (for example, a book or calendar) as a form of recognition.

- If feasible, consider a salary increase or merit pay, perhaps by advancing the individual a step up in the pay scale.

---

grateful to people and thank them for their assistance. The program was an enormous success and a morale and team builder.

More formal and systematic personnel practices, such as performance reviews, must also be in place to encourage people to work to the best of their abilities. Performance reviews should be carried out as part of a carefully defined and described process. The more clarity and openness there is about how the system works, the more those affected by it are likely to cooperate and work with it. Most important, demystifying the evaluation process will reduce the tension and anxiety that naturally accompanies it. One key aspect of performance review is performance measurement, a subject sufficiently complex to merit its own chapter (see Chapter Ten).

The CEO defines the performance evaluation process and sets the tone. When performance review is seen as a diagnostic tool, one that documents achievement and identifies areas for improvement, the person being evaluated may view the report as balanced and fair. If the review is seen as punitive, people will obviously respond to it negatively and defensively. The CEO must declare and support the purpose and ensure the fair use of the process. His actions must set a good example for others.

The most difficult situation, of course, is the filing of a negative review, with its possible consequences of probation, demotion, or lack of pay increases. In the worst case, it may trigger a conflict that requires a grievance process, charges made to government agencies, or litigation before it is resolved. Even the leader who believes he is on top of the conflict must take care to draw upon the legal and personnel expertise of those who are familiar with labor law and workplace regulations, such as human resource specialists and attorneys.

One CEO always invites the staff members who report to him to furnish a written self-evaluation to assist his preparation of a review. This enables employees to highlight those actions and achievements that the leader may otherwise overlook. Sometimes a person who needs to improve performance will recognize it himself in a self-assessment, which makes it easier for the leader to address the issue.

Occasionally, the leader may need to sanction an employee for poor job performance, place an employee on probation, or even terminate employment. The leader needs to be aware that what he does in these situations, as in many others, will set an example for the organization. Subordinate managers and supervisors are likely to follow his example in making tough personnel calls. This is one of the most unpleasant and unrewarding aspects of the leader's job. It should be as handled as discreetly and confidentially as possible, and involve only the leader, the employee, and perhaps the employee's supervisor.

The leader should give a full hearing to the individual who faces discipline, listen to all sides of the story with an open mind, and be prepared to be very specific about expectations. It is most important that the process be conducted fairly and with compassion to minimize resentment and preserve the individual's dignity and self-esteem.

It is to be hoped that these occurrences will be rare. More often the nonprofit leader acts as a personal coach for individuals in the organization, trying to encourage them and help them improve their performance. For example, the executive director of a medium-sized arts organization found that she could strengthen relationships with colleagues by inviting them to accompany her to evening performances in the local arts community. The invitations were prized by the staff as an opportunity to have some quality time with the CEO. Sometimes she would ask a small group or department to accompany her and take them out to dinner as well. This simple practice built trust and goodwill in the organization and made her a more sympathetic and understanding coach.

A more difficult case arises when the person whose performance is at issue is a volunteer, perhaps even a leader among the volunteers, who give their time and talent without material compensation. Some grassroots and smaller nonprofits depend upon volunteers for most of their staffing. This is not an employer-employee relationship, so the incentives and sanctions available for use with regular staff do not exist for volunteers. Yet feedback is at least as important for volunteers as for regular staff.

Volunteers appreciate knowing how well they are doing in the eyes of others, especially those who are supervising their activities or leading the organization. Words of encouragement and constructive advice are likely to be welcomed by the volunteer, who is not participating to earn a living or advance on a career ladder. Indeed, this type of feedback is one of the major ways a leader can acknowledge that a volunteer is doing a good job and benefiting the community.

Sometimes staff or volunteers take advantage of a CEO's accessibility. In one organization a staff member started calling the leader at home with what could only be described as personal problems. The CEO referred the colleague to the organization's employee assistance program, which was one of the benefits under its health plan. Leaders might have reasonable differences of opinion about how much responsibility a nonprofit organization has or should assume for dealing with the personal problems that people bring to the workplace. It may depend upon the size of the organization or its culture, what people have become used to and expect. Among the more problematic areas in today's nonprofit organizations are labor issues, potential grievances, and even litigation arising from the claims of some employees that the workplace exacerbates their particular problems. This is a large and complex issue that we cannot delve into here, but the leader should be aware of the minefield that such matters may present to the organization.

In larger nonprofits a good human resource manager can anticipate such problems and stay current with the law. In smaller organizations an updated set of personnel policies and practices can be designed to handle such contingencies and deal with them fairly and discreetly. There is probably no area of leadership responsibility that causes more apprehension among boards of directors than personnel disputes, which can be legalistic, stressful, and expensive. Exhibit 7.4 lists some steps designed to prevent little episodes from becoming huge crises.

Fostering Growth in the Organization

With the larger interests of the team always uppermost in mind, there are many ways that a leader can use the coaching role to nurture individual and collective growth. It starts with setting high standards and expectations and hiring the best people available. Certainly Bill Strickland's achievements at both the Manchester Craftsmen's Guild and Bidwell Training Center could not have happened without his ability to attract and hold competent staff and volunteers who could follow in his footsteps and carry on the work of the organization as it grew.

The leader should also do everything possible to help staff increase their knowledge, improve their skills, expand their outlook, and work toward higher levels of performance. There are many ways to do this, including formal mentoring programs, networks and support groups,

---

Exhibit 7.4. Keeping the Lid on Legal and Employment Issues.

- Update the personnel policies (consult a specialist if there is no personnel manager on the staff) to make sure that they conform to the latest legal requirements and that everyone affected by them understands them.

- Establish policies and practices for handling grievances, putting the emphasis on conflict resolution, mediation, and arbitration.

- Solicit feedback from staff and volunteers frequently to obtain early warning of personnel problems before they become critical; then deal with them promptly.

- Put the improvement of people skills on the agenda for staff retreats and training.

- Invest in an employee assistance plan, or identify other resources that can be used to help employees who are struggling with such problems as alcoholism, depression, or serious family matters.

---

and job rotation. Many organizations support their people by reimbursing them for formal education such as returning to school to complete a degree or to obtain a new credential or certificate.

Leaders have a special responsibility for seeking to develop multiculturalism and diversity among staff. In social and human services agencies this is an old story because their client populations can often best be served by staff members who share the clients' language, cultural background, and ethnic origins. However, diversity has proven valuable in all types of organizations in generating innovative ideas; broadening the appeal of the organization; expanding its network of donors and volunteers; and making it more open, flexible, and responsive.

For example, the CEO of a small environmental organization was concerned that relatively few young people of color were being attracted to environmental causes or were working professionally for them. Determined to maximize opportunities for young people of color, this leader captured the interest of a local foundation. The foundation supported internships at the nonprofit to give high school and college graduates the opportunity to learn the field and work closely with senior people in the profession.

The leader who is trying to coach his teammates toward their fulfillment might also consider providing some research and development financial support, time, and space for those with promising ideas. By showcasing results that deserve recognition, and quickly adopting those that can improve organizational performance, the leader reinforces his commitment to innovative ideas and practices.

Finally, effective leaders know that guided self-discovery is one of the most powerful forces for staff development. Therefore they use every long-range planning exercise or retreat with the staff as an opportunity for self-discovery and team building. For example, as an organization contemplates its future challenges and opportunities or examines possible future scenarios, the staff can engage in fruitful exchanges on how the organization ought to respond to the new circumstances and what it needs to do to get ready. As participants learn about what they might be called upon to do in the future, they become aware of new skills or technologies they might need to master in order to be more successful at their jobs. The vision retreat process described in Chapter Four is also very useful for this purpose.

For example, one CEO who spent many years in a health organization stimulated his staff and those of other health providers by organizing an annual conference at which participants read scripts devised to encourage exploration of alternative scenarios that might occur in the community in the future. These scripts were always designed to reflect the current controversies and hot issues and were an impetus for an intensive and fruitful exchange.

In the end, leaders can be effective only when their staffs are effective, so the responsibility of the leader as coach is to ensure that everything is done to enhance staff effectiveness. As we have discussed in this chapter, that means igniting the passion; creating the right kind of organizational culture; building trust, loyalty, and mutual support between the board and staff; and taking every opportunity to develop the capabilities and enhance the performance of staff members.

As one writer puts it, leaders need to develop organizations "that are functioning well, that give the individuals within them a purpose and an identity, not through molding them into conformity but through challenging them to become active, innovative, responsible, and thus happy persons because they understand what they are doing and why it is important" (Bellah, 1991, p. 50).

8

Leader as Politician
Advocate, Troubleshooter, and Spokesperson

*Knowledge of human nature is the beginning and end
of political education.*

Henry Brooks Adams

Marian Wright Edelman, founder and president of the Children's Defense Fund, has been an outspoken advocate for poor and disadvantaged Americans throughout a long and distinguished career. A graduate of Spelman College and Yale Law School, Edelman was the first black woman admitted to the bar in Mississippi, where she led the NAACP Legal Defense and Educational Fund office in Jackson. She also campaigned for civil rights with Martin Luther King Jr. and came to Washington, D.C., as counsel for the poor people's march that King began organizing just before his assassination in 1968.

Edelman grew up in Bennettsville, South Carolina, the daughter and granddaughter of Baptist ministers. Her community was a highly segregated one, but in her father's church she was taught a powerful lesson about social justice. As Edelman writes in *The Measure of Our Success* (1992), "The message of my racially-segregated childhood was clear: let no man or woman look down on you, and look down on no man or woman" (p. 3). This philosophy helped fuel Edelman's passion for civil rights for all people. The imperative for service that was part of her upbringing would also eventually translate into her own lifelong quest for a better society.

Edelman was especially committed to children, remembering what she and millions of other blacks had experienced growing up in the South. In 1973, after years of work in the civil rights movement, she began the Children's Defense Fund (CDF) "to provide a strong and effective voice for all of the children of America, who cannot vote, lobby, or speak for themselves."

Edelman forged an organization whose programs and policies affect large numbers of children. CDF gathers data, disseminates information on key issues, monitors the development and implementation of federal and state programs, and provides education and support to a large network of other child advocates, service providers, public and private sector officials, and national, state, and local leaders concerned about the welfare of children.

Perhaps what CDF has become best known for is the unrelenting pursuit of its legislative agenda in the U.S. Congress and in state legislatures. Edelman emerged in the early 1990s as part of the kitchen cabinet of the wife of the governor of Arkansas and future first lady Hillary Rodham Clinton. When Bill Clinton was inaugurated as president in January 1993, one of his first legislative commitments was to the top priority on the CDF agenda, the passage of a bill that would provide immunization against such preventable childhood diseases as tetanus, polio, and measles for millions of children in low-income families.

Marian Wright Edelman personally lobbied that bill into existence. She met with numerous members of Congress, pressed the facts on them in an avalanche of reports and testimonials, and enlisted the active endorsement of every leader who could be persuaded to join in the CDF crusade.

CDF works closely with other private and government programs "to ensure that no child is left behind and that all American children have a Healthy Start, a Head Start, a Fair Start, a Safe Start, and a Moral Start in life" (Children's Defense Fund, 1997, p. I). It has a presence and mounts programs in virtually every state, with dedicated workers inspired by Edelman's leadership. She has made the Children's Defense Fund the most powerful children's lobby existing today, with an annual operating budget of over $20 million and an endowment of more than $13 million. Hundreds of foundations and corporations and thousands of individual donors support such programs as Active Child Watch, Freedom Schools, Children's Action Teams, and Children's Sabbath Congregations.

Because of this work Edelman is one of the most recognized and esteemed nonprofit leaders in the United States, the recipient of numerous honors and awards, including a MacArthur Foundation fellowship. For more than a quarter century she has also been a consummate politician, often sparring with more powerful people but knowing how to use her network of contacts and allies to persuade legislators to get the job done. For example, she played a major role in 1990 in the passage of the pathbreaking Act for Better Children, which created two programs providing $5 billion over five years to child care programs, representing the first acknowledgment by the federal government that, as Edelman would say, "children matter."

In acting as an advocate and spokesperson for the cause of children and her organization, she had to be clear about her mission and who would benefit from the programs she so passionately believed were needed. She enlisted allies all over the United States. Her comprehensive knowledge of the issues, solid speaking skills, and low-key manner have all contributed to her success.

Not all nonprofits are overt advocacy organizations like the Children's Defense Fund; nevertheless they all depend to some extent upon the ability of their leaders to form communities of common interest. The key to creating these communities is identifying all those with a stake in the success of the organization or its clients and enlisting them in a cooperative effort to achieve common goals.

The Focus on Stakeholders

Successful CEOs work at relationship building, patiently fashioning over time an extensive network of contacts that includes everyone who has a stake in the efforts and outcomes of the nonprofit organization. The process begins with an inventory of all of the possible individuals and groups that might be considered as stakeholders, including the following:

- *Staff* and members of the *board of directors*

- *Clients and customers,* those who actually use the nonprofit organization's services or goods

- *Volunteers,* those who share their time, energy, dollars, and concern for the organization

- Financial donors, sometimes called the organization's *angels*

- *Advocates,* those who are interested in policies and actions important to the organization

- *Other nonprofits* who are either allies on some issues or who serve similar clients

- *Business and commercial neighbors* and also companies further afield whose employees may be affected by the organization's work

- *Civic organizations,* such as chambers of commerce

- The *press and other media,* which exercise a protective watchfulness over the community interest

- *Government agencies* for whom the organization carries out contracts or that work in the same or related service areas

- The *community and the larger society,* which benefit from the services of nonprofit organizations, allow them to operate tax free, and provide the pool from which advocates, financial supporters, volunteers, and board members are drawn and developed

These stakeholders constitute the political family and supporting infrastructure of a nonprofit organization. In America's increasingly diversified communities, they are likely to include people who vary in race, ethnicity, national origin, and religious affiliation. Nevertheless, all stakeholders share a common interest in the cause for which their organization exists and operates. It is the leader's responsibility to strengthen and sustain ties with them. Here are some of the ways the leader meets that challenge and responsibility:

- By being passionate about the organization's mission and walking her talk

- By developing the trust and integrity that enables others to consider the leader's words as her bond

- By giving colleagues and supporters strong and persuasive reasons for the policies followed, actions taken, and outcomes produced

- By representing the organization in the community, acting as its public spokesperson to articulate the vision and values for which the stakeholders have come together

- By seeking and securing resources to develop and sustain programs that fulfill the organization's mission and that facilitate the involvement of all the stakeholders

- By earning admiration and recognition for the work done by the organization

- By acknowledging the individual contributions and achievements of all the stakeholders, thus building loyalty and long-term involvement

It is daunting to imagine giving appropriate attention to and developing strong working relationships with *all* of these constituencies. Still, this is the real challenge facing the leader who seeks to master the politics of a nonprofit organization. Certainly nonprofit organization leaders have had to be inclusive in order to function as credible spokespeople for diverse interests, maintaining frequent contact and communication with each sector of the coalition that has been shaped so that all its members are pulling in the same direction.

One of the secrets of some leaders' success has been figuring out ways to divide time and attention without neglecting any of the principal functions of the role—and without exhausting oneself. Burnout is a real problem for nonprofit CEOs, and delegating some parts of the political responsibility to trusted staff colleagues or board members is one way to lighten that burden.

One of Marian Wright Edelman's favorite techniques is to promote the talents of colleagues and allies working at the local level for the Children's Defense Fund or for other children's organizations. For example, inundated by speaking requests, she has steered many inquirers to a person or group in whom she has faith and confidence. "Talk to my friend Angela Blackwell in Oakland," Edelman responded to one Bay Area inquiry among the hundreds of speaking invitations she receives every year. "She and I think alike and she will do a good job for you."

When one of the authors of this book was the CEO of a large foundation, he was invited to literally dozens of affairs every month: press conferences, annual meetings, galas and fundraisers, recognition and award ceremonies, facility dedications, community meetings, officer installations, seminars and conferences, breakfast clubs, civic lunches, and many other events. It was *politically* necessary that the foundation be represented and show the flag at each of these events, but he understood that it would be impossible (and unnecessary) to attend everything himself.

So he developed the practice of personally calling the top person in the organization sponsoring the event, excusing himself because of "prior engagements," and saying that he was sending a colleague or board member who would report to him on the proceedings. Sometimes he followed up after the event with a brief note expressing thanks for the invitation and indicating that the report had been duly made. This was calculated political functioning, all part of the practice of sustaining and strengthening the relationships that are indispensable to the success of a nonprofit organization. Other ways to stay in touch are listed in Exhibit 8.1.

One CEO who understands the importance of staying connected is Clark Blasdell, executive director of Northbay Ecumenical Homes, a small nonprofit in Novato, California. Blasdell keeps his network of business leaders and politicians well informed, maintaining regular contact with them over a cup of coffee or a meal.

Exhibit 8.1. Ways to Stay in Touch with Stakeholders and Build a Political Base.

- Publish a regular newsletter sent to all stakeholders.

- Update the nonprofit's Internet web site to feature current developments, provide program statistics, give the addresses of officeholders that stakeholders should call or write to about issues and legislation.

- Host an annual community conference for stakeholders, to articulate current issues and share speculations about future developments.

- Set aside a special day for visiting with legislators; seek press and media coverage for these visits to politicians' offices.

- Periodically urge allies and stakeholders to write letters to the editor to keep their interests in the public view.

- Invite selected individuals or groups to meet privately with the CEO for personal updates and the opportunity to offer feedback.

This offers him the opportunity to share current information on an insider basis and to obtain feedback about his agenda. In addition, should an emergency arise, he would be able to call upon them for advice or assistance.

For example, on one occasion some monies became available to Northbay but they needed to be committed quickly, which meant that the paperwork had to be completed practically overnight. With his superb information network, Blasdell was able to anticipate the situation, respond immediately, and secure the funds for his agency's programs.

A good character, an accessible personality, and an ability to communicate well are highly valued in both political and nonprofit leadership. And political leaders' remarks sometimes show how much these leaders have in common with nonprofit leaders and how much can be learned from them about the political role. For example, Winston Churchill eloquently recognized that his main function as a spokesperson was to forcefully represent the people who actually did the work when he said: "It was the nation that had the lion's heart. I had the luck to be called upon to give the roar." And several decades later, Václav Havel, president of the Czech Republic, offered this more detailed and introspective view of how to be a successful spokesperson:

> It is largely a matter of form: knowing how long to speak, when to begin and when to finish; how to say something politely that your opposite number may not want to hear; how to say, always, what is most significant at a given moment, and not to speak of what is not important or relevant; how to insist on your own position without offending; how to create a friendly atmosphere that makes complex negotiations easier; how to keep a conversation going without prying or being aloof; how to balance serious political themes with lighter, more

relaxing topics; how to plan your official journeys judi-
ciously and to know when it is more appropriate not to
go somewhere; when to be open and when reticent and
to what degree.

But more than that, it means having a certain instinct
for the time, the atmosphere of the time, the mood of
the people, the nature of their worries, their frame of
mind. . . . Qualities like fellow-feeling, the ability to talk
to others, insight, the capacity to grasp quickly not only
problems but also human character, the ability to make
contact, a sense of moderation: all these things are
immensely important in politics [Havel, 1992, p. 11].

These qualities acquire meaning only in context, in a specific
setting in which there is an opportunity not only to hear what an
individual says but to examine his deeds and actions. Sometimes
the leader is confronted with stakeholders who are on opposite sides
of an issue. For example, a community foundation may have to deal
with *development types*, who want to build low-income housing, and
environment types, who in protecting the environment hope that
nothing will be built at all. The most politically astute and sensible
course of action for the leader of a community foundation that supports both low-income housing and the environment is to encourage dialogue and compromise. Leadership in this case calls for
mediating discussions between the two sides to help them reach
outcomes of mutual interest.

In his book *The Good City and the Good Life* (1995), Daniel
Kemmis, director of the nonprofit Rocky Mountain Institute,
describes a process that facilitates finding common ground among
people with diverse interests, experience, and even agendas. As a
state and municipal politician in Montana, Kemmis discovered that
he could not be effective without identifying and employing the
individual strengths of all the stakeholders so that a collective unity

could be fashioned. Knowing just how to make those individual assessments while keeping everyone under the same tent is a valuable skill for nonprofit leaders.

Kemmis realized that the key lay in careful cultivation of stakeholders—building trust, keeping people informed, and especially, reaching out to those with whom one has differences. The consummate nonprofit leader is the one who, as Henry Adams implied, uses human nature to advantage, creating a sense of family and mutual self-interest among the stakeholders.

The Leader as Public Advocate

Although all nonprofit leaders have responsibility for maintaining ties with external constituencies, there are some organizations, like the Children's Defense Fund, whose main purpose is public advocacy. In fact the active espousal of causes has been one of the great hallmarks of the U.S. political system, long admired by foreigners such as Alexis de Tocqueville (in his *Democracy in America*, [1835] 1969).

Literally thousands of interest groups representing millions of people—from small associations like local chambers of commerce to huge national organizations like the American Association of Retired Persons (AARP) with its thirty-three million members—maintain regular contact with their local and state legislatures and with Congress to implore, plead for, promote, urge, and recommend adoption of certain policies, programs, practices, or other courses of action.

Moreover, because government contracts and grant awards are such a prominent part of nonprofit support—up to 90 percent or more in some cases—influencing lawmakers' attitudes is an essential task for those who lead organizations dependent upon this kind of support and regulation. Thousands of programs in such areas as social services, education, environment, housing, transportation, and the arts are in this category at the federal level, and they encounter a similar structure of decision making and funding at the state and county levels. For the leaders of these organizations, advocacy is a major part of the job, affecting not just the level of their funding but the contractual relationships that determine how they operate and whom they can serve.

For the local nonprofit, likely to be a small to medium-sized organization, connections with government are more frequent at the municipal or county level. Advocacy for these organizations takes place at city hall or the county court building. This process is sometimes open—occurring through newspaper ads or political talk shows, for example—and sometimes private—through conversations at dinners or at the shopping mall, for example.

The advocacy process works both ways, connecting the nonprofit leaders to the desires and interests of their constituencies and simultaneously informing them of the needs of their organizations. It provides important information to leaders about what might be feasible in the legislative or bureaucratic climate at any particular time. Exhibit 8.2 lists some ways to build relationships and lobby for one's interests with officeholders.

Exhibit 8.2. Ways to Build Relationships with Officeholders and Politicians.

- Add a personal note to bulletins, newsletters, alerts, annual reports, and other publications that are routinely sent to government offices.

- Prepare a brief outline of key points in support of desired legislation and send it to officeholders.

- Attend community events where a politician will be speaking or appearing and seek a brief opportunity to share views.

- Stay in touch with the chief deputy or assistant in a politician's office and cultivate his or her attention and interest.

- Share letters of endorsement with officeholders, especially letters from business leaders and other prominent people in the community in support of the organization's agenda and priorities.

- Make a financial contribution to a politician's campaign (with your own money, of course, not the organization's).

One CEO, Mimi Silbert of San Francisco–based Delancey Street, an award-winning rehabilitation program that provides education, housing, job training, and new chances for ex-convicts and others with troubled lives, made it a regular practice to communicate her views to her congressional representatives and to update them on the progress of her agency. Silbert developed relationships with both U.S. Senators for her state, members of the House, and a wide range of other officeholders and government officials.

Her efforts enabled Delancey Street to be plugged into the political situation as well as to feed information and ideas to those policymakers. Delancey Street events were always well attended by politicians, business leaders, and other civic supporters. These relationships paid dividends when Delancey Street wanted to build a large new home for its residents and some of its businesses on the San Francisco waterfront. Silbert was able to secure the necessary approvals and her fundraising for the new project was extremely successful.

Being an active spokesperson for a cause requires a variety of skills on the part of the nonprofit leader. Here are some of the most important:

- An *ability to articulate a position*, which requires the leader to know the background (database) of the issues, be aware of both the strengths and weaknesses of the position, have persuasive reasons for adopting the course of action advocated, and understand the challenges of implementing that action.

- A *personal dedication to the underlying cause*, which demonstrates the leader's own full commitment to what is advocated.

- A strong *sense of trust and credibility*, which reassures supporters and others that the data and research used to support the leader's position are valid and that the commitments made in the organization's name will be carried out.

- A *willingness to partner with other organizations* to find the best solution for the larger community, to be part of a team effort, and to avoid the ego battles among agencies that sometimes dilute their effective response.

- A *sensitivity to the timing and means* required to be suitably seen, heard, and noticed. Advocacy is a strategic exercise, and it is more likely to hit the target if audiences are properly alerted, time and place are carefully selected, and the message is clear and succinct.

- A *knowledge of how to use the press and other media* to the organization's advantage, by such means as seeking opportunities to be interviewed on local cable television and going into interviews with one's own idea of what one intends to get across.

Being the advocate or spokesperson for a nonprofit organization can be a twenty-four-hour-a-day responsibility. In addition to scheduled meetings and public events, leaders are often called upon at unforeseen times to speak on behalf of their organizations. For example, a leader should always be prepared to be contacted by the media without warning to offer reactions to some development related to her organization's interests. The politically astute CEO never declines the opportunity to give an appropriate message to a receptive audience.

Every nonprofit leader should consider creating for public consumption at least three basic messages, which can be labeled the generic, the popular, and the political messages. For purposes of illustration, imagine a nonprofit focused upon cleaning up the environment. The *generic* message might be that the organization is a partner in a regional effort with other public and private environmental agencies, including government units dealing with Superfund sites, to reduce heavy metal pollution in the lakes and streams of the state. The organization hopes to find alternative long-term ways of disposing of toxic substances. Field studies are taking place to ascertain safety levels for each of the substances at issue. The generic message is thus one designed for the collegial, professional, and policy level. It has a helpful amount of detail and uses the jargon familiar to the environmental field.

The *popular* message is devised to help the general citizenry understand what is happening. It might go like this: a coalition of public and private environmental organizations has been formed to work in partnership with the industrial companies that are creating or using toxic substances, to find solutions that will work for everyone involved. Its purpose is to reduce the risk to the community's citizenry, especially the children who may be vulnerable. This message focuses on finding answers to the problem rather than on punishing those who could be easily blamed. The popular message is designed for general public consumption, and emphasizes features that would be expected to play well in the media, such as partnering and reducing risk.

Finally, the leader's *political* message might be that her nonprofit organization is entering into an agreement with a consortium of local manufacturers to investigate policies and practices across the country in order to learn how other communities resolve these kinds of environmental conflicts. The investigating group will report to constituents on both sides and endeavor to use the community's overall and long-term interest as the consensus criterion when advocating a solution. It is reserved for those occasions when the CEO has to explain what her organization is actually doing to make progress on the issue. It is the political explanation.

The Leader as Troubleshooter

Perhaps at no point are the leader's political skills tested as thoroughly as when a crisis occurs. This crisis might be triggered by a resignation, termination, or labor dispute involving the staff or board. Certainly, if there are suggestions of financial irregularities or litigation against the organization for any reason, board members will become alarmed and will expect a prompt response by the leader. Sometimes, a mere criticism of the organization by a public official or an adverse story in the press or other media will put the organization in a crisis mode. Other examples of events that can become crises are the loss of a major donation or grant that had been routinely expected, and a charge of sexual harassment or discrimination.

However it happens, at some point in the life of most leaders a crisis will arise that demands the fullest exercise of political talents. In these circumstances the CEO needs to draw upon her instincts and abilities to face the issues honestly, take quick action where required, deflect unwarranted charges, cool the hotheads, and make a credible public response. Although crises are oriented most often to developments outside the organization, political crises can also occur within the organization, with little public interest or involvement. A nonprofit leader's political instincts must be attuned to both the world outside the organization and the internal working environment.

Because many smaller nonprofit organizations are so vulnerable to external threats (existing as they do on short-term government contracts, local donor support, irregular media interest, and the general satisfaction of their clients), they may be seriously harmed by a crisis that would be less than life threatening for larger organizations. In these cases, the leader's ability to function as a troubleshooter may be a survival skill, required for the very existence of her organization.

However, even large national organizations can get in serious trouble. The scandals described in the next two chapters concerning United Way of America and the Foundation for New Era Philanthropy attest to the vulnerability of any nonprofit organization when supporters and the public lose confidence and trust in the organization.

The CEO will be the first person to whom the board turns when trouble erupts. Experience has provided some guidelines for nonprofit leaders in dealing with such problems, including the following:

Face the matter promptly. Bad things seldom improve on their own. It's better to face a small brushfire than a raging conflagration. Recognizing that a problem exists and acknowledging it quickly may prevent it from getting worse, and this action also reinforces the perception that the leader is on top of the problem.

Get all the information and don't rush to a verdict. Most episodes of trouble are multilayered, and there may be extenuating circumstances. Effective leaders take the time they need to make careful assessments and avoid premature judgments. It is also important to understand the issue and be realistic about the organization's ability to respond.

Protect the organization. Leaders need to think beyond momentary damage control to the long-term impact on the organization. They need to focus on a proactive and positive response rather than a defensive one.

Get in touch with stakeholders. The board, staff, volunteers, donors, and community supporters will want to know what is going on. It is wise for leaders not to let others define the story for the stakeholders but to take the initiative in contacting them and reassuring them that everything possible is being done to address the issue.

Expect fallout. Few crises go away quickly. The aftereffects may linger in the form of anxiety, loss, and distrust. Organizations do survive trauma and upheaval, but the rate of recovery depends upon timely actions the leader takes to promote healing. For example, a period of reflection—perhaps a board-staff retreat or just some quiet time to think—might follow the episode to allow people to learn from the experience and ponder how a similar situation could be prevented from occurring again.

Fix whatever is broken. In the aftermath of acting as troubleshooter and crisis manager, the leader needs to be the healer and the architect of necessary changes. Stakeholders will be watching to see if lessons learned provide a stimulus for action.

More than a few leaders have gone through such difficult times. In one example, a patently false and damaging accusation was made in a letter to the editor of a local newspaper about alleged interference by one agency's staff in another organization in the community. Members of the board wanted a prompt public response, believing that the reputation of their agency was at stake. But the cool head of the CEO prevailed. He convinced the board that answering in print would bring another letter and keep the matter before the public. Instead, he marshaled his stakeholders to make telephone calls the next day to several community, nonprofit, and business leaders in order to offer a brief recitation of the facts and rebuttal of the charge. This effectively removed the issue from public concern.

In a second example, a newly hired CEO for a gay rights organization was faced with rebuilding after a financial scandal involving, among other transgressions, large payments made to consultants who basically did no work. Several staff members of the organization lost their jobs, and a number of donors indicated their unhappiness. The new leader quickly moved to repair and replace bridges to the key stakeholders, reassuring donors and others that controls would be put in place to prevent any reoccurrence of financial irregularities. She also mounted an immediate search for a new financial officer and selected an experienced senior individual well regarded in the community. Finally, she looked for opportunities to be out in the field, meeting with clients, other service providers, local government agency heads, and the general public to reassure people and reestablish productive relationships.

Both these leaders understood that the prime directive when things go wrong is to repair and reinforce key relationships with other people and reestablish trust and confidence as quickly as possible. Only then is the organization in a position to move forward again.

The Leader as Spokesperson

Harvard professor Howard Gardner's theory of multiple intelligences describes a form of interpersonal intelligence; it is attributed to people who are good at noticing and distinguishing other people's intentions, motivations, and temperaments (Gardner, 1983, chap. 10). The most effective nonprofit leaders seem to exhibit this form of intelligence. They are able to tune into what people are thinking and saying and to respond in ways that build bridges and connect the work of the organization with the needs and aspirations of the larger community. Their goal is to make the organization and its mission indispensable to the community. They do this by intelligently using information, cultivating people and ideas, and building resources. This activity is a key to effective advocacy and spokesmanship.

Indeed, getting the word out must be a daily preoccupation of the nonprofit leader. It is a mistake to think solely in terms of issuing press releases and making an occasional courtesy call on a local editor. Instead, active CEOs create strategies for keeping the spotlight on their organizations whenever possible. They aggressively pursue every opportunity to tell their story and garner public understanding and appreciation.

Doug Kridler, president of the Columbus Association for the Performing Arts (CAPA), is just such a leader. Founded in 1969, CAPA is the leading presenter of performing arts events in central Ohio. Virtually every night of the week, CAPA lights up downtown Columbus with events featuring nationally recognized artists and entertainers. More than 700,000 citizens in the region annually avail themselves of these offerings. Kridler was so widely recognized as a talented spokesperson for CAPA that he was asked to head up efforts to raise community and financial support for a proposed downtown arena and stadium project. He spearheaded a campaign that raised almost $58 million from the private sector in six months. He was able to put to use for the benefit of the general community the skills of public speaking and persuasion upon which he had built the performing arts center. (In Chapter Nine we will examine more closely the role of the nonprofit leader as campaigner and fundraiser.)

Leaders can use a wide variety of practical techniques to reach out to the community, including the following:

- Identify a reporter from the local press and cultivate a relationship. Feed him or her some good stories, and stay in touch. Suggest a series of profiles of local non-profit organizations, beginning with your own.

- Invite individual citizens in small focus groups to meet with you, other staff, and perhaps members of the board for informal sessions to seek their advice about issues and programs of community interest and concern.

- Use the local access cable television station. Arrange to be invited to appear on one of the community news or political discussion shows that typically are scheduled on such channels.

- Ask a board member with contacts in the business community to offer you as a luncheon speaker for the Rotary, Kiwanis, Lions, and other service clubs that exist in every community. These organizations frequently raise funds for scholarships and other charitable assistance, and they are always looking for interesting speakers.

- Offer to speak to high school groups. The students are the citizens and donors of tomorrow, and recent surveys show that about one-third of all young people contribute time to nonprofit organizations, so students are a potent volunteer labor force.

- Host a lunch for colleagues in other nonprofit organizations and encourage an increased flow of information among those with convergent purposes and programs. This could be the kickoff for the formation of a community leadership council (as discussed in Chapter Three).

- Participate in fairs, festivals, and other community events that provide opportunities for nonprofits to showcase their work. Prepare videotapes of participants experiencing programs and offering testimony about the impacts on their lives to show at these events.

• Use the new information technologies to keep stake-holders current. Use desktop publishing to create news-letters, issue alerts, and annual reports, for example. Develop a Web site on the Internet. Use e-mail to stay in touch with supporters.

This last point is especially interesting in light of recent developments in computers and communications. Information technology may well lead to dramatic new forms of outreach that will change the shape of the political process, with enormous consequence for nonprofit leadership.

The Virtual Leader

One of the most remarkable developments of the computer age has been the explosive growth of the Internet. At the time of this writing, Internet traffic was doubling every hundred days, and about 65,000 new Web sites were being added every hour. By the year 2005, some experts expect no fewer than two billion people around the world will be linked to the World Wide Web.

A single Web site potentially connects a nonprofit organization to millions of people both near and far, providing a global soapbox for its causes.

Personal computers are increasingly ubiquitous in U.S. homes, schools, and businesses. Access to the Internet has created an unprecedented flow of information. The nonprofit community, like other sectors, needs to consider the best ways to use this new capacity. Agencies large and small are finding it cost effective to put information about their programs on a home page, which is easily accessed by anyone anywhere with a modem.

For instance, in Marin County, California, the home page for MIDAS (Marin Information and Data Access System) provides pathways, or *links*, to the home pages of arts and cultural organizations, social services agencies, educational institutions, philanthropic resources, government offices, and other nonprofit venues. The information made available by all these entities can be constantly updated and shared almost instantaneously with individuals, groups, or other organizations inquiring from anywhere on the planet.

This capability can be used by nonprofit leaders in many ways, such as the following:

- To let people know how they can access the organization's services

- To solicit and enlist donor and volunteer support for the organization

- To raise public consciousness and support for societal issues

- To provide quick response to inquiries about the organization's services and programs

- To notify constituencies of changes in programs and policies

- To feature current developments, such as an award or media coverage

- To enable leaders to monitor news reports, conduct polls, and exchange information with other nonprofit leaders

- To offer an interactive forum, such as the Web site chat rooms, in which important issues can be discussed

More than sixty million Americans already have access to the World Wide Web, and many of them are well educated and affluent, making this potential market for nonprofits a large and tempting one. Furthermore as *e-commerce* grows on the Internet, useful applications for the nonprofit sector are bound to emerge. One of these might be on-line fundraising, which is obviously less expensive and less labor intensive than direct mail or phone bank soliciting.

For example, at the Nature Conservancy's Web site, bison named Sweet Pea and Prairie Chief wait to be adopted in exchange for $35 on-line contributions. The American Cancer Society estimates that it currently raises about $144,000 annually in on-line contributions, a small portion of its $450 million annual budget but a portent of things to come. At the moment, philanthropy's brand names (American Red Cross, Sierra Club, Muscular Dystrophy Association, and so forth) pull in the majority of the on-line contributions, but a cottage industry of consultants and technology firms is sprouting up to bring the benefits of the Internet to nonprofits across the board.

In one community a low-income housing provider mounted a public campaign for a homeless shelter and used its Web site to answer questions sent by e-mail by site visitors. This interactive process allowed a broad and inclusive public dialogue around an important community issue, a dialogue that otherwise might have been limited to those who showed up for council meetings or who were good at writing letters to the editor.

The Internet is likely to have many impacts on the ways in which nonprofits do business, especially in the opportunities it provides leaders for promoting their causes. In addition to leading those with whom they have personal contact, nonprofit leaders will become *virtual leaders*, reaching out to potentially interested stakeholders wherever they are.

In such an environment public visibility will be a consequence of the power and appeal of the message rather than the size or affluence of the organization. This will give organizations that cannot afford expensive exposure in newspapers, in magazines, and on television the opportunity to compete for attention and support. It could expand by huge multiples the audiences to which the non-profit leader can appeal as a spokesperson for her organization. It could also connect like-minded people and nonprofit organizations throughout the nation, to facilitate their collaboration.

One organization that has its finger on the electronic pulse of the future is the Pew Charitable Trusts of Philadelphia. The foundation provides extensive data on its Web site, including program guidelines, updates on grantmaking, and reports on other activities. It is likely that Pew and other foundations will also publish their annual reports on the home page rather than print them on paper to be mailed at great cost to the thousands of stakeholders.

With this action, Pew's potential audience has expanded to millions, the information shared has became more current than it had been when it was only published on paper, and the entire process is interactive, with inquiries generated by the material flowing right back to the foundation on its e-mail link. Tens of thousands of dollars have been saved in printing costs, and there are environmental benefits from not having to chop trees down to produce paper for the reports and not having to burn gasoline in trucks in order to deliver them.

Through the new technology, like-minded individuals and groups are forming new networks, working together for reform, change, and opportunity. With new tools like the World Wide Web, nonprofit leaders are better positioned than ever before to be effective advocates, spokespersons, and politicians for their organizations. But as important as these skills are, they will not in themselves sustain an organization unless the leader can leverage them to provide the necessary level of financial support for the organization. The challenge of fundraising is the subject to which we now turn.

9

Leader as Campaigner
Maintaining the Financial Lifeline

*He gives twice that gives soon; he will soon be called
to give again.*

Benjamin Franklin

E laine Chao's résumé shows that she was eminently qualified to
take on one of the greatest challenges in the nonprofit sector,
rescuing the once proud United Way of America. After graduating
from Harvard Business School in 1979 and working for several years
in international banking, finance, and transportation, Chao turned
her attention to public service. By the end of the 1980s, she was
chairman of the Federal Maritime Administration and subsequently
served as deputy secretary of the U.S. Department of Transportation,
an agency with a budget of $30 billion and 104,000 employees.

President Bush then selected Elaine Chao to be director of the
Peace Corps, the world's largest volunteer organization. Her initiatives in that post included establishing the first Peace Corps programs
in the Baltic nations of Lithuania, Estonia, and Latvia and in the
newly independent states of the former Soviet Union. During her
service in the federal government, Chao had become the highest-
ranking Asian American in the history of the executive branch.

In 1992, she was selected from over 600 candidates and appointed president and chief executive officer of United Way of

America, one of the nation's largest and best known nonprofit organizations. Established in Denver in 1887, this organization made its mark by planning, coordinating, and conducting combined fundraising campaigns for thousands of different nonprofit agencies. With well-organized campaigns to attract modest contributions from millions of paychecks, the United Way also established invaluable relationships with the corporate sector, inducing many companies to lend executives to it to run the annual campaigns. By 1987, there were over two thousand local United Way organizations across the country, and in 1990, their combined campaigns raised a dazzling $3 billion. The United Way had become synonymous with community fundraising in America.

Then the troubles started. Chao's predecessor, the long-time CEO of United Way of America, was accused of looting the agency to pay for personal expenses, including exotic vacations and posh condominiums. Even though his compensation was one of the highest of any nonprofit leader in the country, William Aramony had put his girlfriend on the payroll and diverted agency funds to pay his bills, continuing also to collect his pay even though not conducting United Way business. The scandal caused a catastrophic loss of confidence in United Way. Along with two other top United Way of America executives, Aramony was convicted in April 1995 of defrauding the charity.

Chao found herself dealing with the greatest crisis in the history of United Way. To complicate matters for the new CEO, the economic recession of the early 1990s had hurt charitable giving. Downsizing of government and the corporate sector meant fewer dollars available for nonprofits. States also faced huge deficits ($14 billion in California alone), which cut into funds for nonprofits with programs in such areas as social services, education, the environment, and the arts. What Chao did from the start was to focus on two goals: reestablish the credibility of the United Way, and institute the volunteer-driven financial controls that had obviously been lacking. She needed to restore the trust that had led to the singular effectiveness of the organization, and to ensure that funds entrusted to the United Way were properly managed and distributed.

As if the crisis of confidence wasn't enough, there were also other problems affecting the United Way. Attitudes toward philanthropy were changing. Although recognizing the virtues of coordinated fundraising through a single community-based agency, nonprofits in general were experiencing financial pressures that had caused many of them to conduct their own fundraising campaigns—discreetly, hoping not to jeopardize their relationships with the United Way.

Furthermore, a more involved and activist-oriented donor appeared in the 1960s and 1970s, prompting demands for expanding the charitable fields of interest to which the local United Ways had been traditionally committed. For example, a growing environmental consciousness and the development of a veritable industry of nonprofit agencies dedicated to environmental issues put enormous pressure on the local United Ways to include these agencies in their funding universe. Donors were beginning to demand such inclusion, and givers who were displeased sometimes ceased to give through their United Ways and contributed directly to the nonprofits. Nonprofit organizations were also complaining. Traditional nonprofits in the community, such as long-established social services and cultural organizations, appeared to receive permanent entitlements, whereas newer nonprofits were much less successful in competing for United Way funds.

Under Elaine Chao's leadership, the United Way managed to put years of mismanagement and organizational shame behind it and at the same time develop new and better systems for determining community allocations. By the time she left, after only three and one-half years as CEO, Chao had turned the organization around, returned overall fundraising to an upward trend, and restored public confidence in the United Way system. The rapid turnaround was a surprise; ordinarily a nonprofit organization with troubles of the United Way's magnitude would require many years to restore its luster. But Chao was a very special and effective leader who realized that there wasn't time for a long and tortuous rebuilding. Tom Ruppanner, head of the Bay Area United Way, summarizes Chao's approach: "She practiced 'emergency room medicine.' Everybody—staff, donors, civic leaders—was grievously wounded. She stopped the bleeding and set us all on a path to renewal and growth."

She achieved this through sound leadership principles and campaign acumen: listen carefully to the critics and seek common ground, delegate responsibility to colleagues upon whom one can rely, create improved systems for accountability, produce changes that make a difference, and demonstrate through personal commitment and passion the worth of the organization and its programs.

To begin, she worked with volunteers, staff, and professionals to thoroughly reform the national organization. She led the effort to implement new board governance reforms, a fair and equitable personnel system, guidelines for corporate travel and expenses, a new employee ethics committee, and a quality and continuous improvement program. Ms. Chao also visited hundreds of local United Ways, reaching out personally to millions of donors and thousands of staff and volunteers whose trust in the organization had been badly shaken.

What Chao said to people was not political or esoteric. She simply expressed appreciation to them for their years of unstinting effort in service to their communities, gathered success stories in each locale to help restore self-confidence, and let people know how important it was that their good work continue. She reminded them that people don't give to causes as much as "people give to people." She gave her audiences a renewed fervor for the community-building process.

Chao also asked of her associates and supporters throughout the country the tough questions that needed answers if United Way of America was to have a viable future: Can trust be restored? What are the value-added outcomes that make the organization a priceless community resource? How does the organization need to change to be responsive to its constituents?

She then used her findings in instituting the first strategic planning process at United Way of America. The resulting plan sought to capitalize upon the added value that United Way provided, such as its success in leveraging payroll deduction contributions with corporate matching funds. It emphasized the synergy that could be realized in a community campaign in which agencies were not competing but cooperating with one another. It also addressed the long-standing problem of entitlements, grants that were routinely renewed for member agencies based upon such variables as the numbers of people served. Chao championed outcome-based grantmaking, which supports nonprofit organizations that fulfill their goals and actually make a difference in their communities—those that create social goods, organizational capital, and social energy.

The strategic plan, with its new community grantmaking system, donor designation, and other unfamiliar features, was not easily adopted or implemented. With billions of dollars at stake, politics was ever present. But Chao traveled the country, attended scores of strategy meetings and confidence-building sessions with local leaders, and persuaded them that the changes were necessary to revitalize their United Ways.

Although Chao led a very large national organization, the lessons for nonprofit leaders are applicable to organizations of any size. She committed the United Way to at least four principles regarding contributions: multiply or leverage the effects of donors' charitable investments; recognize donors' interests and commitments; fully disclose how donors' contributions are helping the community; and create a bond of partnership and expertise between the donor and the organization.

Elaine Chao's success story at United Way of America is impressive. In less than four years, she and her team rescued what had become a tired and flawed organization. In fact, given the tough odds

facing her at the outset, she may qualify as one of the most successful fundraisers in history. Through her personal leadership, she
showed everyone what campaigning for the soul of a nonprofit organization is all about.

Dimensions of Charitable Giving in the United States

The statistics on philanthropy are impressive. In 1997, total giving
in the United States was almost $144 billion, with nearly $122 billion of that coming from individual contributions and bequests.
Charitable foundations gave more than $13 billion, and corporations
contributed more than $7 billion (American Association of Fund-
Raising Counsel, 1998). That $122 billion figure is an especially
impressive number testifying to the generosity of many Americans.
Yet it represents less than 2 percent of household income in a growing economy, so there is plenty of room for improvement, in terms
of both expanding the base of givers and receiving a higher percentage of income from each donor. The money is there, and the
question for nonprofit organizations is how to get a larger share of it.

It is sobering to realize that there are over a million nonprofit
organizations in the United States competing for a serving of the
overall charitable pie. Religious groups received fully 47 percent of
all contributions in 1997, some $75 billion. Education (primarily
higher education) received the next largest share, some $21.5 bil-
lion or 13.5 percent. Health care received 9 percent, human services 8 percent, arts and culture 7 percent, and environmental
causes about 3 percent. In most cases these sums were supplemented
by income from government contracts, fees for services, and other
forms of support.

Another report offers a profile of the 73 percent of all adults who
make financial contributions. Among all households, the respon-
dents most likely to report household contributions had education
beyond high school, and many were college graduates. They were
married, employed or retired, members of households with incomes

above $50,000, and thirty-five to seventy-four years old. Respondents that reported the highest percentage of household income contributed were likely to be retired and over sixty-five years of age or from households with incomes of $100,000 or more (Hodgkinson and others, 1996).

What makes these donated dollars truly special is that they are untaxed, increasing the benefit to the donors who give them and the organizations that receive them, and they are generally discretionary, which means organizations have more flexibility in their use compared to public funds, which are generally accompanied by strict regulations and a gigantic paperwork burden. Bequests, foundation grants, and corporate support also carry some restrictions and conditions, making them somewhat less flexible than the support provided by individuals.

Taxpayers support nonprofits in two ways: by allowing individual and corporate donations to be deductible and by paying added taxes to make up for the sums that would have been paid by nonprofits if their operations were not exempt from taxation. Note, however, that the wages received by nonprofit employees are fully taxed, as are profits from *unrelated business income*, such as monies from running a gift shop or renting out space.

In addition to providing financial support, many Americans also volunteer their time and talent to nonprofit organizations. In 1993, almost ninety million adults, about one-half the population aged eighteen or older, volunteered an average of about four hours a week, for a total of almost twenty billion hours. This includes both formal time commitments to organizations and hours spent in such informal volunteering as periodically assisting neighbors or working on an ad hoc basis for organizations. The fifteen billion hours of formal volunteering was equivalent to the hours that would have been put in by almost nine million full-time employees at an estimated cost of $182 billion, so the value of this contribution of time exceeds the $144 billion given in the form of philanthropic financial contributions. In addition, of course, many individuals and businesses make *in-kind* donations of food, clothing, auto mileage, office equipment, and other valuable products and services.

Charity Begins at Home

The American tradition of self-reliance is deeply imbedded in the ethos of nonprofit organizations. They have consistently demon-strated over decades of struggle and performance, under sometimes difficult conditions—public apathy and neglect among them—that the success of the organization turns on a sensible balance between dependence and self-reliance.

Small groups of people passionately devoted to a cause have sometimes prevailed with few dollars but much persistence and hard work. They may have labored on behalf of opposing the despoiling of the earth, calling attention to unaddressed societal problems of child and spousal abuse, or getting a fair shake for consumers. When no one else believed in them or in their causes, when the pleas for support fell on deaf ears, they persisted, running tiny agencies on shoestring budgets, accepting financial sacrifices most people would not dream of making, and somehow keeping the issue alive and their commitment steadfast.

But to sustain these good fights, to organize on a scale that makes it possible to mount an effective crusade, the foot soldiers of the greater good need economic support. Agencies cannot run pro-grams solely with volunteers; facilities need to be rented or built, materials and equipment must be purchased, and messages must be gotten out to the public. But contributors will want to know first what the organization is doing to pull itself up by its own bootstraps. Most foundations, for instance, will typically inquire of a grant applicant, What's your board doing to support you? Altruism is pow-erfully stimulated by a sense of others sharing the burden.

In addition to support from its immediate family, a nonprofit must win support from its extended family, such as those who directly benefit from its efforts. Thus environmental organizations are expected to target donors who enjoy the outdoors and use parks, beaches, and trails; social services groups traditionally seek initial support among populations that have used and relied upon their programs; and arts organizations attempt to connect with those people for whom the quality of life in their community includes the use of cultural resources and activities.

One of the central duties of the leader is to seek, cultivate, and protect the financial resources that fuel the organizational engine. Although the CEO should have lots of assistance from board members, staff (especially fund development personnel if the nonprofit can afford them), and supporters, the CEO must be the chief campaigner. That role in fundraising includes the following functions:

- Articulating, in a summary case statement or other document that can be shared with current and potential donors, why the money is being sought

- Balancing near-term needs with longer-term interests in building and sustaining the organization

- Developing and implementing campaign plans that outline a strategy, roles for participants, and a timeline for the fundraising effort (see Exhibit 9.1)

- Hiring and setting priorities for the development staff

- Participating in the *closing* for major donors

- Attracting and productively using fundraising volunteers

- Seeking opportunities in the press and other media to draw public attention and support to the campaign

- Acknowledging and recognizing donors and celebrating success

Exhibit 9.1. Elements of a Good Campaign Plan.

- A well-honed strategic plan that includes organizational values, management commitments, and multiyear plans.

- A clear set of attainable goals for the campaign that defines, among other things, amounts to be raised, duration of effort, and purposes for which funds are to be used.

- A set of roles and functions for everyone in the organization—the CEO, staff, board, and key supporters—involved in the campaign. This part of the plan focuses on leveraging the contacts and networks that members of the organizational family have with potential supporters.

- A list of qualified past and potential donors, with information about their interests and donor history.

- A detailed time plan that outlines the campaign in phases and indicates the different activities that correspond to strategic milestones or goals to be attained.

- A promotional plan that details the use of press releases, media contacts, and promotional materials.

- A backup strategy should the campaign fail to meet its goals and a Plan B is in order.

To avoid burnout the leader will need to allocate varying amounts of responsibility for fundraising to development staff, board members, and volunteers. The role of the CEO in getting the board involved in fundraising is especially critical because the board's financial commitment will be carefully noted by foundations and other potential donors.

The leader's approach to board fundraising often includes the following steps: articulating his clear expectation of the board's responsibility in raising funds to support the organization, setting a specific dollar goal or range for the board, directing the board's efforts toward major donors and the largest donations, apprising the board of significant successes in obtaining important contributions (the board ought to be the first to know), providing training and staff support if needed or requested by the board, and following up and giving due credit to the board's fundraising activities and outcomes.

Some nonprofits have adopted a "give, get, or get off the board" rule, which imposes specific fundraising targets for board members. Large arts, cultural, and educational organizations sometimes operate this way because board seats are considered prestigious and are sought after in the community. Others have focused on a rule of "wealth, wisdom, or work."

Working with (or Without) a Development Staff

The leader's role in fundraising and development also varies according to the size and staffing of the organization. Smaller nonprofits often cannot afford a professional fundraiser or campaigner. In such a case the leader not only is the head of the organization but is also likely to be the chief fundraiser as well. This wearing of many hats tends to drain creative energy from the CEO, as he may become absorbed with hustling for money and preoccupied with worries about meeting the payroll.

Some philanthropies, such as the William and Flora Hewlett Foundation, have helped smaller nonprofits increase their fundraising capacities by sponsoring a development position for a limited time. This is intended to help the recipients build organizational capital as it also demonstrates how much more effectively a nonprofit can operate when the leader has more time to spend on developing a vision and programs as opposed to nonstop fundraising.

Another way for smaller nonprofits to create organizational capability is by establishing a working relationship with a fundraiser on a part-time consulting basis. The National Society of Fundraising Executives (NSFRE) is a source of experienced development professionals who provide part-time consulting to help many nonprofits get started or sustain their fundraising. Exhibit 9.2 lists the types of assignments that such consultants can fulfill. If successful, these consulting arrangements can turn into permanent positions.

Exhibit 9.2. The Role of Consultants and Development Professionals in Fundraising.

- Suggesting goals and helping to chart fundraising strategy
- Developing lists and targeting individual and group donor prospects
- Researching and writing grant applications to foundations and corporations
- Planning and carrying out special fundraising events
- Working with the press and other media to create awareness and interest in the community
- Preparing print or video materials to use with potential contributors
- Monitoring the flow of contributions and following up on pledges
- Helping to maintain morale and productivity among the members of the campaign team

For most nonprofit organizations, fundraising is an ongoing and fundamental activity, somewhat akin to the marketing function in business. Even the best endowed nonprofits are unable to relieve their leadership of the task of campaigning for those charitable dollars.

Only a fortunate few—some of America's great universities, cultural institutions, and medical research centers—have large enough endowments to provide a reliable funding stream for decades to come. Yet because of the size of their operating budgets, even these fortunate few have large and permanent fundraising staffs. They never stop seeking additional contributed dollars for their institutions. These institutions and hundreds of thousands of others, large and small, employ development professionals and allocate substantial budgetary resources to fundraising.

However, no matter how many development people are on the staff, the leader is still the indispensable asset for nonprofit fundraising. For example, the presidents of such universities as Stanford and Yale spend a prodigious amount of their time cultivating donors, despite their staffs of development professionals and multibillion dollar bank accounts. And Elaine Chao, even when she was working on the internal organizational problems afflicting United Way of America, still had to personally reassure major donors that the organization would meet and exceed the requirements of its most valued supporters. The trust instilled through relationships with supporters is a precondition for giving. The average nonprofit operates on a smaller scale than a university or a national organization like the United Way, but the leader of that smaller or grassroots nonprofit is nonetheless engaged in the same process of building trust.

The leader need not attend or be a part of every solicitation, but a personal touch is important. A thank-you letter or call, for example, ought to come from the individual at the top to properly impress and thank the donor. One executive director makes a special point of personally signing every gesture of appreciation that goes out over his name, including form letters for small and routine donations. Many donors mention how meaningful it is to them that the head of the organization takes the time to write a personal note as part of the acknowledgment process.

So one key to successful fundraising is using the board effectively, and another is balance, delegating the more routine responsibilities of fundraising to development staff or community volunteers, without losing sight of the importance of the leader's selective participation. The third key is tailoring the appeal to the different motivations of donors.

The Motives of Donors

Donors are as diverse as any other kind of client, harboring different motives for giving money, time, or talent to the organization. The sources of people's altruism are likely to be deeply personal. Religious belief systems and upbringing, family practice, and conscience are powerful stimulants. Exposure to influential role models, the perceived utility of charitable organizations, and the impact of peers and associates also contribute to a person's charitable impulses.

All of these motives and others need to be recognized and acknowledged, so that the organization can work to meet the donors' needs, just as donors try to meet the essential needs of the organization and the causes it serves. There is a notion of reciprocity here, of some quid pro quo between the nonprofit and each of its supporters. This helps build a businesslike and reliable relationship, one that the leader can leverage to create a tighter bond, stronger interest, and incentives for sustained and even increased giving.

Several scholarly works have attempted to outline the basic forces animating charitable contributors. These forces include the following:

- Good citizenship: giving because it is morally obligatory or socially responsible (for example, donors might give to the United Way, Salvation Army, or League of Women Voters for this reason).

- Ideological commitment: giving because it advances an agenda that the donor cares about (for example, donors might give to the American Heart Association, Mothers Against Drunk Driving, or NAACP for this reason).

- Smart estate planning: giving because it allows the donor to direct the use of his wealth, contributing it to a worthy cause rather than having the government confiscate it through taxation (for example, donors might make a charitable pledge or create an endowment or remainder trust for this reason).

- Noblesse oblige: giving because it is the right and decent thing for those who have been more fortunate to do, and it is emotionally satisfying to help others (for example, donors might give to the American Red Cross, Junior League, or I Have a Dream Foundation for this reason).

- Status consciousness: giving because other people
  whom the donor admires or respects do so; peer pressure can be very effective, and appearances are important (for example, donors might give to the New York
  Philharmonic, Boston Public Library, or Dallas Art
  Museum for this reason).

The following vignettes illustrate how CEOs might respond to
the kaleidoscope of motivations and intentions of donors. Imagine
a nonprofit organization that sponsors international student
exchanges and an executive director who tries to meet donors'
needs by fashioning relationships with them around their own altru-
istic motivations.

- Good citizenship. The donor speaks of his strong sense
  of patriotism. The CEO replies that student exchanges
  help young people who might someday become leaders
  in their own countries come to know and appreciate
  the United States.

- Ideological commitment. The donor lived overseas
  during her own student years and now says she believes
  that such exchanges help build international understanding. The CEO responds by sending newspaper
  items and magazine articles about the flow of people
  and ideas across national borders and how this contributes to more peaceful relations among countries.

- Smart planning. The donor is an international businessman who wants to save on inheritance taxes yet
  also give something back. The CEO suggests sponsoring students from the nations that were the source of
  his prosperity.

- Noblesse oblige. The donor is a woman who inherited a
  large fortune and has benefited from cultural diversity.

The CEO responds that she could sponsor student exchanges to satisfy her feeling it is only right and decent to allow others to experience cultural diversity firsthand as she has.

- Status consciousness. The donor thinks he will impress his neighbors by hosting a foreign visitor. The CEO in turn emphasizes how beneficial living overseas might be for his son's résumé, college prospects, and job opportunities.

Each of these donors has a different motivation with which the leader tries to connect. This knowledge gives the leader leverage and an inside track when appealing for support. In responding to the variety of donors' motives, just as in advocacy for any cause, effective leaders use a combination of passion, self-interest, and common sense. Regardless of their motives, however, all donors want the object of their charity to succeed. The nonprofit leader bears the burden of seeing to it that the choices made by donors are good ones.

Finally, the leader must reinforce relationships with financial contributors and volunteers through various forms of donor recognition, which might include the following:

- Giving testimonials to donors at a special event or celebration

- Featuring a story about a donor in a newsletter or annual report

- Naming a program, scholarship, or facility in a donor's honor

- Awarding donors an honorary degree, a plaque, or other special gift

- Offering donors special privileges, such as expedited entry to a facility, special seating at events, and so forth

A Leader's View of Effective Fundraising

Over the years, effective leaders have discovered what works and what doesn't with prospective donors. There is a large literature about fundraising, and various reviews of that material are readily available (for example, see Nielsen, 1996; Prince and File, 1994; Rosenberg, 1994). Here, we offer some general guidelines derived from the experiences of one of the authors, who raised funds for both small community organizations and a major community foundation:

- *Create a realistic fundraising plan* with achievable goals so that the effort is not set up for failure. So-called pyramid giving (seeking one gift at $100,000, three at $50,000, ten at $5,000, and so on) usually looks better on paper than it works in practice.
- *Stay in touch with donors* through publications, special events, and personal contacts. Supporters expect to be updated on the progress of organizations to which they have contributed.
- *Try to attract larger donors with recognition that is meaningful to them*, to help them feel they are not just run-of-the-mill donors but belong to an elite class of *angels* who are especially appreciated and recognized. Arts organizations can offer preferred seating, educational institutions can name facilities and scholarships for donors, social services agencies can name program components, environmental groups can develop special tours and outings, and so forth.
- *Develop some contacts and interactions with donors* that are not about asking for money (at least not directly). If every conversation is about the financial status of the organization, the donor may come to dread a call from the CEO.
- *Avoid going to the well too often*. Excessive requests pleading for contributions offend many donors and are not effective marketing. Some donors will complain that the organization is spending their donations mainly for paper and postage.
- *Obtain professional advice* from lawyers, tax accountants, and estate planners about handling long-term gifts like bequests, endowments, charitable remainder trusts, and annuities.

- *Show donors why it is a good idea to consider gifting appreciated stock*, because of the enormous tax advantages.
- *Never divulge or share donor mailing lists.* Although donors' names may appear in publicity or publications, the nonprofit should never give out the contact information.
- *Encourage donors to participate in the organization in other ways*, such as serving on the board or on staff committees.
- *Explore with donors how they can establish funds at the local community foundation* to benefit the organization. Through designated agency endowments and *donor-advised funds*, the community foundation is a constructive partner for nonprofits. It offers efficiency (reporting and other administrative tasks are taken care of), reliability, and accountability for long-term charitable giving.
- *Involve donors in long-range planning* by creating a focus group to solicit their feedback and suggestions.
- *Plan an annual thank-you event* for donors, at which they will not be solicited.
- *Avoid building a fundraising campaign around deficits or losses.* People want to feel that something positive is being done with their money.
- *Use simple and straightforward language*, avoid jargon, and keep texts and documents relating to gifts as straightforward and non-legalistic as feasible.
- *Look for items in the press that can be sent to donors* with a personal note. This is an effective way to stay in touch, make contacts personal, and keep supporters updated on information that matters.
- *Never say to anyone else that a donor has given too little.* Such a complaint invariably gets back to the donor and may contaminate the source.
- *Don't bad-mouth the competition.* The nonprofit sector is filled with worthwhile organizations doing important work but ultimately competing against one another for donors' support. Some are better organized and managed than others, and some have a lengthier or more impressive track record. But, unless asked to do so, a leader

should not try to shape a donor's perceptions of that community. Many donors support multiple nonprofits working in any given arena, and they may resent advice about selecting the recipients of their philanthropy.

Working with Foundations

The Foundation Directory defines a foundation as "a nongovernmental, nonprofit organization with its own funds (usually from a single source, either an individual, family, or corporation) and program managed by its own trustees and directors that was established to maintain or aid educational, social, charitable, religious, or other activities serving the common welfare, primarily by making grants to other nonprofit organizations" (Rich, 1998, p. vii).

There are nearly 43,000 foundations in the United States. However, most nonprofits turn their attention to the approximately 8,600 foundations with at least $2 million in assets or gifting more than $200,000 per year. These funders represent fewer than one-fifth of all active grantmakers. However, they hold combined assets of more than $247 billion (88.8 percent of all foundation assets) and award grants totaling more than $13 billion (90 percent of all foundation giving). There are four basic types of foundations:

1. *Independent foundations* (84 percent of the total) are usually endowments established as independent grantmaking organizations by an individual, family, or group of individuals. They are also known as *family* or *private* foundations.
2. *Company-sponsored foundations* (8 percent) are grantmaking organizations legally independent from yet with close ties to the corporation providing the funds.
3. *Community foundations* (4 percent) are publicly sponsored organizations that make grants for various charitable purposes within a specific community or region.

4. *Operating foundations* (4 percent) use their resources to conduct research or provide specific services, in contrast to giving grants to other nonprofits.

When a nonprofit organization raises money from donors, it has to have an attractive cause, express passionate advocacy, and demonstrate the ability to use the money to make a significant impact on target issues or problems. But raising money from individuals is quite different from winning funding from charitable foundations because the latter generally require more thorough and detailed accountability. In general, foundations will require much more from a grant applicant, both before awarding support and after, than individual donors tend to demand because foundation directors are often fiduciaries for someone else's money.

This high degree of accountability is manifest in many ways. At the outset there is a systematic and thorough investigation of the applicant organization, the proposed program or project, and the personnel and budget submitted. Once the foundation is satisfied that the applicant is a worthy recipient, a contract is written that sets out a series of formal terms and conditions for the grant award. After the grant is awarded the foundation often monitors progress and asks for reports assessing outcomes. All of this requires documentation in reports and meetings.

Most foundations interact with applicant nonprofits through their program officers, line professionals who tend to have a specialized background and experience in the grantmaking areas in which they assume cases. Program officers tend to be conversant with the issues and experts in the field, aware of other programs and projects in the local vicinity, and cautious about undertaking new investments. They are likely to be inquisitive about all aspects of the nonprofit's operation and anxious to turn up anything awry that may not have been appropriately communicated in the application, like budget deficits, leadership changes, or loss of funding from long-time sponsors. Exhibit 9.3 lists some further questions that a program officer might ask.

Exhibit 9.3. What Funders Look For.

- How sound is the proposal, and how likely is it that the organization can make a substantial impact on the clients or community it serves? Is the project sustainable over time?

- What steps has the nonprofit taken, and what results does it have to show for its efforts to raise money from its constituency: the board, people who can afford to pay for services, and others?

- Would the requested funds be among the initial monies raised or an over-the-top contribution intended to give the campaign its final boost?

- How beneficial would a matching funds or challenge grant be in the situation? Are there other potentially large donors who might be responsive to leveraging their contributions through a pledge to match their funds?

- Can the funds be paid out over time so as to help the organization meet its needs but also hold it accountable for the goals (including fundraising goals) it has pledged to achieve?

- How will the applicant's performance be measured? What is the track record with similar grants in the past? Is collaboration with other nonprofits an option?

Most program officers want to help nonprofit organizations succeed, and they seek to form a working partnership with the nonprofit leader. The fact is that foundations need nonprofits just as much as nonprofits need foundations, because the money must be given away one way or another. The Internal Revenue Service requires that most foundations distribute no less than 5 percent of their assets annually, but some foundations give away much more, usually depending on how well their endowment has performed in the stock and bond markets. Program officers simply have to ensure that the organization's goals are consistent with the foundation's mission and that the prospects for success are promising as demonstrated by clear objectives, a workable strategy, a realistic timetable and budget, a supportive board, and access to appropriate and ample resources.

Most important of all, foundations want to believe that as a result of the nonprofit's interventions the community will be better off, that in some modest but meaningful way the outcomes of the sponsored program or project will make a difference. It is the CEO's primary task to persuade would-be funders that such is the case and that the investment will pay off. In addition to all this, leaders have to be able to sell themselves to funding organizations. Supporters need to have confidence in both the merit of the program proposal and in the leadership of the organization. Foundations also invest, as Elaine Chao said about individual contributors, in people.

A successful track record is the principal asset a leader has for soliciting the good faith of the funder. After all, unlike a contract in which each party has clearly defined rights and obligations, a grant is riskier. The sponsor takes a chance on the organization in return for pledges of performance and achievement. If the nonprofit grantee does not succeed, the sanction is likely to be nonrenewal of the grant rather than being sued in court for not having performed (as a contractor who builds a leaky house might be). The best assurance the sponsor has is the reputation and prior record of the organization's leadership.

Consider the case of Joe Marshall Jr., the executive director of San Francisco's Omega Boy's Club, a program to help students failing in school acquire the academic skills needed to succeed and graduate. Marshall was a charismatic former high school teacher who was tired of watching kids drop out of school. He built a national reputation for Omega Boy's Club by investing his own considerable talent and energy in kids written off by everyone else. He invited political, business, and civic figures to visit the program and impressed them with its hard-won success. He wrote a book, *Street Soldier* (1996), and fed the media a steady stream of fact-based stories about the successes of kids from inner-city neighborhoods. He courted foundations and corporations eager for workable solutions in this area of community concern and even started a show on National Public Radio to carry the message well beyond his own community.

Grants and gifts followed, and Marshall was eventually selected to receive a MacArthur Foundation genius grant for his outstanding achievements. Marshall's name is synonymous with that of the Omega Boy's Club. His track record is the same as the organization's. When a foundation supports Omega it can have some degree of confidence that the money will be well used. The same can be said of most of the nonprofits featured in this book.

Every nonprofit may not have a charismatic leader like Elaine Chao or Joe Marshall to help it acquire a large reputation and raise financial support, but every nonprofit leader can take some steps to enhance success when applying for foundation grants. One of the authors has been a staff member, CEO, and board member of a half dozen charitable foundations and has read and reviewed literally thousands of grant applications over the years. Exhibit 9.4 lists some generic characteristics that leaders should be sure are part of the proposals to which they sign their names.

Exhibit 9.4. Basic Characteristics of Successful Grant Proposals.

- *Focus and clarity.* Successful proposals are focused so that there is no doubt about goals and strategies. They are plainly written, avoiding professional jargon. Foundations are sophisticated and can see through a proposal that substitutes verbiage for good ideas. If the program cannot be summarized on a single page or two, it is probably too complicated, too ambitious, or too confused.

- *Modesty and incrementalism.* Projects that seem realistic and attainable are more likely to be funded than those that attempt to create excessive expectations. Funders want performance, not posturing, and will respect proposals for taking small steps before large ones. A low-pressure approach is usually best.

- *Collaboration and leverage.* Pooling resources is important when the problem is large, complicated, and has diverse stakeholders. Nonprofits need to work together when their constituencies have overlapping interests and problems. Using success in one area to leverage impact in others is always desirable.

- *Accountability.* Every goal or objective should be tied to a process for ascertaining the extent to which it is achieved, and if it fails, why it did so. It often helps to bring in an independent, third-party observer or evaluator who has no ax to grind. When the organization can both perform and demonstrate the results, such findings become a primary argument for renewal or additional funding downstream.

Some foundations will work closely with the leader or the fund development staff of nonprofit organizations to offer technical assistance to applicants. This might include meeting with the program officer, reviewing concept papers or drafts, or offering the services of consultants. Other foundations may refer applicants to local resources, such as the libraries of the Foundation Center, local councils of agencies, or seminars and workshops for grant writing. All foundations are likely to counsel the generic characteristics in Exhibit 9.4. In the usual competitive environment, in which there is far more demand for foundation dollars than there are dollars available, answering carefully for the use of those funds is especially important. In fact these issues of accountability and measuring results are so important to leadership success that we devote the entire next chapter to them.

Part IV

Making a Difference

10

Measuring Results
Being Accountable

Lord, we're not what we want to be,
we're not what we need to be,
we're not what we're going to be,
but thank God Almighty,
we're not what we used to be.

An African American prayer

Lovett H. Weems Jr., president of the Saint Paul School of Theology, demonstrated that he is an astute judge of religious leaders in his excellent book *Church Leadership*. When we asked Weems to name an outstanding church leader in America today, he suggested that we contact Adam Hamilton, senior pastor of the fastest-growing United Methodist church in the United States.

Hamilton was only twenty-five years old in 1990 when he started the United Methodist Church of the Resurrection in Leawood, Kansas, with nothing but a $3,000 grant and a dream. At the time, he had no building, no land, no congregation, and not even a name for his new church. Only eight years later, more than four thousand people were worshiping at the Church of the Resurrection every Sunday, and members were contributing over $4 million annually to the operating budget. Moreover, some 70 percent of the church members said they were nonreligious or unaffiliated with a church before they met Hamilton. How did all these changes happen?

Hamilton's first step was to articulate a vision, which was to build a new church to which nonreligious and nominally religious people would be attracted and there find God. He allowed this vision to become the driving passion in his life. He fervently believed in what he was doing and was convinced that he could change the world by doing it.

In the first three years, Hamilton spent fifteen to twenty hours a week calling at the homes of first-time visitors to his church, welcoming them and persuading them of the importance of his vision and mission. His weekly sermons, which he viewed as his most important product, were carefully designed to be relevant, scriptural, inspiring, and personally meaningful. He assembled a first-rate professional staff from members of the congregation to help him launch programs that would be attractive to potential members.

When the congregation first began meeting, Hamilton had to borrow the chapel of a funeral home to conduct services. The young pastor's message and vision inspired confidence and the congregation grew. Within two years, the Church of the Resurrection moved to the Leawood Elementary School gymnasium, where it was soon offering three services every Sunday.

The church did not have its own building until December 1994. Membership quadrupled over the next three years. Adam Hamilton found himself conducting six services every weekend. In 1998, the church constructed a large new building capable of seating 1,600 worshipers at a time and including forty classrooms, a separate music wing, a bookstore, café, and prayer gardens. In addition, it acquired another forty-two acres to accommodate further growth.

Today, hundreds of church members participate in music programs that include four adult choirs, four handbell choirs, and five children's choirs. Some 80 percent of the members volunteer regularly at the church. Their thousands of volunteer hours each month are devoted to a wide variety of ministries, including renovating homes for low-income families, feeding the hungry, assisting the homeless, offering community seminars, and serving the needs of every age group from nursery school to the elderly.

When asked how he measured his success as a leader, Hamilton responded that it was difficult for him to separate his personal success from the success of the church as a whole. He elaborated:

> I gauge my success as a leader by looking at the people who have been attending the church for some time: Are they being transformed by God? . . . Are they living out their faith in the world? Are their values, their priorities, and their relationships affected by their faith? . . . I evaluate myself based upon both the impact our church is having on individuals and the community, and based upon the numeric growth of the congregation.
>
> There are a number of indicators by which we evaluate the impact the faith is having on individuals. One of these is registrations for small-group activities and Bible studies. Another is mission outreach to the community. Another is giving—which is a key reflection of one's commitment level. And still another is average worship attendance.

When pressed further on his own role in building the church, Hamilton told us: "In most large churches, the senior pastor is primarily responsible for four things: (1) vision and strategic planning, (2) preaching (usually considered the number one draw for persons to become and stay active in large Protestant churches), (3) inspiring and leading the leaders, and (4) fundraising."

Many factors were responsible for Adam Hamilton's success as a church leader. His passion, vision, ability to inspire and empower others, keen sense of entrepreneurship, effective strategy for building the church, and fundraising skills were among the more obvious qualities that contributed to his success.

However, two other aspects of his leadership were also very important. First, he viewed himself as fully accountable to his religion, his community, and his congregation for all his decisions. He worked hard to earn and retain the trust of all of the church's stakeholders. Second, he carefully measured both his and the church's progress every step of the way so he'd know where his leadership was effective and where changes or additional efforts were required. These two characteristics of successful nonprofit leaders—accountability and measuring results—are the subject of this chapter.

Accountability

Accountability involves issues of professionalism, morality, organizational performance, and responsiveness to the needs and expectations of all the major stakeholders. These are real obligations in nonprofit organizations, not just parts of a preferred leadership style or organizational culture, and they carry serious social penalties for noncompliance.

For example, a nonprofit leader like Adam Hamilton operates within a subtle web of social constraints and responsibilities that he cannot violate without severe adverse consequences. If he shirks his obligations to the community, church members are likely to reduce their financial or volunteer contributions, and some may leave the congregation. If he is not responsive to the board of directors, he may find himself replaced by another senior pastor. If he behaves unethically or is not faithful to his own religious beliefs, he will soon lose the power to serve as a role model and will alienate the very followers upon whom he most relies for his success as a leader.

Most of the leaders of the more than one million nonprofit organizations in the United States understand their obligations and do their work quietly, without much public attention. In recent years, however, a few highly publicized scandals have put the issue of nonprofit accountability squarely in the public spotlight.

The conviction in April 1995 of William Aramony, president of United Way of America, on charges of fraud, filing false tax returns, and money laundering was described in the last chapter. Soon after that, in May 1995, the Foundation for New Era Philanthropy declared bankruptcy. Its president, John G. Bennett Jr., was accused of having attracted millions of dollars from noted philanthropists and nonprofit corporations for what turned out to be a fraudulent investment pool.

More recently, Minnesota Public Radio sold its for-profit sister company, Greenspring, to Dayton Hudson Corporation for $120 million. As part of that deal the president of the nonprofit radio station, who was also president of Greenspring, reportedly received $2.6 million. Also, the general counsel of both the radio station and Greenspring received $1.4 million, and his wife, who headed the catalogue business, received another $2.6 million (Abelson, 1998).

Nor is this the only example of unusually high pay for a nonprofit executive. Citizen's Energy Corporation, a Boston nonprofit started by Representative Joseph Kennedy II, allegedly paid its employees millions of dollars in annual compensation. One manager of the endowment for a prestigious university reportedly received over $10 million for his efforts, more than thirty times the salary of the president of the university.

These incidents and others like them raise serious questions of accountability. To whom were these leaders and the nonprofit organizations they headed accountable? What should they be held accountable for? Is it enough to comply with legal requirements, or must nonprofit leaders be bound by higher ethical standards in order to maintain the public trust? For example, even if it is perfectly legal, is it appropriate and acceptable for nonprofit leaders or employees to reap huge personal rewards from tax-free organizations whose chartered purpose is to serve the public interest?

A recent book cogently argues that accountability includes much more than just reporting to higher authorities such as a board of directors or tax authorities. In addition, it states: "Accountability involves preserving the public trust—being able to account for the organization's implied promises to its constituencies by pursuing its stated mission in good faith and with defensible management and governance policies. . . . People want to know not only that we are doing what we promised to do, or what we are legally obligated to do, but what they expect us to do, what they want us to do, what they think we should do" (Kearns, 1996, p. 40).

Thus, despite the considerable operating freedom that nonprofit organizations appear to enjoy—or perhaps *because* their operating freedom is granted as part of a social contract that requires the organization to be working in the public interest—they are properly held to high standards. Only by being fully accountable can they earn their legitimacy, without which they have little hope of attracting the resources needed to serve the public and the community.

Exhibit 10.1 suggests some types of accountability to which a nonprofit leader may be subject. Given the complexity of the subject, this list is far from complete. Moreover, each nonprofit organization has its own dimensions of accountability. Every leader must carefully assess the obligations and expectations that accompany her role as leader. Kearns (1996, pp. 195–229) offers detailed worksheets for conducting just such an accountability assessment.

Because all leaders are answerable to their constituencies, and are vulnerable to sanctions if they disappoint them, effective leaders establish mechanisms to ensure that high standards are applied throughout the organization. Examples include checks and balances, audits, formal reporting procedures, organizational policies, and performance evaluations. All these mechanisms depend on the nonprofit's ability to effectively measure organizational performance and leadership success.

Measuring Organizational Success

Every organization is on its own journey into an unknown territory fraught with challenges. To help it navigate through these challenges, the leader must constantly measure organizational performance and assess what can be done to improve it. These measures are also of considerable interest to the individuals and organizations to whom the nonprofit is accountable. For example, as Tom Ruppanner, head of

Exhibit 10.1. Examples of Leadership Accountability in Nonprofit Organizations.

Type of Accountability	Examples
Legal accountability	Compliance with tax laws, terms of incorporation, OSHA, contracts and grants, local ordinances, and federal and state regulations; true reporting of performance data
Board accountability	Full and open disclosure of performance, financial status, and actions; follow through on board's decisions; adherence to mission; stewardship of resources; professionalism; efforts to build leadership for the future
Donor accountability	Compliance with donor's intent; efficient and effective stewardship and application of funds; appropriate donor recognition; low administrative cost; disclosure of performance; high impact on community problems
Client accountability	Effective and efficient service delivery; respect for dignity and individual needs of aid recipients; high moral standards; confidentiality of records; reduction of client dependency; avoidance of excessive red tape
Staff and volunteer accountability	Effective leadership, including a clear mission, vision, and policies; respect for individual needs and diversity; effective training; availability of resources to do the job; equitable and just treatment; opportunities for personal growth; recognition and reward for good service
Community accountability	Collaboration in community leadership; effective and efficient service delivery; dedication to community service; high moral standards; stewardship of community resources; high impact on community problems
Institutional accountability	For a branch of a national or regional organization, compliance with central mandates, image, and expectations; full and open disclosure of local activities and performance; assistance to parent organization; maintenance of a favorable image in the community
Accountability to self	Ethical actions; trustworthiness; avoidance of any appearance of impropriety; efforts to build personal leadership skills through lifelong learning; persistence of passion; team building and effective delegation; balancing of work and personal life

the Bay Area United Way, told us, "The days of turnstile counts and happy smiling poor kids are over. Today's donors want measurable results."

In Chapter Two we suggested that the success of a nonprofit organization can be measured primarily by the social goods it provides to its clients and community. Secondarily, it can be evaluated by increases in the organizational capital and social energy it generates, both of which represent the potential for providing greater social goods in the future. The leader's prime responsibility is to help the organization succeed in this fashion, but in a practical sense, how can social good be measured?

Social Good

Sometimes, the measures of social good are straightforward enough. One can count the number of patients at a nonprofit community hospital who have been cured of a specific disease by listing those whose disease has not recurred for at least five years after treatment. A vocational training program can measure its success in terms of the number of students it has been able to move from welfare to full employment at wages that allow them to be fully self-supporting. A Red Cross chapter can measure the number of lives saved by those it trained in first aid and CPR. An environmental organization can measure the number of polluted lakes and rivers it has cleaned up.

Where such direct indicators of social good are available, they are clearly the most powerful indicators of performance in a nonprofit organization. In many cases, however, social good is much more difficult to measure, for several reasons:

• The measures may be diffuse, complex, and multidimensional. In the case of the Church of the Resurrection, for example, social goods include a vast array of benefits to the community such as spiritual nourishment for churchgoers, food for the hungry, recreational opportunities for teens and singles, education for parents, community assistance in disasters, musical programs, community beautification, and aid to underdeveloped countries. It is difficult to conceive of a single measure of social good, or even a small set of measures, that would encompass all these results and more.

- From the point of view of a community, social good may be an amalgam of goods received from a variety of sources. For example, suppose there is a decrease in teen delinquency in Leawood, Kansas. How much of the credit for this social good should go to the youth-oriented Underground Café established by the Church of the Resurrection as a place where teens can hang out safely and keep out of trouble?

- Similarly, from the point of view of the individual recipient of services, his or her needs may be satisfied from a variety of sources. For example, a homeless person may feed her family at the church's soup kitchen three days a month, but use food stamps or other sources of assistance the rest of the month. Does this mean that the church can take only 10 percent of the credit for the social good of feeding this family?

- There may be several steps between the provision of a service and a favorable social outcome. For example, the Church of the Resurrection has a program called Building Better Moms to teach parenting skills to young mothers. A lesson taught this year may not be used by some of the parents for several years, if at all, and measurable beneficial effects on the children may not be seen for years after that.

- Some clients may require a range of services such as food, clothing, health care, and housing. Any one service provided by a nonprofit organization, although valuable in itself, may not greatly improve the life of the individual without further contributions from other entities, both public and private. Because most nonprofit organizations are not chartered or equipped to provide the full range of services required, it would not be fair to judge their performance on criteria that assume such treatment.

Thus, although nonprofit organizations would prefer to measure social good in terms of the direct impact of their activities on the lives of their clients or on the vitality of the communities they serve, it may be very difficult to do so. In these cases social good has to be measured not by direct impact but by program outputs or the number of people served.

For example, Adam Hamilton would be pleased to have a direct measure of how religious members of his congregation are becoming, but that would be quite difficult to assess. The next best thing is to count those who participate in overtly religious church activities, looking at average worship attendance, the number of people attending Bible classes, or the number of cassettes of Sunday sermons requested by congregants, for example.

Similarly, museums can count membership or attendance at arts programs. Mothers Against Drunk Driving (MADD) can measure the frequency of media messages on the dangers of driving after drinking. The League of Women Voters can total the numbers of voters registered by their members. A Red Cross chapter can count the pints of blood donated in local blood drives. A local food kitchen can note the pounds of food collected and distributed monthly. In all these cases it is assumed that favorable social impacts will follow—for instance, increased cultural sensitivity, fewer deaths caused by drunk drivers, or greater citizen involvement in public issues—but these results can be measured only indirectly, through indicators of program output.

Organizational Capital

The second indicator of the success of the organization, increases in organizational capital, is usually easier to measure than social good. In a church, for example, the level of annual donations, the growth of the building fund, the number of educational programs offered, the number of skilled professional staff, and improvements in the image or reputation of the church in the community are all measures of its organizational capital, or in other words, its capacity for providing more services to its congregation and community in the future.

Among the various measures of organizational capital, financial indicators, such as growth in endowments, contingency funds, grants received, and paid memberships, are often viewed as key measures of the health and viability of nonprofit organizations. Fortunately, they are readily available and relatively easy to measure in most cases. For example, when we asked a sample of larger community foundations to identify their key measures of success, the most frequently cited indicators were the range, quality, and impact of grants made; asset growth; gifts received; and investment performance—all of which are easily measured.

Just behind the financial indicators of organizational capital are measures of the increase in *human capital*—program skills and training, management abilities, technical competence, and the like. Nonprofits vary widely in their ability to assess human capital and to make effective use of the talents they have. Apart from financial and human resources, organizational capital also includes increases in facilities and equipment, the number and contributions of strategic alliances, the quality and effectiveness of operating systems, and the stature of the organization in its community.

Social Energy

The third indicator of organizational success, increases in social energy, is still more difficult to measure. Social energy involves such elusive variables as levels of satisfaction, commitment, morale, and enthusiasm. In a church, increases in the commitment and enthusiasm of members of the congregation might be indirectly evaluated by counting the number of volunteers for ministries and the participation of members in community activities; conducting surveys of member satisfaction and commitment to the church's mission; measuring teen attendance at Sunday school; and assessing increases in the effectiveness and involvement of the board.

In some cases, social energy is almost a proxy for leadership effectiveness because it measures the number of followers and the level of participation of those most committed to the purpose of the organization and the vision of the leader. Martin Luther King Jr., for example, may be remembered as a great leader by future historians more for the passions he aroused and the vast numbers of followers he attracted to the civil rights movement than for the actual improvements he was able to realize in race relations in his lifetime, improvements that were slow to come and attributable to many factors besides his leadership.

Beyond these three key measures of organizational success—social good, organizational capital, and social energy—leaders often try to find other indicators of long-term institutional viability. These may include the presence of an effective plan for leadership succession, organizational strengths compared with others who provide similar services, peer group respect, and growth in community need or support for the services being offered.

All these are primarily measures of organizational success, but as Adam Hamilton said, it is difficult for leaders to separate their own success from that of the institution. Because no leader can be considered successful if the organization she leads is not, measures of organizational success are also useful as indicators of leadership effectiveness. Indeed, organizational success may be the primary measure of leadership effectiveness, because leaders are inherently results oriented and the leader's results are achieved through the organization. However, it is also true that there are measures of leadership success that go beyond institutional successes.

Measuring Leadership Success

In the first chapter we defined the leader of a nonprofit organization as a person who marshals the people, capital, and intellectual resources of the organization to move it in the right direction—that is, toward the greater good. The three measures just discussed (social good, organizational capital, and social energy) measure *what* the leader has accomplished. For a more complete appraisal of a leader, however, three additional measures are needed to assess *how* the leader has realized these accomplishments: the way the leader has changed the organization to improve its effectiveness, the quality of the relationships she has created with key stakeholders, and the professional competence with which she has led the organization.

Organizational Change

Chapter Six discussed the leader's role in organizational renewal and transformation. Leaders can be judged on the extent to which the changes they set in motion actually improved the ability of the organization to serve its clients and community.

For example, Robert Gard Jr. served as president of the Monterey Institute of International Studies from 1987 to 1998. During that time he reorganized the institute several times, recruited new faculty, established the Nonproliferation Studies Center and the Center for Trade and Commercial Diplomacy, and introduced several new programs including master of arts degrees in environmental policy and in commercial diplomacy. His changes energized the faculty and attracted new funding and students. By the time he retired after twelve years in office, the size of the faculty had increased 120 percent, enrollment was up 62 percent, and the size of the campus had tripled. In addition, the reputation of the institute had soared, and its graduates were much in demand. As these measures show, Gard had clearly renewed and transformed the organization (Hucklebridge, 1998, pp. 4–5).

The leaders highlighted at the start of each chapter in this book all tell a similar story. These leaders did not merely assume stewardship for the financial and human resources in their organizations. They also took responsibility for changing their organizations in dramatic ways so that they became energized and progressively more responsive to the needs of their clients and communities.

Measuring the effectiveness of a leader as a change agent often requires some qualitative judgments. Has the leader responded in a timely fashion to changes in client and community needs? Has the leader promoted innovative programs to deal with these needs and followed through to see that changes are well executed? Has the leader created a sense of urgency for change, effectively overcoming inertia and gridlock? Has she attracted good people to the organization and fostered effective teamwork to make things happen?

Quality of Relationships

Success in nonprofit leadership depends crucially on the quality of relationships established with a variety of stakeholders—the board of directors, clients, donors, volunteers, staff, and the community at large. Some relationships can be measured quantitatively. For example, Adam Hamilton was able to measure the commitment of his congregation to his leadership by plotting the growth in church membership over time, staff and board turnover, contributions to the various activities of the church, and the number of volunteers for church missions. He could also have arranged for surveys to measure each key stakeholder group's level of satisfaction with his leadership as senior pastor.

Some nonprofits use an annual review process to assess how staff and volunteers feel about the leader. They may be asked about their morale and their confidence in the future of the organization, the extent to which their views are sought and valued by the leader, and their motivation and satisfaction with the way the organization is being led. Similarly, clients, donors, board members, and other stakeholders may be polled to assess the quality of their relationships with the leader.

Some relationships can be measured only indirectly. For example, the inspirational power of Adam Hamilton's message might be reflected in the fact that the church sold over six thousand cassettes of his sermons in 1997. Confidence in his leadership is also evident in the fact that he was able to raise more than $5 million for a new building, over and above regular giving in the congregation.

These measures can be supplemented with qualitative judgments about the leader's effectiveness in building relationships. Is she able to engender mutual trust and high morale among board and staff members, and does she have their full support? Does she actively participate in or lead committees to address community problems? Can she transmit her confidence and optimism to others, energizing them and raising their hopes and aspirations?

Professional Competence

The advice of Confucius to a leader of his own time was never more appropriate. "Do not worry about holding high position," he said, "worry rather about playing your proper role." This entire book has been about the proper roles of leaders of nonprofit organizations. Professional competence means that these roles are well executed, with great integrity and in the best interests of both the institution and the clients and community it serves.

Professional competence can be measured only qualitatively, with the leader's performance ranked on such variables as the following:

- Has the leader developed and secured commitment to an effective vision and mission statement for the organization?

- Has the leader developed and implemented an effective strategy for the future development of the organization?

- Has the leader communicated well with all the stakeholders and been an effective spokesperson, advocate, and negotiator for the interests of the organization?

- Has the leader maintained high ethical standards throughout the organization and served as a role model for the staff and volunteers?

- Has the leader exercised good judgment in decision making?

- Has the leader organized effectively, avoiding excessive bureaucracy and red tape?

- Has the leader made effective use of the board of directors and been responsive to their concerns?

- Does the leader have a succession plan and has she developed other leaders in the organization?

All these measures—of social good, organizational capital, social energy, organizational change, quality of relationships, and professional competence—come into play whenever a CEO is being evaluated by her board. The board has every right to ask tough questions about the leader's performance. Indeed, many believe that except for fundraising, overseeing the leader's performance is the most important role of board members. Moreover, it is their continuing responsibility, not just a role they exercise once a year at the annual review to set compensation levels for the CEO.

Many would argue that beyond monitoring and rewarding the leader, board members should also provide all the advice and support they can to help the CEO improve her effectiveness as a leader. Many board members have themselves been leaders of organizations and have much wisdom to offer on the subject of leadership.

In developing a good working alliance between the CEO and the board, nothing is more important than a clear mutual understanding of what is expected of the leader, how her tenure as a leader will be evaluated, and how her leadership can be improved. The six measures we have described in this chapter provide a good starting point for such an agreement.

Conducting a Performance Audit

Leaders need to know not just what the organization's present level of performance is but also how it compares to past performance, current needs, and future trends; how it relates to budgets and strategies; and what all these measures mean in terms of possible decisions and actions that might be taken. Where does all this information come from?

There are at least four different kinds of performance audits that may be conducted by a nonprofit leader, each with its own purposes and characteristics: legal performance audits, operational audits, situational audits, and leadership audits.

Legal Performance Audits

Every nonprofit organization must keep an accurate set of books that records its transactions according to generally accepted accounting principles. These records are required for a variety of tax and legal purposes: to separate taxable from nontaxable transactions; to determine social security and pension contributions; to calculate unemployment and vacation benefits; to trace the flow of funds, including contributions to reserves; and to comply with the regulatory requirements of governments at every level. Such records are regularly audited by independent public accountants to ensure their accuracy and to prevent fraudulent or improper uses of funds.

Although accounting records are sometimes also used for performance measurement in areas other than legal accountability, most leaders recognize their limitations for these purposes. For example, the social good produced by the organization does not appear in the accounting records at all. In addition, the true value and usefulness of physical assets like buildings and land may be grossly distorted by legal requirements for depreciating those assets.

Another type of legally required performance audit is the formal evaluation report often mandated in contracts and grants from government agencies and foundations. Many nonprofit organizations, especially those providing human and social services, receive the lion's share of their funding from these sources. These nonprofits routinely include an evaluation component in their proposals for funding and often agree in advance to explicit criteria by which they expect their performance to be judged.

Every program evaluation is unique because it must be tailored to the individual circumstances of the grant recipient and the population being served. Where possible, funding agencies prefer measures of client or community impact, but in many cases, they will accept measures of program output instead: the number of clients served, classes offered, meals served, job seekers placed, and so on. They may also insist that the evaluation be conducted independently by objective outsiders. An entire industry of evaluation consultants and academics has grown up to provide these services.

Unlike accounting records, program evaluations often measure *soft* variables. The evaluation attempts to discern whether the services provided were competently provided, adequate, and in line with community expectations and needs. For example, a homeless shelter may be evaluated on such criteria as client satisfaction or the quality of the housing it provides. An educational program designed to reduce teen pregnancies may be evaluated in terms of changes in participants' attitudes or reported use of safe sex practices.

Where such soft variables are the only ones that can reasonably be assessed, nonprofit leaders need to protect their organizations by making sure the criteria are carefully specified in advance and agreed to in writing by the funding agency before the program begins. There have been cases where disappointed officials of funding agencies have terminated their contracts with nonprofit organizations and even sued them to recapture funds already spent because of unfortunate and largely preventable disagreements over the criteria that should be used to evaluate performance and the ways these indicators should be prioritized.

Operational Performance Audits

All leaders strive to establish ground rules or policies to guide the operations for which they are responsible. For example, shortly after George Bush took office as president, he issued these marching orders to his staff and cabinet: "Think big. Challenge the system. Adhere to the highest ethical standards. Be on the record as much as possible. Be frank. Fight hard for your position. When I make a call, we move as a team. Work with Congress. Represent the United States with dignity" (Safire, 1990, p. 31).

In a nonprofit organization the operations encompass all the people, systems, and processes used to deliver services to clients and the community. They might include information systems, the training and deployment of volunteers, procedures for interviewing prospective clients, methods of monitoring service delivery, and many other activities.

At Goodwill Industries, for example, the operations at the local level include soliciting and sorting public contributions of clothing and other goods, transporting these items to warehouses, employing physically or mentally challenged people to repair them, and managing retail outlets to sell them back to the public. The operations also include the information systems used by Goodwill to monitor the flow of goods through the organization, the outreach system used to locate volunteers and employees, and the management procedures needed to maintain quality and efficiency.

Nonprofit leaders must be able to assess how cost effective their organizations are, both in overall terms of delivery of services to clients and in each separate operational aspect. For example, imagine that the head of a local Goodwill office has the funds to hire an additional staff person. She needs information to determine whether the organization and the community benefits most from adding another truck driver, another factory supervisor, or another retail clerk or, indeed, whether the money would be better spent in some other way, like training more volunteers or upgrading the accounting system.

An operational audit seeks to provide this information. It assesses how effectively resources are being used throughout the organization. Some large national organizations also provide benchmarks that help local leaders compare the performance of their organizations with the performance of similar ones elsewhere in the country. In addition, leaders can search their own data for trends and ratios, such as increases in the average cost or time to serve a client.

Situational Audits

The most powerful forces driving change in a nonprofit organization tend to arise outside the organization itself. They include changes in client needs, community expectations, funding possibilities, and the state of the art of service delivery. Thus it is important from time to time for a nonprofit leader to assess the performance of the organization in relation to external trends, threats, and opportunities.

Situational audits fulfill many purposes. They enable the leader to judge the adequacy of existing programs relative to community needs. They are useful in developing new strategies and policies. They help the leader in her role as politician to understand the needs of other actors with whom she may have to collaborate or negotiate in the interests of the organization. Moreover, by providing an early warning of shifts in the organization's social, economic, or political context, situational audits extend the leader's lead time for repositioning the organization to adapt to change.

In smaller nonprofit organizations, leaders tend to monitor the external environment informally and personally. They do this mainly through their frequent interactions with board members, clients, and community leaders and with the people they meet through serving on other boards and participating in professional associations and peer networks. Most effective leaders are highly sensitive to external information. They are good listeners and voracious readers, ever alert to subtle clues about new developments or emerging issues that may have implications for their organizations.

In a few larger nonprofit organizations, like the United Way and some major foundations, a situational audit may be a more elaborate process. It may involve systematic information scanning and trend monitoring, sometimes engaging dozens of volunteers or consultants. For example, in the early 1980s, one of the authors was retained as a consultant by the American Institute of Certified Public Accountants (AICPA) to help its staff and a committee of distinguished practitioners assess the evolving position of the accounting profession in the United States. The association was particularly interested in the implications of societal forces for the future scope and mix of accounting services. It also wanted to begin deliberations on new professional and regulatory practices and standards that might be needed in the coming years.

After many meetings across the country and several commissioned studies, the committee prepared a report titled *Major Issues for the CPA Profession and the AICPA*. The report identified fourteen major evolving issues, assessed the importance of each, described the driving forces behind them, and listed both current initiatives and new options available to the accounting profession to deal with them. Several hundred thousand copies of the report were distributed to local chapters, professional accountants, educators, government officials, and others to stimulate discussion about needed changes in the profession.

Leadership Audits

Because one of the main responsibilities of a nonprofit leader is to develop other leaders, it is helpful from time to time to assess the quality of leadership throughout the organization. A leadership audit can have many purposes: to evaluate leadership strengths and weaknesses, to identify potential change agents, to locate individuals who can be depended on to lead successful programs in the future, and to uncover leadership gaps that may need to be filled by recruiting or training. A leadership audit may also be useful for the board of directors as it contemplates succession plans.

The six major measures of leadership performance discussed earlier in this chapter can all be applied to nonprofit leaders at any organizational level. In doing a leadership audit, however, three additional variables are of interest. The first is strategic fit, or the extent to which each leader's style, competence, personality, and interests are congruent with the particular assignments she has been given or may have in the future. Some leaders seem to be so versatile that they can fit into a variety of situations, as Dwight Eisenhower did as military leader, university president, and finally president of the United States. However, an individual can be an effective leader without such a high degree of versatility when there is a good match between the person and the position.

The second added variable in a leadership audit is the leader's track record, her record of accomplishment. One of the best indicators of leadership potential is a record of past successes as a leader. Leaders can be judged by the number of leadership positions they held successfully in the past and the accumulated experiences they would bring to a new position.

The final additional variable is readiness, or the extent to which lower-level leaders are prepared to move into higher levels of responsibility. Although this is largely a judgment call, readiness might be demonstrated objectively by, for example, successful service in a deputy role or the enthusiastic endorsement of peers and superiors.

In the end all these forms of measurement and assessment are useful in enabling leaders to act effectively on behalf of their organizations. Abraham Lincoln, in his own eloquent fashion, acknowledged the importance of measurement to a leader when he said, "If we know where we are and something about how we got there, we might see where we are trending—and if the outcomes which lie naturally in our course are unacceptable, to make timely changes."

11

Leaving a Legacy

There is a strange charm in the thoughts of a good legacy.
Miguel de Cervantes

Sitting prominently on a hill overlooking much of Los Angeles, the J. Paul Getty Trust is not an average nonprofit organization. Although it is clearly dedicated to charitable purposes—"to more fully understand, experience, value, and preserve the world's artistic and cultural heritage"—the material assets of the Getty bear a family resemblance to those of a large, multinational corporation: worldwide operations, billions in the bank, and architectural showpiece headquarters. The Getty is one of the nation's foremost cultural institutions, featuring two world-class museums and an endowment with which to fill them with the rarest art treasures.

Yet ultimately even the Getty, with its many advantages, depends upon the character and quality of the people who lead and sustain it. Presiding over the Getty Trust for seventeen years, from 1981 to 1998, was Harold Williams, the former dean of the Anderson School of Management at the University of California–Los Angeles, president of the business conglomerate Norton Simon, Inc., and chairman of the Securities and Exchange Commission during the Carter administration. The Getty board selected Williams to develop and implement an audacious plan to diversify the trust beyond the works of art and the small museum in Malibu bequeathed by J. Paul Getty.

With a vision of a major museum complemented by research institutes in such fields as education, conservation, and humanities scholarship, Williams set about building a first-rate staff and developing the Getty infrastructure. He understood from the beginning that this was an opportunity, in what would probably be his last large professional undertaking, to create an institution that would have enormous, long-lasting consequences.

There is ample evidence of his success. The Getty manifests its presence all over the world. The conservation program is responsible for numerous good works to protect the world's artistic heritage, including restoring ancient tombs in China, preserving wall paintings in Egyptian pyramids, and repairing medieval stained glass windows in European churches. The education institute is a leading resource in the effort to develop quality arts education programs in U.S. schools. The humanities program supports diverse scholarly research and invites people from all over the world to study at the Getty Center in Los Angeles. The museum has made major acquisitions that moved it into the front rank internationally in such curatorial areas as antiquities, medieval illuminated manuscripts, and photography.

Every leader needs to look to the future from day one and presuppose that he will enjoy a lengthy tenure with the organization. Only by making the assumption that one has a future as a leader can one be expected to invest heart and soul in being a leader. A long-term perspective is important if one is to think about, at the appropriate time down the road, bequeathing a legacy, handing over the past to the future.

Harold Williams proved to be an exceptional person who left an exceptional legacy, including a spectacular new *city on the hill*, the Getty Trust's museum and cultural complex on a promontory overlooking the Los Angeles basin. Williams's legacy to the Getty, and to nonprofit cultural institutions in general, includes the following:

- A unique vision and mission to create world-class museums complemented by additional programs that contribute to the conservation, study, exhibition, and extension of the world's artistic heritage

- A set of strategic goals that includes service to other art institutions, a global presence, and the full use of technology

- A philosophy of leadership based on hiring good people and granting to them a large measure of trust and autonomy, in order to encourage the fullest exercise of their own abilities

- An organizational infrastructure consisting of various research institutes that can grow and develop into effective contributors to their respective domains

- A sound financial structure that involves professional management of the endowment, long-term support for the new buildings, and sustaining ongoing programs

- A tradition of high standards and professionalism throughout the organization

- An international network of individuals and organizations affiliated with the Getty and sharing common values and aspirations

Harold Williams's legacy is a multifaceted one, embracing the entire organization, spanning both the larger picture and the smaller details. In a sense his signature is on every service and product. But Williams went one step further. He hired outstanding professionals and supported their growth as leaders in their own right. He became a leader of leaders. And all these leaders in turn are leaving their own legacies for the individuals who succeed them.

As an illustration, consider one of the programs he fathered, the Getty Education Institute for the Arts (with which one of the authors was affiliated as senior program officer from 1987 to 1989). Its mission is to increase the status and quality of arts education in the nation's K–12 schools. To lead this effort Williams recruited Leilani "Lani" Lattin Duke, an experienced arts professional who had been a staff director at the National Endowment for the Arts and the executive director of the California Confederation of the Arts. When Duke arrived there were literally no staff at the Getty outside the museum personnel.

Over the next eighteen years, Duke led the creation of a program that has had widespread impact on the field of arts education, affecting many school districts and millions of students all over the country. A summary list of the achievements of the Getty Education Institute would include the creation of new theories and paradigms for teaching and learning in the arts, establishment of professional training institutes, development of a national network of cooperating organizations for arts education advocacy, formulation of new curriculum and instructional materials for programs in schools, and establishment of national standards for student and teacher accountability.

Williams inspired and mentored Duke to set high standards and seek the best-quality people and programs, to work closely in partnership with other institutions, and to become accountable for her performance. In turn, Duke used well the assistance that Williams was willing to provide. She featured him at national conferences, leveraged his participation on the prestigious President's Committee on the Arts and the Humanities into an advocacy asset, and sought his advice on various aspects of the program. Williams also participated regularly in the institute's advisory committee meetings, which provided feedback and counsel from professional colleagues, practitioners in the arts and education, and business leaders from the outside community.

Thus Lani Duke established her own leadership legacy with the help of Harold Williams. In her turn she mentored and empowered other leaders in the Education Institute for the Arts. The same thing happened all over the Getty organization, so by the time Harold Williams retired in 1998, there were many strong and experienced leaders in various fields at the Getty, each having earned recognition through his or her own accomplishments. Williams had made the Getty into a leadership incubator in the cultural arena.

Williams also demonstrated the orientation to the future that is indispensable to successful nonprofit leaders. He realized early on that his organization, with its huge stock and bond portfolio, stood as good a chance as any of remaining around for the duration. This facilitated the long-term thinking appropriate to an enterprise that has excellent prospects of surviving well into the next century. Williams was also able to use the advisory committees for the trust's various programs as sources of unfiltered feedback and speculation about the Getty's future.

Williams demonstrated his sensitivity to the future in the first place by encouraging diversification through the creation of research institutes in the visual arts and humanities. He appreciated that the endowment was more than sufficient for the maintenance of the museum alone and sought other ways to use the Getty Trust's assets. He invested in people and then got out of their way to let them do their jobs, inspiring his colleagues with his quiet but formidable determination to make the Getty the very best of its kind.

But he also had the vision to undertake a huge building project that would provide the trust and its various programs a world-class headquarters, the Getty Center in Los Angeles designed by the award-winning architect Richard Meier. More than a decade in the making, the new Getty opened to the public in December 1997, only a month prior to Williams's retirement. Harold Williams made the mountaintop facility a key part of his legacy and worked for most of his tenure as Getty's CEO to implement his dream.

Every nonprofit leader's legacy will not be as elaborate or as publicly visible as Harold Williams's Getty Center. But to create a legacy, whether it be grand or modest, the leader will always require a sense of a future for the organization, of what its needs and opportunities will be. A basic optimism and passion furnishes the bedrock: the leader's belief in the good work of the organization, the organization's viable standing in the larger community of organizations that have similar or related purposes, and the leader's own identification with the institution.

Preparing Others to Be Leaders

Perhaps one of the most effective ways to strengthen the organization, ensure continuity, and preserve the leader's achievements is to help prepare others to be leaders as well. By actively encouraging others toward their own professional development, the outgoing leader increases the chances that someone within the organization or close to it might be prepared to step into the leader's shoes.

Most nonprofit leaders do not have the opportunity to handpick their successors. Perhaps the fact that this is seldom done in the nonprofit sector is one reason it is led as well as it is. Nevertheless the leader can help prepare others by furnishing them the opportunity to exercise their own leadership.

He can do this in a variety of ways, including

- Developing a succession plan for all leadership positions in the organization

- Putting a potential leader in charge of a new program and giving him full authority for building it to a significant size

- Delegating to subordinates and colleagues the authority and responsibility for making decisions or giving them control of programs or budgets

- Absenting himself from the organization for an extended period for holiday or leave

- Offering the resources for a special project that will give visibility and attention to potential leaders

- Working with a facilitator in a retreat setting, and exchanging roles with colleagues

- Involving subordinates and colleagues in high-level meetings, and taking other steps that demonstrate trust of these potential leaders

In addition, leadership development might be made a part of such ongoing professional training opportunities as seminars, workshops, and tuition subsidies for degree programs. The organization can also provide support materials such as books, videos, and Internet access and can sponsor informal learning activities such as brown-bag lunch discussions and book clubs. In a large nonprofit organization, younger leaders can be encouraged through internship, summer training, and apprentice programs.

For example, the San Francisco Foundation, through its Koshland Fellows program, provides young people of color the chance to become leaders in the nonprofit community by working in areas of significant impact. Participants function alongside program officers, attend seminars and workshops covering various aspects of foundation and nonprofit work, are mentored by their more experienced associates, and eventually assume responsibility for managing selected cases. This is invaluable training for later work in the nonprofit sector.

Other opportunities for leadership development are available in the form of postsecondary education training programs, commercial seminars, and books and tapes. Many communities feature leadership development training as part of adult or continuing education courses or credential programs offered through a local college or university. For example, the Center on Philanthropy at Indiana University sponsors and operates the Fundraising School, which provides nonprofit leaders and development staff with skills and techniques for maintaining a nonprofit's financial lifeline. Jay Conger, executive director of the Leadership Institute at the University of Southern California, has identified some of the essential new leadership skills that effective training programs should address, and these are listed in Exhibit 11.1.

Knowing When to Leave

The long-term oriented and responsible leader must consider how and when it will be best to pass the baton to another. For some the triggering event will be retirement, but for others there will be different reasons for knowing it is time to leave. When we speak to nonprofit leaders who have made a positive decision to step down, they typically offer one of these reasons:

- I laid out a clear agenda when I came, and never intended to stay any longer than it would take to complete that work and meet my goals.

- I've been in this business a long time, and I realized that I was getting tired of certain aspects of it. I wanted something else to look forward to for the rest of my career.

- I see people all around me getting into new settings and changing jobs, so I figured why not give it a try?

- It's the money; I still have young kids, and I just need to go make some money for awhile.

- I feel good about what I've accomplished, but I also feel that there's not much more that I can do for this organization. I have no wish to be a caretaker.

- Frankly, I'm just tired of all the small stuff. My skin's not as thick as it used to be. I can handle it, but there must be an easier way to make a living, or at least one easier on my blood pressure.

- I need a new challenge, something to excite the molecules and reenergize me. I want to feel again the way I did when I started out in this organization.

Exhibit 11.1. Some Trainable Leadership Skills.

Shaping Strategic Visions
- Developing a future orientation
- Challenging the status quo
- Mastering future industry trends and demographics
- Conceptualizing strategic initiatives into a vision

Aligning the Organization
- Communicating strategic vision
- Role-modeling
- Developing a leadership philosophy and value set
- Leading organizational change
- Directing decentralized units
- Persuading

Mobilizing the Troops
- Building trust
- Empowering
- Developing inspirational speaking skills
- Harnessing human resource systems
- Building effective teams

Source: Adapted from Conger, 1996.

Nonprofit leaders who take the initiative and decide why, when, and how to step down are in an excellent position to shape that event and perhaps even their legacy. A voluntary resignation allows a leader to declare the reasons for his departure, thereby preempting what others might read into the situation. He can time his departure for his own convenience, perhaps phasing out in order to allow time to secure other employment rather than leaving abruptly.

A voluntarily departing CEO is also better situated to design the transition period for his successor and may even be permitted to help select that individual. This approach allows for a process of disengagement that may benefit both the old leader and the staff. The leader who chooses to leave can also set a positive tone that can be healthy for the organization. By doing so, he is asserting that no one is indispensable, that the institution will benefit from fresh energy and ideas, and that this is the right time to enable the organization to move on to its next phase.

One well-known charitable foundation switches its program officers, who are often leaders in their respective specialized fields of grantmaking, every seven years. There is no tenure at this foundation; policy dictates that the program officer role requires periodic turnover to ensure renewal and guarantee a fresh infusion of talent and energy on a regular basis.

Harold Williams decided many years ago that he would retire on his seventieth birthday. By that time he hoped to have completed the new Getty Center. Everything happened on schedule, a happy ending to a successful career for the man and the nonprofit organization.

Facing the Music

Even excellent leaders can wear out their welcomes. The turnover typical in the leadership ranks (for example, every four to five years for a university president) testifies to the difficulty of such assignments, the toll they can take on individuals, and the risks one runs in accepting the challenges of meeting high and unrelenting expectations from a board, staff, clients, donors, and community.

Sometimes a person has simply been on the scene too long and has lost some of the vigor and dynamism that were so much in evidence in an earlier era. Dealing with a once charismatic leader or a founding executive director who exhibits no signs of letting go even after many years is a particular challenge for a nonprofit board. In one social services agency the reluctance of the long-time CEO to stand aside for a person clearly better suited to the changing environment paralyzed the organization. Ultimately this led to her forced removal, as the board and her staff supporters acknowledged that the struggle further undermined her effectiveness as a leader.

Such an inglorious end might have been avoided if she had the ability to sense that it would be best for her organization as well as herself if she stepped aside.

It is not easy for anyone to face the fact that a time may come when the best option is a definite but dignified exit. Holding onto a job in which either one's powers or effectiveness may have become critically diminished is itself a precipitate cause of leadership decline. But mustering the resolve and courage to move on before being compelled to do so enables the reflective leader to more successfully manage his own career rather than to surrender that task to others. Exhibit 11.2 lists a number of warning signs that it may be time to move on.

A CEO confronting signs of disaffection or impending dismissal needs to recognize his plight and take strong action to remedy or otherwise resolve it. Here are some tactics for owning up to the problem and facing the music:

- Meet with the board chair and ask for an honest, no-holds-barred assessment of the leadership issues and what the board may be considering as its options.

Exhibit 11.2. Red Flag Queries for Nonprofit Leaders.

- Has the board indicated its intention to conduct a performance evaluation of the leader outside the normal sequence or schedule?
- Are executive sessions of the board, as best as the leader can determine, occupied with discussions of the current leadership?
- Are the media calling for the leader's removal?
- Has staff morale plunged or has dissatisfaction mounted to an open and visible rebellion in the ranks?
- Have client troubles or complaints risen to a crescendo?
- Do members of the board take a long time or fail to return the leader's calls?

- Determine what's being said on the internal grapevine, the informal network that often knows what's going on before the principals who are being talked about.

- Consult with colleagues in the field to ascertain whether the external grapevine in the community is suggesting the leader is in trouble.

- Review the last year and prepare, for the chair's or the board's eyes only, a candid self-assessment of one's performance, providing a critique that requires improved performance and indicates what steps are needed to meet expectations.

If, after consulting others and making a self-assessment, it is clear that the leader will have to either step down or be fired, there are advantages for the leader in taking the initiative and striking the best possible deal in return for resignation. This can turn out to be in the self-interest of both the departing leader and the organization. A board faced with the unhappy task of discharging a once valued leader may be particularly sympathetic to doing whatever it takes to help the leader resign rather than face a messy termination. Board members may be more generous in such matters as severance pay, continuing medical benefits, and a decent letter of recommendation. In addition, a voluntary divorce usually offers more flexibility in both the timing of the action and exactly what is to be said for public consumption.

Preparing for the Succession

The extent to which a departing leader will be able to help prepare the organization for choosing a successor will depend upon several factors: the circumstances under which the leader's tenure is being concluded, the trust in and reliance on the leader that the board has developed, the existence of any precedents from former transitions, and the need or desire to expedite the process and have someone ready to step into the leader's role without delay, at least on an interim basis. A leader can take a number of steps to help prepare for a successor:

- Groom internal candidates with board support.

- Offer to organize the search process (although this will usually be a board prerogative).

- Meet informally and individually with board members to offer information about prospects for a successor, especially in-house candidates.

- Profile other recent leadership changes in similar organizations to provide a sense of the market and the competition for suitable candidates.

- Obtain current compensation and benefits information.

- Identify a transition team to carry on if the successor cannot take charge promptly.

- Offer to be available for consultation with the successor.

There are also some administrative and housekeeping items that departing leaders should attend to. Leaving the office in good order, disposing of unimportant papers, and conveying what is left in reasonably good shape will be appreciated. Completing all staff performance reviews will help the new leader maintain the documentary record and protect the organization in the event of any dispute over employment. A departing leader might create a briefing book containing the organization's basic papers, such as the mission statement and bylaws, organization chart, backgrounds of the board members, operating policies, donor lists, recent board minutes, personnel manual, program descriptions, and budgets.

Finally, once a successor has been selected, it is time for the old leader to cede the spotlight and step away gracefully. If there are farewell events it is appropriate for board and staff to acknowledge what has been accomplished under the departing leader, express satisfaction with the outcome of the search for a successor, and declare confidence in the organization's future. A personal note from the old leader to the new and an open invitation to consult should the need arise are also friendly, supportive, and welcoming gestures.

Leaving a Legacy

The departure of a valued leader who has been closely identified with the development and success of a nonprofit organization can be stressful for colleagues on the board and staff and for clients and others in the community. After all of his years running the J. Paul Getty Trust it was understandably difficult for many staff colleagues to accept the fact that they would no longer have the steady and capable hand of Harold Williams at the helm.

But the transition to new leadership will likely be much smoother when that departing leader, like Harold Williams, has a legacy worth leaving. The CEO who has led the vanguard for the organization, who has been publicly passionate for its advancement, and under whose leadership progress and achievement took place, may continue to have an impact even after leaving the post. It depends upon his track record in office, the well-being of the organization, and the goodwill that has been built up over the years of relating to people and caring about those relationships. Some organizations bear the imprint of a former leader's influence for a long time, even as new leaders undertake to move the organization forward and adapt to a changing environment.

The nonprofit leader can help ensure that when the history of the organization is prepared, a little foresight and planning will have preserved data that reveal a solid understanding of the life and culture of the organization. Putting an oral history on audio- or videotape is a low-cost way to capture and preserve remembrances in a simple, archival fashion for future use.

For example, one of the authors, while running a large charitable foundation, decided it was important to leave to the future a more complete record of his foundation's origins and early development than was provided in the official texts of minutes, annual reports, press releases, and internal policy papers. The organization had a rather idiosyncratic history, with its origins in litigation. The court record offered an official picture of what had transpired, but there was much more to tell. Through individual interviews with those who had played a part in this drama, he was able to preserve on videotape firsthand accounts of the early years of the philanthropy. This became part of the legacy at the foundation, manifest in some two dozen filmed interviews. Such information might prove useful to future leaders and help them maintain the organization's sense of history.

The Future of Nonprofit Leadership

As the twenty-first century begins, the size, complexity, and influence of nonprofit organizations in virtually every area continues to grow. A century ago the nonprofit sector was established but relatively young, although there were several venerable colleges and universities, some celebrated libraries, museums, settlement houses, and symphony orchestras. In that era before the rise of the modern charitable foundation (which began in the first decade of the 1900s) and the establishment of the federal income tax (instituted by the Sixteenth Amendment in 1913), nonprofit organizations were often small, community-based entities, frequently dependent on church charity and almsgiving. Few were organized to conduct national campaigns or operate throughout the nation.

The evolution of nonprofit organizations has been a great success story of the twentieth century. Colleges and universities, medical research centers, social services agencies, arts and cultural institutions, neighborhood and community development organizations, environmental groups, volunteer cohorts of all kinds—these have become fixtures on the American landscape, valued resources in the struggle to improve the human condition and enhance the quality of life for everyone. Public libraries, the yellow fever and polio vaccines, educational television, and the hospice movement are all examples of what has been achieved in the nonprofit sector in the past century. What will the next one bring?

Peter Drucker and other observers of organizational culture have remarked upon the impressive outcomes that so many nonprofits produce with very limited resources. For example, the grant funds available from the larger foundations in the United States, representing almost all grant monies awarded, total enormous sums but it's a small fraction of the profits of the Fortune 500 and much less than 1 percent of the federal budget. Yet these special funds leverage additional tens of billions of dollars to create new organizational capital and marshal social energy to meet the challenges of this nation.

There is little reason to believe that the needs to which nonprofit organizations respond will vanish or even significantly decline. Shoring up the public school system, dealing with the scourge of racism, assisting frail senior citizens, mentoring troubled adolescents, cleaning up polluted rivers and lakes, ridding our neighborhoods of crime and violence tied to poverty and despair—these goals will remain on the national agenda for many decades to come. Those who have the vision to guide and direct America's diverse nonprofits may face intense pressures, especially in the near term, as disillusionment and dissatisfaction with government's approach to societal issues expedites federal and state withdrawal from the commitments made over the last half century by the New Deal and the War on Poverty. Even the largest institutions of higher education and health care face escalating costs that cannot be met without either implementing basic changes in their operations or dramatically amplifying their fundraising, both requiring exceptional leadership.

Philanthropy will be hard-pressed to keep up with these escalating costs and challenges. There is likely to be increasing competition for the philanthropic dollar. Having a just cause, as we have shown, is not enough to attract sufficient charitable donations. Donors, volunteers, and others are increasingly demanding competent, cost-effective performance and full accountability from grant recipients. Moreover, members of a new class of donors—young, successful entrepreneurs—are insisting on an active role in determining where their philanthropic dollars go and how they are spent.

One certainty is that leaders in the private sector, the government arena, and the nonprofit community will have to work together. Public-private partnerships will become more common. They already exist in such fields as low-income housing, job training, community development, and protection of the environment, and they are likely to be extended to such other areas as the creation of cultural and recreational facilities, the improvement of K–12 education, and management of international affairs.

For example, there is already a great deal of reciprocity and interdependence among the university-based research community, the pharmaceutical companies, and the National Institutes of Health, which is the primary source of public funds for the fight against cancer, AIDS, and other diseases. But government and industry have a vested interest and huge investments in mainstream medical therapies. Nonprofits can be more adventurous. A case in point is the new Osher Center for Integrative Medicine at the University of California at San Francisco, established in 1998 to search for the most effective treatments for patients with a variety of ailments by combining nontraditional and traditional approaches that address all aspects of health and wellness—biological, psychological, social, and spiritual. A private charity, the Bernard Osher Foundation, is contributing a $10 million endowment to support the program. Harvard University has established a similar organization, the Center for Alternative Medicine Research and Education.

It is likely that other similarly imaginative and ambitious projects will spring forth from the nonprofit sector. They will result from leaders accepting the risks and seizing the opportunities to initiate potentially boundary-breaking approaches. Sometimes the nonprofit organizations themselves, subject to such forces as deregulation and pressures toward collaboration and merger, will be reinvented to more successfully address the challenges of tomorrow: such impediments to the full realization of the American dream as disease, poverty, racism, and the alarming gap between the haves and have-nots. Nonprofits will continue to be the fount of enterprise, experimenting with creative approaches that would be too risky for others. They will continue to build and reshape our cultural institutions and enhance the quality of life in the communities in which we all live.

The field of nonprofit leadership is in its relative infancy. As a professional discipline in its own right, nonprofit leadership is slowly developing a body of knowledge, a code of ethics, recognized standards of practice, and an academic specialization. There is the Jepson School of Leadership Studies at the University of Richmond and the James MacGregor Burns Academy of Leadership at the University of Maryland, among others. Over a thousand colleges and universities, including Harvard and Stanford, offer leadership courses or minors. And the subject is addressed in thousands of other degree programs in the management of hospitals, churches, arts institutions, and education. For example, Rowan University, part of the state university system in New Jersey, offers a Ph.D. program in educational leadership.

Within the next several decades many more academic programs will be established in universities and colleges in response to a growing interest in and need for professional preparation. There will be opportunities for both degree and continuing education programs, for further development of research in the field (to be reported in such periodicals as the *Journal of Nonprofit Organizational Management*), and for expansion in organizations of nonprofit academicians and researchers. Exhibit 11.3 lists some of the typical components of an academically based professional program for nonprofit leaders.

Exhibit 11.3. Typical Components of an Academic Professional Leadership Program.

Topics

- The philosophical, historical, and legal basis for nonprofit organizations and the role of the board of directors
- The nature and scope of nonprofit activity in U.S. society, and of its principal areas of activity
- The best literature on leadership, historical studies of great leaders, theories of leadership, and the findings of current research in nonprofit leadership
- Relevant theories in sociology, organizational behavior, psychology, and leadership ethics
- Current issues in nonprofit leadership, including issues of diversity, community development, and philanthropy
- Communications, human behavior, financial analysis, and information systems

Experiential Learning

- Apprenticeship to a nonprofit leader in the community, with the opportunity to be in charge of a group project
- A self-development program for the postdegree period

To this list we would add the following specific kinds of knowledge needed by leaders to perform successfully in each of the different roles we have been discussing:

- Leader as visionary: knowledge of the role of vision in organizational success, future analysis and forecasting, ways to develop a vision, organizational assessment, creativity and innovation, values analysis, and trend monitoring.

- Leader as strategist and change agent: knowledge of transformational leadership, strategic planning and policy, decision-making models and styles, entrepreneurship, organizational development and design, coalition building, change management, budgeting and financial analysis.

- Leader as coach: knowledge of theories of leader-follower interaction, group processes, organizational dynamics, conflict resolution, theories of power, modes of influence and authority, leadership development and selection, team building, organizational culture and learning, performance measurement, and motivation.

- Leader as politician and campaigner: knowledge of public speaking, stakeholder analysis, advocacy and persuasion, networking, negotiation, dealing with boards and public bodies, fundraising, media relations, community development and activism.

For those nonprofit leaders who want to be at the cutting edge, the challenge is to incorporate the lessons and experiences of those who preceded them and found success and satisfaction running such organizations. We have attempted to draw on that collection of information, insights, skills, and techniques in this book.

As we look ahead, we see many changes in the state of the art of nonprofit leadership, some of which are summarized in Exhibit 11.4.

Just as nonprofit leadership is becoming more professional, so is leadership in the business and public sectors. In fact, there is a growing convergence of interest and sharing of information among leaders in all three sectors. In the future we expect that more leadership careers will, like that of Harold Williams, straddle all three sectors. This could have important implications for nonprofit organizations, quite apart from greatly increasing the pool of potential leaders. Some businesses, for example, have experimented with sabbaticals for their mid-level executives to allow them to head community efforts such as running a fundraising campaign for the American Cancer Society or the United Way. Others encourage their senior executives to serve on nonprofit boards or lead efforts to solve community problems.

Exhibit 11.4. The Next Stage of Nonprofit Leadership.

From	To
Having few leaders, mainly at the top; many managers and administrators	Having leaders at every level, including volunteers; fewer administrators
Leading by goal setting: for example, controlling costs, fundraising, and so forth	Leading by vision; creating new directions for long-term growth and service
Seeking efficiency; benchmarking for low-cost, high-quality services	Seeking effectiveness; creating domains of uniqueness and distinctive competencies
Leading by allocating scarce resources	Leading by creating strategic alliances and new resources
Being reactive; adaptive to change	Being anticipative; creative of futures
Being a designer of hierarchical organizations	Being a designer of flatter, distributed, more collegial organizations
Directing and supervising staff and volunteers	Empowering and inspiring individuals and also facilitating teamwork
Having information held by a few decision makers	Having information shared with many internally and with outside partners
The leader, acting as boss, controlling processes and behaviors	The leader, acting as coach, creating learning communities
The leader, serving as stabilizer, balancing conflicting demands and maintaining the culture	The leader, serving as change agent, creating agendas for change, balancing risks, and evolving the culture
The leader, being responsible for developing good administrators	The leader also being responsible for developing future leaders

Source: Adapted from Bennis and Nanus, 1997.

Nonprofit organizations benefit from this, of course, but so do the businesses, and not just because they are hoping to establish reputations as socially responsible corporations. Businesses are finding this an excellent way to develop the leadership skills of their executives, skills that can later be employed in business. For example, when younger business leaders participate in nonprofit activities, they learn how to lead teams, inspire others, develop their communication skills, network with other corporate executives, and broaden their perspectives.

The implications of this trend for nonprofit organizations are enormous. Not only do they get highly qualified free help but their own leaders and managers have much to learn from business leaders about leading-edge practices in such areas as management information systems and quality assurance. Moreover, nonprofit leaders may develop valuable contacts in the business community for future support.

Summary and Conclusions

In this book we have tried to distill the essence of leadership success in nonprofit organizations. The stories of exceptional leaders with which we begin each chapter deliberately present a wide range of personalities and contexts. To the uninitiated, it might seem that the founder of a local church in Leawood, Kansas, would have little in common with the president of the Getty Trust or the Children's Defense Fund. What, they might wonder, is it about directing a large national organization like the United Way or Second Harvest that is also useful in leading a health center for Native Americans in Minneapolis or a small children's museum in Marin County?

But as we have shown, all these leaders have a great deal in common. Although there may be many ways to fail as a nonprofit leader, there are only a few ways to succeed. We hope we have demonstrated that all these leaders share certain key skills and talents and that these characteristics have been directly responsible for their effectiveness as leaders.

All of them have seen themselves as leaders, not managers and certainly not mere stewards or caretakers of their organizations. They have been builders. They built their organizations and they built new relationships with a multitude of others in positions to help their organizations. And when they were finished, they left legacies far greater than the ones they found when they arrived.

These leaders have sought to change things, to move their organizations in new and more effective directions. They all have been innovative and entrepreneurial, whether that meant franchising the Regis College approach to adult education or starting new institutes at the Getty or securing the involvement of pension plans in low-income housing at BRIDGE Housing. All have been responsive to changes in their environments. Indeed, most of them have aspired to nothing less than changing the world in their own areas of concern through the actions of their organizations.

All these leaders have been passionate about the causes of their organizations. These have not been just men and women trying to do a good job. They have been personally committed to improving society and their communities, whether that means housing for people who otherwise couldn't afford it, food for the hungry, or greater prospects for peace in Eastern Europe. They have cared deeply about what they do, and their commitment has inspired others to work together to increase the amount of social good their organizations could deliver.

Their vision and passion have been prime movers in creating exciting places to work and attracting volunteers and donors to their cause. They have been able to further inspire their staff and volunteers with their sensitivity, intelligence, organizational competence, communication skills, and ability to get along with others. In all cases these leaders have been able to increase the organizational capital and social energy in their organizations and to raise organizational performance to a new, higher level—a greater good for their organizations, for the people who benefited from these organizations, and for all their communities.

Every one of these leaders has mastered the six key roles of leadership. They have all been visionaries, strategists, change agents, coaches, politicians, and campaigners of the first order. Few of them had formal instruction in any of these roles, but they all have learned how to exercise the necessary skills to perform well in each capacity. In doing so, they have proved their competence to their followers both inside and outside their organizations, thereby gaining their confidence and respect.

Although every nonprofit organization is quite different and each faces its own unique set of challenges, not one can succeed without an effective leader. In their turn, effective leaders face their own daunting set of challenges, but the point of this book is that the challenges are masterable—indeed, must be mastered—if nonprofits are to fulfill their proper function as a key pillar of society.

Great rewards await leaders who are able to guide their organizations successfully toward the greater good. Nonprofit organizations offer their leaders a chance to make a contribution to people's lives and to their communities that few individuals in other sectors could ever hope to achieve. William James once said that "the great use of life is to spend it for something that outlasts it." The nonprofit leader, living for something that outlasts life itself, lives for the greater good.

References

Abelson, R., "Suddenly, Nonprofit Work Gets Profitable." *New York Times*, Mar. 29, 1998, p. WK3.

American Association of Fund-Raising Counsel. *Giving USA 1998: The Annual Report on Philanthropy for the Year 1997*. New York: AAFRC Trust for Philanthropy, 1998.

Arsenault, J. E. *Forging Nonprofit Alliances*. San Francisco: Jossey-Bass, 1998.

Barry, B. W. *Strategic Planning Workbook for Nonprofit Organizations*. St. Paul, Minn.: Amherst H. Wilder Foundation, 1986.

Bartling, C. E. *Strategic Alliances for Nonprofit Organizations*. Washington, D.C.: American Society of Association Executives, 1998.

Bellah, R., and others. *The Good Society*. New York: Random House, 1991.

Bennis, W. *On Becoming a Leader*. Reading, Mass.: Addison-Wesley, 1989.

Bennis, W., and Nanus, B. *Leaders: The Strategies for Taking Charge*. (2nd ed.) New York: HarperCollins, 1997.

Bryson, J. M. *Strategic Planning for Public and Nonprofit Organizations*. San Francisco: Jossey-Bass, 1995.

Burns, J. M. *Leadership*. New York: HarperCollins, 1978.

Carver, J. *Boards That Make a Difference*. San Francisco: Jossey-Bass, 1990.

Children's Defense Fund. *1996 Annual Report*. Washington, D.C.: Children's Defense Fund, 1997.

Conger, J. "Can We Really Train Leadership?" *Strategy and Business*, Winter 1996, pp. 52–65.

Cronin, T. E. "Reflections on Leadership." In W. E. Rosenbach and R. L. Taylor (eds.), *Contemporary Issues in Leadership*. (3rd ed.) Boulder, Colo.: Westview Press, 1993.

De Pree, M. *Leadership Is an Art*. New York: Doubleday, 1989.

Drucker, P. *The Five Most Important Questions You Will Ever Ask About Your Nonprofit Organization*. San Francisco: Jossey-Bass, 1993.

Edelman, M. W. *The Measure of Our Success*. New York: HarperCollins, 1992.

Etzioni, A. *The Spirit of Community*. New York: Crown, 1993.

Foundation of the American Society of Association Executives. *The Personal Equation: A Critical Look at Executive Competency in Associations*. Washington, D.C.: American Society of Association Executives, 1989.

Gardner, H. *Frames of Mind: The Theory of Multiple Intelligences*. New York: Basic Books, 1983.

Gardner, H. *Leading Minds: An Anatomy of Leadership*. New York: Basic Books, 1995.

Gardner, J. W. *On Leadership*. New York: Free Press, 1990.

Havel, V. *Summer Meditations*. New York: Knopf, 1992.

Hodgkinson, V. A., and others. *Nonprofit Almanac 1996–1997*. San Francisco: Jossey-Bass, 1996.

Hucklebridge, M. "Robert Gard Leaves the Monterey Institute with a Legacy of Vision, Growth, and Success." *Monterey Institute of International Studies Alumni Bridge*, Spring 1998, pp. 4–5.

Kearns, K. P. *Managing for Accountability: Preserving the Public Trust in Public and Nonprofit Organizations*. San Francisco: Jossey-Bass, 1996.

Kemmis, D. *The Good City and the Good Life*. Boston: Houghton Mifflin, 1995.

Knauft, E. B., Berger, R. A., and Gray, S. T. *Profiles of Excellence: Achieving Success in the Nonprofit Sector*. San Francisco: Jossey-Bass, 1991.

Koteen, J. *Strategic Management in Public and Nonprofit Organizations*. New York: Praeger, 1989.

Kouzes, J. M., and Posner, B. Z. *The Leadership Challenge*. San Francisco: Jossey-Bass, 1987.

Kouzes J. M., and Posner, B. Z. *Credibility: How Leaders Gain and Lose It, Why People Demand It*. San Francisco: Jossey-Bass, 1993.

Leavitt, H. J. *Corporate Pathfinders*. Homewood, Ill.: Business One Irwin, 1986.

Lipman-Blumen, J. *The Connective Edge*. San Francisco: Jossey-Bass, 1996.

Marshall, J., Jr., and Wheeler, L. *Street Soldier: One Man's Struggle to Save a Generation One Life at a Time*. New York: Delacorte Press, 1996.

McLaughlin, T. A. *Nonprofit Mergers and Alliances: A Strategic Planning Guide*. New York: Wiley, 1998.

Nanus, B. *Visionary Leadership*. San Francisco: Jossey-Bass, 1992.

Nanus, B. *The Vision Retreat: A Facilitator's Guide*. San Francisco: Jossey-Bass, 1995a.

Nanus, B. *The Vision Retreat: A Participant's Workbook*. San Francisco: Jossey-Bass, 1995b.

National Assembly of National Voluntary Health and Social Welfare Organizations. *A Study in Excellence: Management in Nonprofit Human Services.* Washington, D.C.: National Assembly of National Voluntary Health and Social Welfare Organizations, 1989.

Nielsen, W. *Inside American Philanthropy: The Dramas of Donorship.* Norman: University of Oklahoma Press, 1996.

"The Nonprofit Sector: Love or Money." *The Economist,* Nov. 14, 1998, p. 68.

Nutt, P. C., and Backoff, R. W. *Strategic Management for Public and Third Sector Organizations: A Handbook for Leaders.* San Francisco: Jossey-Bass, 1992.

O'Toole, J. *Leading Change: Overcoming the Ideology of Comfort and the Tyranny of Custom.* San Francisco: Jossey-Bass, 1995.

Prince, R., and File, K. *The Seven Faces of Philanthropy: A New Approach to Cultivating Major Donors.* San Francisco: Jossey-Bass, 1994.

Rich, E. (ed.). *The Foundation Directory.* New York: Foundation Center, 1998.

Rosenberg, C., Jr. *Wealthy and Wise: How You and America Can Get the Most out of Your Giving.* Boston: Little, Brown, 1994.

Rothschild, W. E. *Risktaker, Caretaker, Surgeon, Undertaker: The Four Faces of Strategic Leadership.* New York: Wiley, 1993.

Safire, W. "Bush's Cabinet: Who's Up, Who's Down?" *New York Times Magazine,* Mar. 25, 1990, p. 31.

Schein, E. H. *Organizational Culture and Leadership.* (2nd ed.) San Francisco: Jossey-Bass, 1992.

Senge, P. *The Fifth Discipline: The Art and Practice of the Learning Organization.* New York: Doubleday, 1990.

Tocqueville, A. de. *Democracy in America.* New York: HarperCollins, 1969. (Originally published 1835.)

Watkins, B. "Successful Colleges Found Headed by Presidents Who Are People-Oriented, Doggedly Persistent." *Chronicle of Higher Education,* June 4, 1986, p. 20.

Weems, L. H., Jr. *Church Leadership.* Nashville, Tenn.: Abingdon Press, 1993.

Yukl, G. *Leadership in Organizations.* Upper Saddle River, N.J.: Prentice Hall, 1994.

Additional Readings

Boulding, K. E. *Human Betterment*. Thousand Oaks, Calif.: Sage, 1985.

Clark, K. E., and Clark, M. B. *Measuring Leadership*. West Orange, N.J.: Leadership Library of America, 1990.

Clemens, J., and Mayer, D. *The Classic Touch: Lessons in Leadership from Homer to Hemingway*. Homewood, Ill.: Business One Irwin, 1987.

De Pree, M. *Leading Without Power*. San Francisco: Jossey-Bass, 1997.

Dilts, R. B. *Visionary Leadership Skills*. Capitola, Calif.: Meta, 1996.

Drucker, P. *Managing the Nonprofit Organization*. New York: HarperCollins, 1992.

Duca, D. D. *Nonprofit Boards: Roles, Responsibility and Performance*. New York: Wiley, 1996.

Eadie, D. C., and Shrader, A. (eds.). *Changing by Design: A Practical Approach to Leading Innovation in Nonprofit Organizations*. San Francisco: Jossey-Bass, 1997.

Ellis, S., and Noyes, K. *By the People: A History of Americans as Volunteers*. San Francisco: Jossey-Bass, 1990.

Firholm, G. W. *Values Leadership*. New York: Praeger, 1991.

Fisher, K., Rayner, S., and Belgard, W. *Tips for Teams: A Ready Reference for Solving Common Team Problems*. New York: McGraw-Hill, 1995.

Hargrove, R. *Masterful Coaching: Extraordinary Results by Impacting People and the Way They Think and Work Together*. San Francisco: Jossey-Bass/Pfeiffer, 1995.

Herman, R., and Heimovics, R. *Executive Leadership in Nonprofit Organizations: New Strategies for Shaping Executive-Board Dynamics*. San Francisco: Jossey-Bass, 1991.

Herman, R. D., and Associates. *The Jossey-Bass Handbook of Nonprofit Leadership and Management*. San Francisco: Jossey-Bass, 1994.

Hesselbein, F., Goldsmith, M., and Beckhard, R. (eds). *The Leader of the Future*. San Francisco: Jossey-Bass, 1996.

Ingram, R. *Ten Basic Responsibilities of Nonprofit Boards*. Washington, D.C.: National Center for Nonprofit Boards, 1991.

Jackson, P. M., and Palmer, B. *Performance Measurement: A Management Guide*. Leicester, England: University of Leicester, Management Centre, 1992.

Joseph, J. A. *Remaking America: How the Benevolent Traditions of Many Cultures Are Transforming Our National Life*. San Francisco: Jossey-Bass, 1995.

Kanter, R. A., Stein, B. A., and Jick, T. D. *The Challenge of Organizational Change*. New York: Free Press, 1992.

Leigh, A., and Maynard, M. *Leading Your Team: How to Motivate and Inspire Teams*. London: Brealey, 1995.

Light, P. C. *Sustaining Innovation: Creating Nonprofit and Government Organizations That Innovate Naturally*. San Francisco: Jossey-Bass, 1998.

National Commission on Philanthropy and Civic Renewal. *Giving Better, Giving Smarter: Renewing Philanthropy in America*. Washington, D.C.: National Commission on Philanthropy and Civic Renewal, 1997.

O'Neill, J. *The Paradox of Success: When Winning at Work Means Losing at Life: A Book of Renewal for Leaders*. New York: Putnam, 1993.

O'Neill, M. *The Third America: The Emergence of the Nonprofit Sector in the United States*. San Francisco: Jossey-Bass, 1997.

Oster, S. M. *Strategic Management for Nonprofit Organizations: Theory and Practice*. New York: Oxford University Press, 1995.

Powell, W. W., and Clemens, E. S. (eds.). *Private Action and the Public Good*. New Haven, Conn.: Yale University Press, 1998.

Rejai, M., and Phillips, K. *Leaders and Leadership: An Appraisal of Theory and Practice*. Westport, Conn.: Praeger, 1997.

Renesch, J. (ed.). *Leadership in a New Era: Visionary Approaches to the Biggest Crisis of Our Time*. San Francisco: New Leaders Press, 1994.

Salamon, L. M. *America's Nonprofit Sector: A Primer*. New York: Foundation Center, 1992.

Shekerjian, D. *Uncommon Genius*. New York: Viking/Penguin, 1990.

Skloot, E. *The Nonprofit Entrepreneur: Creating Ventures to Earn Income*. New York: Foundation Center, 1988.

Tichy, N., and Devanna, M. *The Transformational Leader*. New York: Wiley, 1986.

Van de Ven, A. H., and Ferry, D. L. *Measuring and Assessing Organizations*. New York: Wiley, 1980.

Wuthnow, R. *Acts of Compassion: Caring for Others and Helping Ourselves*. Princeton, N.J.: Princeton University Press, 1991.

The Authors

Burt Nanus is professor emeritus of management at the Marshall School of Business of the University of Southern California, where he served on the faculty from 1969 to 1994. While there, he founded the university's Center for Futures Research and served as its director for sixteen years. Later he helped start the USC Leadership Institute and served as its first director of research.

In the ten years prior to joining USC, Nanus held positions as manager of advanced educational techniques at the Sperry Rand Corporation, senior technical adviser to management at the System Development Corporation, and president of his own consulting firm, Planning Technology, Inc. He holds an undergraduate degree in mechanical engineering from the Stevens Institute of Technology (1957), an M.S. degree from the Sloan School of Management at MIT (1959), and a D.B.A. degree from the University of Southern California (1967).

A noted speaker on leadership, Nanus has addressed tens of thousands of executives at major national and international conferences of such organizations as, most recently, Goodwill Industries, the Jewish Community Centers of North America, the Association of Higher Education Facilities Officers, and the Larger Community Foundations Association. He has also consulted with numerous nonprofit, government, and business organizations on strategy and leadership. He has served on the editorial boards of five journals and on the board of directors of the Los Angeles Private Industry Council.

He is the author of ten books, seven of them on leadership, including *Leaders: The Strategies for Taking Charge* (with Warren Bennis), named by the *Financial Times* as one of the "top 50 business books of all time." His book *Visionary Leadership* was a selection of the Book of the Month Club and the Fortune Book Club and has been translated into six languages. His two books for facilitators and participants in vision retreats have been used by many nonprofit leaders as part of the process of redirecting their organizations for the next decade.

Stephen Mark Dobbs is the executive vice president of the Bernard Osher Foundation of San Francisco. He served for seven years as president and CEO of the Marin Community Foundation, one of the nation's largest foundations, with assets approaching $1 billion. He formerly served as program analyst for the John D. Rockefeller III Fund, senior program officer at the J. Paul Getty Trust, and executive director and CEO of the Koret Foundation. The *Chronicle of Philanthropy* named him one of "a new generation of foundation leaders."

Dobbs, the recipient of both a B.A. degree in philosophy (1964) and a Ph.D. degree in education (1972) from Stanford University, also had an earlier career in the academic world. He served as professor of arts and humanities at San Francisco State University and director of the university's Center for Experimental and Interdisciplinary Arts. He has also been a visiting professor at Stanford and the University of Washington and a visiting scholar at Harvard University, the University of London, and The Carnegie Foundation for the Advancement of Teaching.

During his professorship, Dobbs was a faculty member for the summer Fulbright Program and served as director of the summer Humanities Institute at the Kennedy Center in Washington, D.C. He is a former editor of a national education journal, a member of the National Faculty for the Humanities, and the author of six books and some ninety other scholarly publications. He is the recipient of the Charles D. Perlee Award for Distinguished Contributions to Humanities Education.

Dobbs has worked as a community volunteer and board of directors member for numerous grassroots and local nonprofit organizations, including a major hospital and medical center, an independent school, an organization for the disabled, and a theater company. He currently serves as a director of the nonprofit Mount Zion Health Systems, Guide Dogs for the Blind, and Words on Dance and sits on the president's advisory board of San Francisco State University. Dobbs lives in San Rafael, California, with his wife, Victoria, and their four sons.

Index

Strategy: defined, 99–100; effective, criteria of, 110–114; implementation, 117; and leadership success, 100; new, stimulus for, 115; vision statement and, 101–102

Strategy process, 115–119; board's role in, 105; determination of thrust and issues in, 102–105; documentation in, 114; implementation plan in, 109; needs assessment in, 108; organizational self-assessment in, 106; shared leadership of, 116; strategic factor in, 108–109; time horizon in, 107; top-down versus bottom-up approach in, 105–106; vision development in, 99–102

Strickland, B., 145–148, 154, 163

Succession, leader's role in, 250–252

System Development Corporation, 132

T

Tax exemptions, 197

Team building, 148–150, 152, 155

Termination, 248–250

Terner, D., 3–5, 16, 20

Think tanks, 36

Thoreau, H. D., 75

Tocqueville, A. de, 176

Trust: establishment of, 55; of new leader, 60, 63; in public advocacy, 178–179

U

United Methodist Church of the Resurrection, Leawood, Kansas, 217–219, 224–225

United Way of America, 47; fraud and crisis of confidence in, 191;

restoration of public confidence in, 192–195; strategic planning process at, 195

University of Southern California's Leadership Institute, 245–246

V

van Hengel, John, 27–28

Virtual leader, 188–189

Vision, 17; defined, 78; and mission statement, 81–82, 83–85; motivational effects of, 79–80; and organizational transformation, 132; shared, payoffs of, 80–81; statement, 82–86

Visioning process: audit phase of, 88–90; four-phased approach in, 86, 87; group process in, 86–88; implementation strategies in, 94–95; mapping exercise in, 92; strategy development in, 101–105; vision context phase of, 91; vision retreat in, 86–87; vision scope phase of, 91

Volunteer workforce: contributions of, 197–198; evaluation of, 161–162; size of, 33, 46; working relationships with, 11–12

W

Watkins, B., 137

Wattleton, F., 131

Weems, L. H., Jr., 217

Williams, H., 239–243, 248, 252

Windsor Village United Methodist Church, Houston, Texas, 126

World Wide Web, 186–189

Y

Yukl, G., 21